**Studia Fennica**
Folkloristica 15

THE FINNISH LITERATURE SOCIETY (SKS) was founded in 1831 and has, from the very beginning, engaged in publishing operations. It nowadays publishes literature in the fields of ethnology and folkloristics, linguistics, literary research and cultural history.

The first volume of the Studia Fennica series appeared in 1933. Since 1992, the series has been divided into three thematic subseries: Ethnologica, Folkloristica and Linguistica. Two additional subseries were formed in 2002, Historica and Litteraria. The subseries Anthropologica was formed in 2007.

In addition to its publishing activities, the Finnish Literature Society maintains research activities and infrastructures, an archive containing folklore and literary collections, a research library and promotes Finnish literature abroad.

EDITORIAL OFFICE
SKS
P.O. Box 259
FI-00171 Helsinki
www.finlit.fi

Pertti J. Anttonen

# Tradition through Modernity

*Postmodernism and the Nation-State
in Folklore Scolarship*

Finnish Literature Society · SKS · Helsinki

Studia Fennica Folkloristica 15

The publication has undergone a peer review.

VERTAISARVIOITU
KOLLEGIALT GRANSKAD
PEER-REVIEWED
www.tsv.fi/tunnus

The open access publication of this volume has received part funding via
Helsinki University Library.

A digital edition of a printed book first published in 2005 by the Finnish Literature Society.
Cover Design: Timo Numminen
EPUB: eLibris Media Oy

ISBN 978-951-746-665-3 (Print)
ISBN 978-952-222-814-7 (PDF)
ISBN 978-952-222-815-4 (EPUB)

ISSN 0085-6835 (Studia Fennica)
ISSN 1235-1946 (Studia Fennica Folkloristica)

DOI: http://dx.doi.org/10.21435/sff.15

A free open access version of the book is available at http://dx.doi.org/10.21435/sff.15 or by scanning this QR code with your mobile device.

BoD – Books on Demand, Nordestedt, Germany

# Contents

# Part 2 Tradition, Modernity and the Nation-State

# Preface

This book deals with the relationship between tradition and modernity and the modernness of objectifying, representing and studying folklore and oral traditions. The first section focuses on modern and tradition as modern concepts, and the conception of folklore and its study as a modern trajectory. The second section discusses the politics of folklore with regard to nationalism, and the role of folk tradition in the production of nation-state identity in Finland.

My discussion of these issues emerges from selected perspectives on postmodernism and postmodernist thinking. These were topical, and in some circles radical issues in the early 1990s, when I was taking graduate courses at the Department of Folklore and Folklife at the University of Pennsylvania in the United States and writing my doctoral dissertation. I am aware that today, more than ten years after, postmodernism seems like out-dated rhetoric, but I can excuse myself by saying that I have an antiquarian interest in things postmodern. The first section of the book draws heavily on literature from the 1980s and early 1990s because that part was originally written for the dissertation. I have used it here – changing in places the present tense to the past and adding newer references – with the belief that it still functions as a theoretical and research historical orientation to the discussion on the politics of folk tradition in the second section. I also believe that many of the points made in conjunction with postmodernism continue to deserve consideration. This is especially so in the field of folklore studies, which was never saturated with the postmodernist critique of modernism. There are academic environments in which such 'postmodernist' issues as reflexivity and representation and their implications for both ethnographic and archival research still await discovery.

In addition to my doctoral dissertation, the research conducted for this book has encompassed four different research projects and networks which all have been concerned with the politics of identity and the construction of tradition, history and heritage. Some of them have dealt directly with the topic of the present book, while others have also served as frameworks for enhancing and developing my parallel research on a multi-faceted and controversial item of political mythology and heritage production in Finland: the folklore-based narrative construction of the birth of the nation and the killing of its allegedly first foreign visitor. I will be presenting the results of this study in a forthcoming publication.

The first of my formative research projects and networks was 'Europe and the Nordic Countries: Modernization, Identification, and the Making of Traditions and Folklore', launched in 1992 with me as the project leader and sponsored by the Nordic Institute of Folklore. The work of the project culminated in the book *Making Europe in Nordic Contexts* (1996), which I edited. I hereby wish to extend my thanks to the other members of this project: Eyðun Andreassen on the Faroe Islands, Jan Garnert in Sweden, Stein R. Mathisen in Norway and Gísli Sigurðsson in Iceland.

The second international network to help me push my research forward was the project 'National Heroes: Construction and Deconstruction', sponsored by the French Ministry of Culture and Mission du Patrimoine ethnologique in Paris, together with L'Ecomusée du Creusot-Montceau (Le Creusot, France), Deutsches Hygiene-Museum (Dresden, Germany), and Verein für Volkskunde (Vienna, Austria). The network comprised of approximately 30 scholars from across Europe, culminating in three seminal meetings in 1995 and 1996 in Le Creusot, France, in Dresden, Germany and in Vienna, Austria, respectively. The project work was finalized in the book *La Fabrique des Héros,* edited by Pierre Centlivres, Daniel Fabre and Françoise Zonabend, and published by the Mission du Patrimoine ethnologique in 1998.

Between 1998 and 2001, I was a member of the coordinating committee for the Nordic research network and project 'Folklore, Heritage Politics, and Ethnic Diversity'. While the network received funding from the Nordic Academy of Advanced Study (NorFa), the Joint Committee of the Nordic Research Councils for the Humanities (NOS-H) financed my own research. In addition to these two organizations and their generosity, I wish to express my appreciation to our networkers of many nationalities as well as my fellow members in the steering group: Academy Professor Anna-Leena Siikala; Professor Barbro Klein, Director at the Swedish Collegium for Advanced Study in the Social Sciences (SCASSS) in Uppsala, Sweden; and Associate Professor Stein R. Mathisen at Finnmark College in Alta, Norway. The work of the network and project is well represented in two books. *Folklore, Heritage Politics, and Ethnic Diversity: A Festschrift for Barbro Klein* was published in 2000 by the Multicultural Centre in Botkyrka, Sweden. The second book, *Creating Diversities: Folklore, Religion and the Politics of Heritage,* was published in 2004 in the Studia Fennica Folkloristica series.

For three months in the fall of 1999, I had the pleasure to work as a guest researcher at the Centre for the Study of European Civilization (Senter for Europeiske Kulturstudier, SEK) at the University of Bergen in Norway. I hereby wish to express my gratitude to Professor Siri Meyer for inviting me to participate in the SEK project 'Det Nye' (The New). From among the many colleagues in Bergen, I especially wish to thank Professors Bente Alver and Torunn Selberg at the Department of Cultural Studies and History of Art (Institutt for Kulturstudier og Kunsthistorie, IKK). My thanks also go to the initiator of my visit, Line Alice Ytrehus, and her husband Hans-Jakob Ågotnes. Since the beginning of 2001, I have been able to concentrate full-time on my research as an Academy Research Fellow at the Academy of Finland. I thank the Research Council for Culture and Society at the Academy for granting me this position, and Academy Professor Anna-Leena Siikala for including me in her group of researchers in the project 'Myth, History, Society. Ethnic/National Traditions in the Age of Globalisation'.

In addition to those already mentioned, I wish to thank the following persons for being sources of inspiration, support and recognition: my wife Mikako Iwatake (University of Helsinki), my brother Veikko Anttonen (University of Turku), Pasi Saukkonen (University of Helsinki), Leila Virtanen, Lotte Tarkka, Ulla-Maija Peltonen and Laura Stark (University of Helsinki), Senni Timonen (Finnish Literature Society Folklore Archives in Helsinki), Seppo Knuuttila (University of Joensuu), Jorma Kalela (University of Turku), Bo Lönnqvist (University of Jyväskylä), Roger D. Abrahams (University of Pennsylvania), Alan Dundes (University of California, Berkeley), Orvar Löfgren and Jonas Frykman (University of Lund), Regina Bendix (Universität Göttingen), and Ülo Valk (University of Tartu).

An earlier version of Chapter 1 was published as 'Folklore, Modernity, and Postmodernism: A Theoretical Overview' in *Nordic Frontiers: Recent Issues in Modern Traditional Culture in the Nordic Countries*, edited by Pertti J. Anttonen and Reimund Kvideland. NIF Publications No. 27. Pp. 17–33. Turku: Nordic Institute of Folklore, 1993. Chapter 5 was first published as 'Nationalism, Ethnicity, and the Making of Antiquities as a Strategy in Cultural Representation' in *Suomen Antropologi – Journal of the Finnish Anthropological Society* 1/1994 (vol. 19/1): 19–42. It has been revised. Chapter 6 was first published as 'Introduction: Tradition and Political Identity' in *Making Europe in Nordic Contexts*, edited by Pertti J. Anttonen. NIF Publications No. 35. Pp. 7–40. Turku: Nordic Institute of Folklore, 1996. It has been revised and it also contains material from the article 'Nationalism in the Face of National and Transnational Integration and European Union Federalism', published in *Identities in Transition: Perspectives on Cultural Interaction and Integration*, edited by Jarmo Kervinen, Anu Korhonen, Keijo Virtanen. Publications of the Doctoral Program on Cultural Interaction and Integration. Pp. 67–84. Turku: Turun yliopisto, 1996.

Chapter 7 was first published as 'What is Globalization?' in *Norveg, Journal of Norwegian Folklore* 1/1999 (Vol. 42): 3–18. It has been revised. Chapter 8 was first published as 'Cultural Homogeneity and the National Unification of a Political Community' in *Folklore, Heritage Politics, and Ethnic Diversity: A Festschrift for Barbro Klein*, edited by Pertti J. Anttonen in collaboration with Anna-Leena Siikala, Stein R. Mathisen and Leif Magnusson. Pp. 253–278. Botkyrka, Sweden: Multicultural Centre, 2000. It has been revised. Chapter 9 was first published as 'Folklore, History, and 'the Story of Finland' in the book *Dynamics of Tradition: Perspectives on Oral Poetry and Folk Belief. Essays in Honour of Anna-Leena Siikala on her 60th Birthday 1st January 2003*, edited by Lotte Tarkka. Studia Fennica Folkloristica 13. Pp. 48–66. Helsinki: Finnish Literature Society, 2003. The revised version also contains material from the article 'Tradition, Modernity and Otherness: On the Political Role of History, Ethnic Diversity and 'Folk Tradition' in the Making of Modern Finland', published in *Forestillinger om 'den andre': Images of Otherness,* edited by Line Alice Ytrehus. Pp. 58–83. Kristiansand, Norway: HøyskoleForlaget / Norwegian Academic Press, 2001.

Despite the fact that most of the chapters are based on previously published articles, this book is not an anthology. The chapters are meant to form a monographic entity consisting of a theoretical foundation and an empirical application aiming to formulate a general argument concerning the topic in question, the concepts of tradition and modernity in folklore scholarship and the historically specific, sociopolitical context of its practice. I thank the two anonymous referees for the valuable insights that helped me finalize the textual framework. I also thank Leila Virtanen for checking the language and Maria Vasenkari for compiling the name index. I am honored to have the book published by the Finnish Literature Society in the Studia Fennica series.

Helsinki, 22 June 2004.
*Pertti J. Anttonen*

# A Short Introduction

Discussing the concept of 'nation', Eric Hobsbawm points out that "concepts are not part of free-floating philosophical discourse, but socially, historically and locally rooted, and must be explained in terms of these realities" (Hobsbawm 1990: 9). One of the main purposes of this book is to apply this proposition to the idea and concept of tradition, especially in the ways in which it has been used and circulated in folklore scholarship. In taking up this task, I wish to continue the 'tradition' well represented in Finnish folklore studies by Jouko Hautala: the examination of scholarly concepts (see Hautala 1957).

When studying social practices that are regarded as traditional, we must reflect upon what we mean by traditional, which is usually seen as an element of meaning in the practices that we are studying. Whose meaning is it? Is it a meaning generated by those who study tradition or those who are being studied? In both cases, particular criteria for traditionality are employed, whether these are explicated or not. The individuals, groups of people and institutions that are studied may continue to uphold their traditions or name their practices traditions without having to state in analytical terms their criteria for traditionality. The political charge inscribed in the idea of tradition does not require the explication of its cultural logics. This is a familiar phenomenon from classic nationalism and the use of traditions to legitimate the consolidation of territorial and administrative control. In recent decades, the notion of tradition has gained attention for being introduced in postcolonial arenas as a political strategy for creating (or inventing) a past that serves to legitimate aspirations for indigenous rights (see e.g. Linnekin 1983; Keesing 1989; Briggs 1996).

The licence to keep the criteria for traditionality inexplicit cannot apply to people who make the study of traditions their profession. This especially concerns those engaged in the academic field of the 'science of tradition,' a paraphrase given to folklore studies (e.g. Honko 1983; Kirshenblatt-Gimblett 1996: 252). Although interest in oral tradition, as I have written elsewhere, "usually means interest in the specimens of oral tradition, the scholarly study of oral tradition cannot do without analytical reflection on the theories of tradition and traditionality that are applied in the selection, construction, and representation of such specimens" (Anttonen 2003: 116–117). Traditions call for explanation, instead of being merely described or *used* as explanations for apparent repetitions, reiterations, replications, continuations or symbolic linking in social practice, values, meaning, culture, and history. In order to explain the concept of tradition and the category of the traditional, we must situate its use in particular historically specific discourses – ways of knowing, speaking, conceptualization and representation – in which social acts receive their meanings as traditional.

Obviously, I do not presume to be the first to draw analytical attention to the concept of tradition. Important works have been written on the subject not only in folklore studies but also in anthropology, sociology, history and philosophy. In folklore, as mentioned by Regina Bendix, tradition is "a core term" (Bendix 2002: 110). Richard Bauman writes that "Few concepts have played a more central role in the development and practice of anthropology than tradition" (Bauman 2001: 15819). In folklore studies, the coreness of this concept means that it is frequently used to both denote and qualify the folklorists' research object, oral traditions and traditional culture. But it becomes apparent in Bendix's discussion that the idea of coreness may also come to mean that the concept is somehow the property of the folklorists, as if marked by their inherited ownership. She writes that a mixture of "unease and amazement pervaded in the early 1980s" when *Tradition* by the sociologist Edward Shils (1981) and *The Invention of Tradition* by the historians Eric Hobsbawm and Terence Ranger (1983) attracted wide attention, but "Neither book acknowledged folklorists' extensive work on, or perhaps more accurately, *with* the concept of 'tradition'" (Bendix 2002: 110). Bendix may have a point in lamenting the tendency that "the labors and insights of the small discipline of folklore" seem to go unnoticed by representatives of other fields (see also Ben-Amos 1998: 272). But I wish to put more stress on the last comment in the quotation, which suggests that the concept of tradition is in frequent use in the vocabulary of folklorists, but to a much lesser degree in the focus of their scholarly analysis.

In taking up the agenda of studying tradition here, my purpose is not semantic, in the sense of mapping out the various ways in which the concept has been, can be or should be used. Instead, the approach that I have adopted emerges from an interest in epistemology and phenomenology, on the one hand, and political analysis, on the other. My starting point is that the concept of tradition is inseparable from the idea and experience of modernity, both as its discursively constructed opposition and as a rather modern metaphor for cultural continuity and historical patterning. For this reason, the discussion of the concept of tradition as well as those social processes that are regarded as traditional must be related to and contextualized within the socially constituted discourses on modernity and modernism.

The same applies to the concept of folklore, which especially in folklore scholarship conducted in languages other than English is commonly, and often without methodological reflection, treated as a synonym for the concept of tradition. Folklore as a Western and English-language concept has its foundation in the modern interest in objectifying the past and the non-modern, both temporally and spatially defined, and in documenting and conserving selected types of communication discovered in that cultural otherness. In the course of this documentation and conservation process, representations are produced mainly in entextualized form in literary collections, to be kept in such modern institutions as museums, archives and universities.

To call such representations traditions is a discursive practice that operates with particular criteria for traditionality, such as those incorporated into the discourse on nationalism, heritage, indigenous rights, or the taxonomy of folklore genres. This may – possibly intentionally – limit the discussion on traditionality to those phenomena that are classified as folklore and/or incorporated into the political rhetoric of heritage making. My preference, however, is to contextualize the folkloristic use of the idea and concept of tradition in a variety of other discourses on tradition. I realize that this is a larger undertaking to which this book can only provide a small contribution.

I wish to emphasize that my discussion on the concepts of tradition and folklore do not strive to formulate a theory of tradition, which has been called for by Pascal Boyer (1990). I am more concerned here with the constitution of the category of tradition within the discourse on the modern than in a cognitive analysis of repetition. I also wish to emphasize that I am not taking a stand in the debate concerning the so-called crisis of the field of folklore, regarding its institutional marginalization, the constraints and negative connotations of its name, and the gap between the name and its present-day scholarly signification (Bendix 1998; Kirshenblatt-Gimblett 1998a). I would contend that folklore is a rhetorical construction that has possibly outlived its modernist agenda, but still, I see its value in identifying a discursive field that makes the production of tradition and traditionality its main target of scientific analysis. Surely, its best legacies could be continued under a different name, but as a particular type of a modernist project, folklore lives and dies with the term.

Regarding my approach in discussing tradition as a category constituted within discourse on the modern, I wish to emphasize that it is not my aim to argue for the newness of that which has been claimed old, or to argue for the inauthenticity of that which has been claimed authentic. I have not set out to reveal misconceptions or 'myths'. I align myself with the so-called Hobsbawmian perspective in considering traditions as modern constructions, attributed to Hobsbawm because of his seminal book, but this perspective by no means applies literally to everything that is defined or researched as traditions. Many of the selected cultural products and practices that are studied in folklore scholarship and conserved in textual representations have a long history behind them. Their circulation is not necessarily a modern invention.

I will, however, argue that since the concepts of tradition and modern are fundamentally modern, what they aim to and are able to describe, report and denote is epistemologically modern, as that which is regarded as non-modern and traditional is appropriated into modern social knowledge through modern concepts and discursive means. While modernity, according to the classic tenet, destroys tradition, it – epistemologically speaking – creates tradition and makes tradition a modern product. For this reason, both tradition and its representation are modern, even if they signify that which is not modern.

Modernity cannot represent non-modernity without modern mediation, which therefore makes the representations of non-modernity also modern. In other words, that which is regarded – and literally, gazed at – as a specimen of non-modern traditionality does not receive its cultural meanings merely from its own history. As an object of modern study, such a specimen is inseparable from modern discourses on non-modernity. Since non-modernity can only be discussed as modernity's otherness, modern discourses on non-modernity are at the same time modern discourses on modernity. Hence the title: tradition through modernity.

# Part 1
## The Modernness of the Non-Modern

# 1. Folklore, Modernity and Postmodernism: A Theoretical Overview

*What is Postmodernism?*

In the late 1970s and early 1980s, modernism as a historical period and an ideological current of modernist ideas and ideals became an object of criticism in a topic of discourse called postmodernism. This critical discourse came into fashion especially in the visual arts, media, architecture, theater, literary studies, philosophy, and the social sciences.

Some of the major issues raised in conjunction with postmodernism were the call for cultural and semantic heterogeneity, multivocality, and the questioning of what was perceived as positivistic universalism, identified with the belief in unilinear progress, the Enlightenment ideology as the pursuit of a unified and rational image of the human being, absolute truths, universal structures, totalizing discourses and master narratives (see e.g. Harvey 1989). The discourse on postmodernism is probably best known for the French post-structuralists' emphasis upon discontinuity and difference in history (Foucault 1972), the deconstruction of metanarratives about universal historical development (Lyotard 1984) and the deconstruction of the metaphysics of language, writing and signification (Derrida 1976, 1981).

Semantically, postmodernism would imply temporal succession to modernism, and some postmodernists actually declared 'the end of modernity' in the sense of modern progress having become routine and lost its teleological basis as a movement forward (Vattimo 1988). The new is no longer qualitatively different from what precedes it, and thus signals the end of history. Another perspective would emphasize postmodernism as a new perspective on modernity and modernism, rather than being something that succeeds the modern in a temporal sense. Indeed, modernity continues to prevail while postmodernism provides reflexive distance from the premises of particular 'modernist' modes of experience, lifestyles, art styles, values, theories, and politics. For Zygmunt Bauman, postmodern stands for an opportunity; the potential for tolerance and solidarity and coming to terms with the ambivalence and ambiguity of modernity (Bauman 1991). Rather than ending modernity, postmodernism objectifies the modern age and the ideology of modernism for critical analysis by bringing into the center of attention that which modernism is regarded as having marginalized. For Néstor García Canclini, in a similar manner, postmodernity is not a stage or tendency that replaces the modern world, but rather "a way of problematizing the equivocal links that the latter has formed with the traditions it tried to exclude or overcome in constituting itself" (García Canclini 1995: 9). Matei Calinescu (1987) calls postmodernism another face of modernity.

Postmodernism has never been a strictly defined style, dogma, or ideology, and in fact, those who have participated in the discourse on postmodernism have not only found its contents or characteristics disputable but might have called into question the very existence of the postmodern as a category. Therefore, it is not surprising that postmodernism soon lost much of its rhetorical force as well as its popularity and function as an umbrella term for the critique of the modern. In fact, many of the protagonists of perspectives discussed under the umbrella of postmodernism never considered themselves postmodernists, or their perspectives in any way postmodern. The term had a certain fashionable and cliché-like ring to it, which many scholars wished to avoid. The fact that the term was even applied to mutually contradictory and exclusive perspectives added to its lack of specificity.

Since the postmodern has mainly stood for the critique of the modern, the question of what is postmodern depends on what is counted as modern. If, for example, postmodernism argues that reality is socially constructed and social categories cannot be defined 'objectively' as lists of essential traits and characteristics, such a perspective would have to be applied to the category of the postmodern as well. Since postmodernism is constructed as distinct from modernism because of its critical stance, the postmodern critique of modernism constructs modernism with its own critical gaze. As is pointed out by P. Steven Sangren, "The creation of the category 'postmodern' itself necessarily creates an 'other'" (Sangren 1988: 413).

For example, since for Jean-François Lyotard postmodern stands for incredulity toward metanarratives (see Lyotard 1984, xxiii–xxiv), any metanarrative that is found to exist represents modernism. Similarly, the Enlightenment has been evoked in postmodernism as the archetype of a one-dimensional and uncontested modernity (Calhoun 1993: 75). Indeed, modernity must itself be seen as a multivocal discourse embedded with elements or 'roots' for many of the postmodernist arguments. In addition, modernity must be seen as containing and even encouraging both critical and uncritical sentiments in conflicting, paradoxical, and often dialectical relationships to each other, which for their part contribute to the quite diverse characterizations and definitions that the postmodern as a critique of the modern has received. Consequently, in terms of political arguments, postmodernist ideas have at the same time been antimodernist and promodernist, progressive as well as counter-progressive. Bruno Latour makes a point by characterizing postmodernism as a symptom, not a fresh solution. "It lives under the modern Constitution, but it no longer believes in the guarantees the Constitution offers." (Latour 1993: 46.)

The 'ideological' concept of postmodernism is closely related to the 'cultural' concept of postmodernity. Postmodernity has generally been used to denote the culture of post-industrial societies and late capitalism, presupposing, in the words of Fredric Jameson, "some radical difference between what is sometimes called consumer society and earlier moments of the capitalism from which it emerged" (Jameson 1988: 103). Postmodernization would thus stand for a cultural shift from an industrial to a post-industrial information society, from 'high modernity' to 'late modernity', including a movement from centralized mass production towards 'post-Fordism', decentralized individualized production, and a myriad of 'taste cultures' (see e.g. Bell 1976; Featherstone 1987; Albertsen 1988; Harvey 1989).

Such a trend has, among other things, been linked to the idea of postmaterialism, which includes such elements as the rise of quality-of-life issues, new social movements such as those evolved around ecological and environmental concerns, women's and minority rights, alternative life-styles, etc. (Inglehart 1990; Dalton & Kuechler 1990). In urban areas, postmodernity came to stand for the gentrification of industrial neighborhoods, especially the changing of waterfronts from docks and factories into parks, residential areas and centers of cultural activity, as well as for the landscape of consumption in the gentrified city (Smith 1987).

## Phenomenological Hermeneutics and the Social Construction of Reality

In social scientific and humanistic research, postmodernization basically came to stand for approaches that reject the Cartesian-Kantian epistemology, which modeled social logics and the social and humanistic sciences after the positivistic natural sciences. Newer approaches were sparked off especially by Thomas S. Kuhn's perspectives on the structure of scientific culture and its revolutions (Kuhn 1962). Another major impact came from the 'phenomenologization' of social philosophical theories. In addition to the French post-structuralists, this trend included the reappraisal of William James' pragmatism (see e.g. Rorty 1979; Abrahams 1985; Mechling 1985) and Aristotelian rhetoric (see e.g. Edmondson 1984; Ricoeur 1986; White 1987), the rediscovery and recentralization of Giambattista Vico, Friedrich Nietzsche, early phenomenologists such as Edmund Husserl, Maurice Merleau-Ponty and Alfred Schutz, the phenomenological hermeneutics of Wilhelm Dilthey, Martin Heidegger, Hans-Georg Gadamer, Paul Ricoeur, etc., as well as the critical theory and neopragmatism of Jürgen Habermas and Richard Rorty.

According to the philosopher G. B. Madison, the postmodernization of philosophy and the emphasis on rhetoric and interpretation shuffled relations between two competing traditions, of which the previously marginalized one was now put in the center. In what he calls the metaphysical tradition of philosophy, from Plato through René Descartes and Immanuel Kant to Georg Wilhelm Hegel and Edmund Husserl, philosophy has been considered 'serious business', thus claiming the status of Science. This came to be contested by what he calls the counter-tradition: the Greek sophists and rhetoricians, the

19

Pyrrhonian skeptics, Michel de Montaigne, Søren Kierkegaard and Friedrich Nietzsche (Madison 1988: 106).

Similar 'lack of seriousness' or a playful spirit of negativity, deconstruction, suspicion, unmasking, satire, ridicule, jokes and punning, is claimed by Richard Bernstein to pervade in postmodern philosophy, for instance in the writings of Richard Rorty, Paul Feyerabend and Jacques Derrida (see Bernstein 1986: 59). Indeed, in its agenda to question established modernist constructions, postmodernism has often been understood as playing with categories that modernism has purported to keep separate, such as authentic and inauthentic, art and kitsch, real and fake (cf. also such folkloristic categories as 'folklore' and 'fakelore'). However, instead of merely for the fun of it, postmodern perspectives, rather seriously, challenge representations that are claimed to be authentic and thus call attention to their constructed and rhetorical character.

Accordingly, some of the most important perspectives in the study of social phenomena that followed the shift in the philosophical, epistemological and ontological premises of social sciences concern the study of social life – instead of universal structures – as processes of social praxis (Pierre Bourdieu, Clifford Geertz), experience (Victor Turner, Roger Abrahams), performance (Erving Goffman), language, dialogue, and polyphony (Mikhail Bakhtin), and intersubjectivity and intertextuality (Roland Barthes, Julia Kristeva). Other contributing insights concerned the growing emphasis on narration and rhetoric in the social construction of reality. In what has been called postmodern reflexivity, there was a turn "away from positivist and formalist epistemologies to an epistemology that sees reality as created, mediated, and sustained by human narratives" (Mechling 1991: 43; see also Clifford 1986).

Thus, instead of objectivism and positivistic empiricism, which would make claims for 'true representations of objective reality', social processes came to be analyzed from a hermeneutic and constructivist perspective, according to which reality and human categories are socially constructed and reconstructed in a continuous process of interpretation and contextualization. As emphasized by Hans-Georg Gadamer, all understanding is interpretation instead of a correct representation of an objective state of affairs (Gadamer 1976: 350). As a pragmatic process, the understanding of a given text is inseparable from its application (Gadamer 1975: 264, 274), which also signifies that understanding is transformative, producing new meanings.

Accordingly, as meaning lies in the realm of the existential-practical, that is, in the transformations that texts produce in the reading and interpreting subject, the study of meaning came to concern such questions as what a text has to say here and now, in a particular historical moment and situation for a particular individual or a group of human agents. Yet, this would not deny textual history, as the history of a text and its existence as a transtemporal entity is part of its meaning in a particular interpretative context.

The phenomenological fact that there is always a context for a text – whether a written text or a social act that is 'read' in the sense of interpreted – anchors it in social reality and allows it to have decidable meanings. Thus, in phenomenological hermeneutics, the object of understanding has a temporal mode of being, for which reason it is never something static or time-less but always historically specific and changing, in a process of becoming. For this reason, as claimed by Gary B. Madison, phenomenological herme-neutics provides models for the theoretical and methodological grounding of interpretation as practical reasoning, rhetoric or persuasive argumentation (Madison 1988: 114).

It must be stressed in this connection that when discussing hermeneutics, one should make a distinction between the 'classical' hermeneutical tradition of Friedrich Schleiermacher, Emilio Betti, and E. D. Hirsch, which is founded upon logical positivism, and the phenomenological hermeneutics of Gadamer and Ricoeur. Gadamer distances himself from classical hermeneutics by not creating a method or technique for reading and interpreting texts, as is the case in classical hermeneutics, which seeks better ways of determining the correct meaning of texts (Madison 1988: 110). Dialogic anthropology is based on Gadamerian and phenomenological hermeneutics (see e.g. Crapanzano 1990; Maranhão 1990). Its point about the dialogical nature of the creation of meaning can be juxtaposed with Aristotelian rhetoric, which emphasizes how logos – text – never receives its meanings independently – that is, in abstraction – but as situated knowledge created by ethos and pathos; ethos denoting how the speaker makes him or herself authoritative and persuasive, and pathos, how the speaker adopts particular ways to speak to a particular audience (see e.g. Edmondson 1984; Ricoeur 1986; Kalela 1993).

## Politics, Poetics and Reflexivity

The awareness of the interpretative and rhetorical basis of social action, and therefore also of the rhetorical basis of the *study* of social action – that is, social and humanistic sciences, including folklore research – has meant, in the language of postmodernism, not only the end of objectivism but the end of totalizing discourses. Modernist innocence, in accordance with Cartesian dualism, claimed independence for the subject from the object, as well as mind from body, spirit from matter. Modernist innocence also claimed im-partiality for the scholar. This innocence has in postmodernism been replaced by what could be described as a Merleau-Pontian duality between the object and the subject, the exterior and the interior, the corporeal and the psychic – and by the awareness of the fact that far from being innocent and non-ar-gumentative, all social scientific and humanistic research makes statements and can therefore be utterly argumentative and political.

In the duality and dialectics of matter and spirit, verbal expressions receive their meanings in relation to material objects and socially constructed space, and conversely, matter receives its meanings in relation to verbal construc-tions in social discourses. Thus, the rejection of Cartesian dualism can also be regarded as a call to the relativization of the academic division between social and natural sciences. Within research into culture – including studies of traditional culture – this would mean the deconstruction of its conventional division into studies of 'spiritual culture' and 'material culture'.

Similarly, instead of regarding time and space as mere settings for social action, or spatial and social relations as epistemically separate, postmodern perspectives emphasize the dialectical relationship between the spatial and the temporal in the constitution of the social and in the construction of social and cultural meaning. Spatiality in social action is not a representation of spatiality as a mental ordering (Soja 1985: 102), but instead, social relations create spatial relations and spatial relations create social relations (Gregory & Urry 1985: 3). Since spatiality is reciprocal and dialectic with temporality, the temporality of social life is rooted in spatiality and the spatiality of social life is rooted in temporality (Soja 1989: 129–130).

Such perspectives on the spatiality and temporality of social processes have questioned the idea of cultures as holistic systems, and called for a re-evaluation of cultural boundaries as not fixed but flexible and questionable, as blurred (see e.g. Geertz 1980). The task of cultural research is no longer to 'discover' overarching, functionalistic, structuralistic, or metaphysical systems behind observable representations but, from a hermeneutic perspective, to describe the social praxis in which culture is continuously recreated and reconstructed through public symbols and symbolic behavior by actors making interpretations (see e.g. Geertz 1973), producing social transformations (see e.g. Turner 1969, 1974) or playing games (e.g. Goffman 1959, 1974, 1981).

While for Lévi-Strauss, for example, scientific anthropology meant abstaining from making judgments, both at home and in the field (see Lévi-Strauss 1967: 384–385), today the ethnographer's attempt to be objective and impartial is deemed impossible, since knowledge is understood to exist in direct relationship with power (see e.g. Foucault 1980). As "objects of knowledge are not things-in-themselves but discursive objects which are the products of rules of discourse" (Turner 1984: 174), for the ethnographer, the truth about "how things really are out there", or, for the historian, "wie es eigentlich gewesen" cannot exist independently from the discursive character of knowledge and its production. "No history is innocent of the purposes of its author", writes Peter Hamilton (2000: 21). In a social sense – as already pointed out by Giambattista Vico in the late 18th century (see e.g. Herzfeld 1987; Dick 1989) – truth cannot be anything but a construction and a representation, and as such, subjective, interpretative, rhetorical, and political.

The awareness of the rhetorical and political character of scholarship and the discursive nature of knowledge, based on particular relationships between the subject and the object, has been part of the heightened interest in reflexivity, that is, consciousness of being conscious, thinking about thinking (Myerhoff & Ruby 1982: 1; see also Babcock 1980; Klein 1993). The awareness of looking at oneself looking at the other, and how these simultaneous gazes qualify and construct each other, has made the anthropologist / ethnologist / folklorist aware of how ethnography is in a fundamental way an act of representation that cannot be independent of the discursive processes in which the objectified other is made an object. In addition, the objectified social processes of the other are in essential ways mediated through the subjective processes of the self. Therefore, the study of social action as processes of interpretation cannot take place without the scholar's awareness of his or her own or other scholars' processes of interpretation when trying to make sense of and report on other people's behavior. From this perspective, reflexivity about the metalevels of signification has become virtually synonymous with being scientific (Myerhoff & Ruby 1982: 28), and conversely, ignorance of such matters and aspects of meaning is doomed to produce quasi-science.

The call for reflexivity about knowledge claims as a criterion for scientific validity has paralleled the so-called linguistic turn in philosophy and social sciences, which has foregrounded language as discourse in all social studies. Meaning, from this perspective, is actively produced in discursive practices, in processes of language use. In accordance with this trend, scholars have become reflexive about how they themselves 'invent' their objects through their own discursive and metadiscursive processes. This has meant, among other things, the understanding of how scholarly analyses of social life are intrinsically works of textualization and writing. In anthropology, this awareness has led to the understanding of ethnography as a text-making activity and a particular literary genre (Marcus 1980; Marcus & Cushman 1982; Sperber 1987). From a phenomenological perspective, this means that the observation of culture is inseparable from the ways in which one both structures experience and reports on that experience. Writing thus constructs the culture and social reality that is being depicted. Therefore, instead of 'telling as it is', the ethnographer 'invents' and 'writes' culture (see Clifford & Marcus 1986; Kirshenblatt-Gimblett 1988; Clifford 1988b; Sanjek 1990).

As a literary genre with its particular generic features and means of argumentation and persuasion, ethnography – as practiced in anthropology, folklore studies and other cultural sciences – produces narratives that are evaluated and authorized according to how they employ the particular generic requirements expected from such literary products. Since such products are made to exist because of particular motivations and argumentative purposes, which are both academic and non-academic, claiming them as scientific calls for the explication of the ways of writing – the poetics and aesthetics – as well as the motivations and meanings – the politics – of the ethnographic practice and the entire research process as a process of objectification.

Such explication can be said to be essentially important in folklore studies, which not only employs particular literary and rhetorical means in the production and publication of research, as do other disciplines in cultural sciences, but studies verbal artistry through texts often created – entextualized into writing – by the scholar him or herself. This does not only call for the problematization of entextualization and transcription, as has been done in ethnopoetics (see e.g. Briggs 1988; Anttonen 1994a), but makes it essential to see how orality, in the process of adopting oral products into a folklore taxonomy, is transformed into literature, following models that are taken from literary categories and traditions (see also Tarkka 1993).

In anthropology, in which there has been a great deal of reflexive discussion on the poetics and politics of research for a couple of decades now, ethnographic accounts have lost the epistemic power that was earlier attached to them as objective truths, as testimonies of those 'who were there'. As a consequence of understanding this, anthropology faced a crisis of representation, which caused scholars to call for research that would relocate its epistemic power, without claiming to represent the cultural subject in any 'real' or 'objective' manner but emphasizing its own selective and political nature. Similar discussion in folklore studies was called for by, for example, Margaret Mills, who urged folklorists to reflect upon

> the verbal constructions of ourselves and others and the rhetorics that frame them as the products of our particular historical positions (macro as well as micro) and of the distribution of power within our social groups, which makes certain rhetorical strategies count as 'truth' (i.e. 'convincing representation') and others not. (Mills 1990: 7.)

Such reflexivity on the politics of representation and argumentation is an epistemological question, but it is often also seen as a question concerning ethics and morals. As regards the difference between ethics and morals, sometimes used interchangeably, it is suggested here that ethics refer to the issues of accurateness and fairness in representation and reconstruction, while morals refer to the scholar's rhetorical and political purposes and goals in relation to his or her audience and the society and community in which he or she lives and functions. In other words, the way in which scholars reconstruct the sociocultural reality they have studied and the way they represent (speak for and give voice to) the people involved is an ethical question. The way in which scholars use their knowledge and social position as mediators and interpreters of this knowledge for their own ends is a moral question. Such a perspective is, of course, based on the notion that knowledge always exists in a rhetorical context, both in relation to its source and its target (audience), and therefore, all scholarship finds its motivation and argumentative basis from being an activity that produces knowledge for a purpose. For this reason, these varying purposes can and should be reflected upon.

Anthropology is a field of scholarship that has traditionally focused on non-Western cultures, thus representing a scholarly interest that is at the same time embedded with an exoticizing gaze extended from the West to the Rest, as well as from 'modernity' to 'tradition'. There is also an undeniable racialist aspect in this, as emphasized, for example, by William S. Willis, Jr. He says in his "minimal definition of anthropology" that "To a considerable extent, anthropology has been the social science that studies dominated colored peoples – and their ancestors – living outside the boundaries of modern white societies" (Willis 1974: 123).

Anthropology's issue with representation has not only been academic but also concerns the people and communities that anthropologists make as their objects. Indeed, one of the most important features of postmodernization in anthropology has been the critique of modernism as an epistemic system that has supported Western hegemony over the non-Western as a cultural and political subject. Not only are non-Western peoples today contesting the authority with which Western ethnographers have represented them, but anthropologists themselves have sought to deconstruct the discipline's colonial encounter (e.g. Asad 1973; Said 1978; Crapanzano 1980; Clifford &

Marcus 1986). A postcolonial and 'postmodern' ethnography acknowledges a 'postmodern world system' based on new kinds of global relations, in which the decline of Western hegemony and the growing influence of non-Western countries and non-governmental interest groups in global economics and politics challenge the center–periphery structures that the colonizing West established in its modernization and industrialization process (see e.g. Breckenridge & van der Veer 1993; Appadurai 1996; Hall 2000b).

Postmodernity and the subsequent new global relations have resulted in, among other things, the deconstruction of the ideological practice that separated the anthropologist's present from the objectified non-Western cultures not only in space but also in time. Johannes Fabian showed in his book *Time and the Other* (1983) how by constructing the 'ethnographic present', in which a culture is depicted in its imagined state prior to its 'corruption in modernization', anthropologists have distanced their research objects from coevalness and co-existence, from participating in the same space and time relations of the present with the anthropologists and their societies. According to Fabian, there has been "a persistent and systematic tendency to place the referent(s) of anthropology in a Time other than the present of the producer of anthropological discourse" (Fabian 1983: 31). Fabian's arguments are also essential when discussing the practices by which the discipline of folklore – with its allochronic synonym of 'tradition research' – has made its objects.

To be sure, folklore research has been moving towards the aforementioned perspectives ever since the 1960s. It is the adoption of phenomenological thinking by way of William James's pragmatism that led many folklorists to reconsider, for example, Saussurean structural linguistics as the foundation for the study of language and linguistic phenomena. Pragmatistic folklore research also emerged to replace the traditional item-centered notion, according to which folklore in performance is a manifestation of folklore as a system, as language is for the structuralist. One of the scholars responsible for this development is Dell Hymes, under whose influence many American performance-school folklorists moved closer to sociolinguistics and the ethnography of speaking, which emphasize language and linguistic phenomena as constructions that receive their forms and meanings in social interaction, in use, praxis, and application. Accordingly, the pragmatic approach adopted by such scholars as Richard Bauman, Roger Abrahams and Dan Ben-Amos is based on the understanding that social life is communicatively constituted in practice, and therefore that which is called folklore is the situated use of particular communicative means in the accomplishment of social life (Bauman 1989: 177).

For many folklorists in the 1970s and 1980s this trend came to mean a focus on 'folklore in context', with a general emphasis on context dependence in the understanding of cultural phenomena and their meaning. Yet, a more pragmatistically oriented approach would call attention to the ways in which texts and performances are embedded with cues for their decontextualization, entextualization, and recontextualization (Bauman & Briggs 1990; Briggs & Bauman 1992; see also Bauman & Briggs 2003: 312). Instead of focusing on how folklore is context-dependent, such scholars as Charles Briggs and Richard Bauman, following Mikhail Bakhtin's dialogical approach to language (see Bakhtin 1981; Todorov 1984a), would look at elements that make it possible for folklore to be detached from particular contexts and attached to others. These are factors that make folklore transmissible and therefore usable as formalized arguments in social interaction.

The change of perspective in which folklore has come to be studied in terms of its argumentative purposes and rhetorical means – in terms of politics and poetics – may not seem 'postmodern' to all scholars involved. Yet, it is not without foundation to conceive of the adoption of sociolinguistic, phenomenological and pragmatistic perspectives as a way to oppose the modernist project of folklore studies as an inheritor to Romantic Nationalism on the one hand and positivism on the other, and as an unreflected ideological servant to the identity politics of the nation-state.

Whether postmodern or not, a great deal of present-day folklore research follows the theoretical premises established as a result of the linguistic turn in philosophy, sociology, and anthropology. This should not, however, be seen as a one-way street, since these perspectives have led cultural analysis in general, and sociologically oriented cultural studies in particular, to the expressive forms that have been of special interest to folklorists. As stated by Alessandro Duranti, "a theory of culture can be expressed not only in the symbolic oppositions found in ritual performances or in the meta-statements about what counts and what doesn't count, or what is appropriate and what is not appropriate, but also in the words and turns exchanged among people while teasing, arguing, instructing, gossiping, joking, or telling – rather, co-telling – narratives of personal significance." (Duranti 1993: 215–216.)

It is the strong belief of the present writer that scholars in folklore studies would raise the analytical level of their field if they paid even more attention to the ideological, theoretical and methodological premises of folklore scholarship, to the way it makes its object, the rhetorics of its practice, and its assumed role and contribution in the making of modernity and modern society. To be sure, folklore studies became its own branch of social and academic discourse not only through its focus on particular expressive forms known among a particular section of the population (poetry, memory, or lore of 'the folk', which in Europe has generally meant the non-elite, especially the peasant class), or through dealing with these in particular methodological ways. Folklore studies became its own branch of scholarship through particular argumentative and ideological positions in the modern and modernizing societies in which it was practiced. One of the main purposes of this book is to try and show how postmodernism and postmodernity provide apt frameworks for discussing the discipline and how the assignments and expectations set for it are fundamentally entwined and embedded in modernism and the experience of modernity. Another main purpose is to apply this understanding to a particular historical setting where representations of vanishing folk traditions have served the production of modernity.

# 2. Tradition In and Out of Modernity

*Modern and Traditional – A Contradiction in Terms?*

The word 'modern' is simultaneously an old word and a modern word. Meaning 'recent', 'up-to-date', 'new' or 'fashionable', it is derived from the Latin adjective and noun *modernus,* which was coined during the Middle Ages from the adverb *modo,* meaning 'just now' (Calinescu 1987: 13; see also Williams 1976: 174; Wallgren 1989: 36). Since the Middle Ages, it has taken root in many modern languages and become one of the most important concepts in the categorization of time and in the perception of temporal change. As a temporal category, the word 'modern' predicates the present, that which is 'just now'. Discourse on the modern is discourse on the present, about making propositions concerning that which is now, what the present arguably is like. Yet, since the adverb 'modo' is the ablative form of 'modus', meaning measure or manner, modern as a temporal category does not merely predicate time but measures it as well. As such, it creates relations.[1]

Indeed, one of the key elements in the word 'modern' is that it is a temporal category that also constructs its own otherness. It is not only used to predicate the present, but also to mark how this predication draws a distinction between the present and the non-present. It emphasizes that the present – meaning both the present time and the present moment – represents a fundamental break from the past, the past time and the past moment. 'Modern' in the sense of 'just now' breaks away from that which is not 'just now'. It does not simply indicate succession, but emphatically separates the present from the past, from that which is not modern. Bruno Latour notes that 'modern' – in the sense of a new regime, an acceleration, a rupture, a revolution in time – is doubly asymmetrical, as "it designates a break in the regular passage of time, and it designates a combat in which there are victors and vanquished" (Latour 1993: 10).

Yet, instead of denoting any given break between any given moments of the present and the past, the concept of modern has come to denote a particular historical period, style, socio-cultural formation and mode of experience. It is Western modernity, the post-medieval era in the history of European or Western civilization that is regarded as being intrinsically different from what precedes it in time and space. This is called the 'modern age' or the 'modern period', signifying a stage of cultural development called Modernity. According to Stuart Hall, David Held and Gregor McLennan, modernity "is that distinct and unique form of social life which characterizes modern societies" (Hall et al. 2000: 426). This is regarded as being markedly distinct from all other eras before it as well as from coevally existing civilizations, cultures, or ways of life elsewhere in the world. In this regard, 'modern' is both a temporal and a spatial concept – a reified category of time, history, civilization and development.

The discourse on modernity is discourse on change, accelerating change (Wallgren 1999: 195). As such, it is discourse on the surpassing, even rejection, of that which prevailed prior to a given change, or what seems to have suspended this change. Within this discourse, the changes in lifestyles and values, social organization, styles in artistic expression, technology, etc., that have taken place due to modernization, industrialization, enlightenment, the rationalization of society, the secularization of political power and sciences, nationalization, market capitalism, the development of parliamentary democracy, etc., have been conceptualized in ways which have emphasized the uniqueness of modernity in human history. Modernity is regarded as being fundamentally different from all previous times – and by conclusion, from all previous modernities.

The inclusion of such changes and processes in the category of the 'modern' is not merely descriptive. Calling them aspects of modernization and/or manifestations of modernity 'premodernizes' earlier social institutions and practices in more than temporal ways. The distinction constructs a qualitative difference. Conveying the meaning of improvement and advance, modernity is conceived of as modern in relation to the non-modern, which is attributed with a variety of denominations, labels and characterizations. These include premodern, old, antique, old-fashioned, conservative, classic, classical, primitive, feudal, and traditional.

The discursive practice of creating and constructing difference makes modernity not only an arena of perpetual novelties but also a perpetual process of comparison. The discourse on modernity is a comparative discourse that does not merely register apparent differences between that which is regarded as modern and that which is categorized outside the sphere of the modern. Instead of merely registering differences, discourse on modernity constructs these differences in accordance with their argumentative position to that which is regarded as modern. Modernity and the modern are, consequently, constructed through their constitutive others. The observed or discovered spatiotemporal cultural differences outside the sphere of modernity receive their meanings through these discursive comparisons – through the discourse of difference.

In the context of Western or European modernity and civilization, the cultural otherness of the non-modern has been projected onto at least four domains of knowledge: The earlier times in European history; the non- or semi-Christian socio-cultural formations, beliefs and practices in the geographically marginal areas of Europe and its high culture; the non-Western societies, cultures and civilizations outside of Christian Europe and its extensions in North America; and human childhood, making the mental and cultural development from childhood to adulthood appear a process of modernization. The story of European modernity is a story about these hierarchical oppositions. The discourse on modernity aligns cultural distinctions with other hierarchical oppositions such as universal versus singular, form versus substance, and sensible versus sensuous.

In the Renaissance a contrast was established between 'modern' and 'ancient'. Western history came to be divided into three eras: Antiquity, the Middle Ages, and Modernity. This division indicated a historical development that was characterized and evaluated with the metaphors of light and darkness, as well as wakefulness and sleep. Light as a metaphor for knowledge, reason and intellect was adopted from Aristotle, but it was also one of the key symbols of Christianity. Such language symbolism associated classical antiquity with resplendent light, conceived of the Middle Ages as the nocturnal and oblivious 'Dark Ages', and made modernity a time of emergence from darkness, a time of awakening and 'renascence' (Calinescu 1987: 20). The Enlightenment ideology continued this symbolism in its very name (see e.g. Hulme and Jordanova 1990: 3–4) as well as in viewing pre-Christianity as 'pagan darkness'.

The symbolism of light was not only applied to temporal but also to spatial relations. Modern Christian Europe, especially its predominantly Protestant countries, together with their civilizational extensions in North America, came to be seen as representing the time and space of light. Europe was synonymized with Christendom, while in contrast, the 'dark', pagan and medieval ages found a cognitive parallel with the 'Dark Africa'.

The establishing of the roots of the Renaissance and Enlightenment symbolism of light in the philosophical tradition of Hellenic Antiquity created a civilizational genealogy that was yet another indication of the changing view on European history and its periodization. While in the Middle Ages *antiquus* had denoted anyone in the undifferentiated past, whether Christian or not, in the early Renaissance 'antiquity' came to denote a privileged and exemplary portion of the past: the pagan classical times and the authors of Greece and Rome (Calinescu 1987: 59). Antiquity and classicism as temporal others were regarded as sources of inspiration for the making of the Renaissance present.

This relationship continued in 19th-century Romanticism and Neo-Humanism and it is still present in the idea that the core of Europe (including the present-day European Union) and its civilizational identity lies in its Latin and Hellenic heritage. The politics of such heritage making has been discussed by, among others, Jonathan Friedman, according to whom Greece, throughout European development after the Renaissance, was incorporated into an emergent European identity as a legitimate ancestor, making the Greeks primordial Europeans. In this process, Europe came to be imagined as a cultural landscape in which its claimed heritage drew a genealogical link to that which was regarded as modernity's temporal other, antiquity. Simultaneously this heritage line would deny a link to its spatial others: the symbolic systems and constructions of Islam and the Orient. The heritage of Antiquity (now with a capital A) would contribute to making Europe the sphere of modernity, while its spatial otherness came to signify the lack of modernity. In addition to becoming a political opposition whose influence must be monitored and controlled by Christian Europe, Islam became – in a discourse that Edward Said in his ground-breaking work (1978) termed Orientalism – an exotic, romantic and mysterious Other.

As modernity became a synonym for the European and the Western – in a process that Dipesh Chakrabarty (2000) discusses as the deprovincialization of Europe – it denied modernity elsewhere and privileged the West in being modern in more than temporal sense. In addition, it also served to indicate how 'modern' is an ideational and as such, an ideological category, a product of Western modernism. From this ideological perspective, non-Western cultures or civilizations are not modern unless they *become* modern by adopting features of Western modernity. Modernity is thus a Western export product.

This perspective has also resulted in producing the present-day tendency to view both the political conflicts and cultural differences between, for example, Islamic countries and Christian Western countries as collisions between tradition and modernity. Tradition here means, among other things, a close link between religion and politics while modernity is regarded as being characterized by secular politics. A recent example of this in current world politics is the characterization of Islamic fundamentalism and anti-American terrorism as antimodernism. Such a proposition is based not only on the synonymization of modernity with Western civilization, which allegedly makes a clear distinction between religion and politics, but also on the equation of modernity with given economic and global policies by governments and multinational enterprises representing countries within the sphere of Western civilization. From this perspective, political, religious and moral opposition, for example, to the international or global interests of the United States or American commercial enterprises might be regarded as a refusal to adopt Western modernity, a refusal to modernize.

Let me take a couple of recent statements as cases in point. The first one is from the American political scientist Francis Fukuyama, whose teleologically oriented book – as well as his famous 1989 article – on the end of history and the victory of modern liberalist democracy after the collapse of Soviet Communism gained wide publicity in the early 1990s (see Held 2000: 442–447). After the September 2001 attack on the World Trade Center towers in New York City, Fukuyama asked whether there is something inherent about Islam that makes Muslim societies "particularly resistant to modernity" (Fukuyama 2001; also quoted in Dyer 2001). For Fukuyama, modernity has its cultural basis in Christianity and its universalism. By definition, this approach categorizes all cultural production within the Islamic sphere as modernity's otherness.

The second example comes from Arthur Schlesinger, Jr., who served as a special assistant to the U.S. presidents John F. Kennedy and Lyndon B. Johnson in the 1960s and is a recipient of two Pulitzer Prizes. He said in a widely publicized interview that Islamic civilization today conveys "a great resentment of modernity" (Katsuta 2002: 1). The terrorists who attacked the World Trade Center with airplanes and communicated with transistor radios and by email were, according to Schlesinger, "using the instruments of modernity against modernity" (loc. cit.).

## Modernity's Temporal Others

In the late 17th century, modernity and the modern were polarized against the ancient in a cultural debate – or a Culture War (see DeJean 1997) – that is generally known as the Quarrel between the Ancients and the Moderns. Those identified as the Ancients preferred to continue valorizing Antiquity and the classical literary models, while those identified as the Moderns did not. According to Matei Calinescu, such thinkers and writers as Montaigne, Francis Bacon, Descartes, Charles Perrault and Fontenelle attempted to liberate reason from medieval Scholasticism as well as from what has been described as the Renaissance idolatry of classical antiquity. In this project, modernity represented rationalism and progress against antiquity's authority, on the one hand, and its barbaric customs, on the other (see Calinescu 1987: 23ff.; see also Levine 1999).

The so-called discovery of the American Continent and of non-European cultures elsewhere during the 15th, 16th and 17th centuries created an awareness of ways of life that differed or were felt to differ from those known in Europe at the time (see Cocchiara 1981; Todorov 1984b; Sörlin 1986; Lopez 1986; Hall 2000b). Most of these discoveries were legitimated with economic, political, religious and ideological (self-)interests, which, among other things, included the argument for Europe's central position in the world (see Hall 2000b: 197–201). In addition to the Eurocentric worldview, the discoveries as well as the eventual colonization of the discovered created a new way of talking about the modern, and provided for new cultural positions against which the modern was conceptualized. In addition to a temporal category, with which modernity had been distinguished from earlier forms of European civilization, modern also came to denote a spatial category that was used to distinguish Western civilization from coeval non-Western socio-cultural formations.

Because of an evolutionary framework, the other socio-cultural formations were not only regarded as belonging to spatial otherness. Since they were seen as representing earlier phases in the allegedly linear development of mankind, they were regarded as belonging to temporal otherness as well – regardless of their coevalness. Non-Western societies were distinguished from Western modern societies by characterizing them as 'traditional' or 'primitive' – and eventually as 'developing' – thus referring not only to their alleged simplicity or crudity but also to their belonging to an earlier stage in the human development towards modernity. Especially for the evolutionist anthropologists in the 19th century, the customs of contemporary primitives were of interest only because these were regarded as primeval (Leach 1970: 10). One hundred years later, the anthropologist Claude Lévi-Strauss wrote how "I went to the ends of the earth in search of what Rousseau called 'the barely perceptible advances of the earliest times'" (Lévi-Strauss 1967: 310).

The evolutionary scheme of modernity has also characterized the historical process in which the culture of the European lower classes, and especially the cultural practices of the rural and other marginal populations, have become objects in a similar 'discourse of discovery' (see e.g. Cocchiara 1981). Much of the scholarly interest in folk and peasant cultures has been historical and has been aimed at the reconstruction of past social knowledge. But in addition to historical reconstruction, this process has entailed historical *construction* in the political context of producing modernity. In the historically specific process of making modern Europe and its others, the culture of selected marginal groups, for example the material objects, ritual practices and 'lore' of those that are called the 'folk', has received much of its meaning as an object of discovery. The objectified cultural practices and products have not only provided representations of difference and otherness but they have also functioned as prerequisites for constructing the category of the modern from which they are separated.

In addition to being objects of historical interest, the cultural practices and products of selected marginal groups have become objects of a 'discovering gaze' that does not merely discover but appropriates the 'discovered' into discourses on application. I will discuss in later chapters how the use value of the discovered as ethnographic discoveries and sources of collectibles is determined on the basis of their capacity to yield symbols and tokens of both difference and historical progression – especially for the making of the modern nation-state and its modern discourses on national symbolism. The subjects of traditionality are thus both objects and subjects of modern nationalism and the modern practice of ethnography. The collectibles from non-modernity, as specimens of antiquities and historical documents, speak for the modernness of the societies that collect and display them.

For this reason, the motivation to 'discover' has a crucial effect on the meaning and value that is attached to the objects of the said discovery. When social and cultural practices in particular historically specific contexts become objects of research through being objects of discovery, the discourse on discovery becomes an essential framework in the conceptualization of such practices. Accordingly, their status and meaning as objects of research cannot be discussed independently from their status and meaning as objects of discovery. Indeed, any study of cultural and social practices is inseparable from the ideological and political motivations that draw the scholar's attention to such practices and thus transform them into study objects.

Another aspect of this issue is that the modern discoveries of the non-modern do not merely discover but also cover up, just as the projection of light onto one spot casts a shadow on another. The discoveries can be metaphorically characterized as gazes, and like light, gaze creates difference. Conceptualized as modernity's otherness, the culture of the people in the rural and pre-industrial societies of Europe and in other, perhaps more 'exotic' societies elsewhere, has in modern times become key material for a discourse on difference, which is also a discourse on the standard and the deviation. A classic example of such discourse on difference is the idealization of the non-moderns, for example in Montaigne or Rousseau's tradition, as 'free peasants' or 'noble savages' (see e.g. Cocchiara 1981: 13–28; Hall 2000b: 217–219; Mathisen 2004). Their communities in 'primitive happiness' have been regarded as being free from private property and other Western and modern 'corruptions'. Such ideas correspond to the tendency of viewing modernity as a site of inauthenticity, of which Dean MacCannell writes as follows: "For moderns, reality and authenticity are thought to be elsewhere: in other historical periods and other cultures, in purer, simpler lifestyles." (MacCannell 1989: 3.)

In accordance with this tendency, modern people continue to locate positively charged aspects of cultural continuity and collectiveness in places or chronotopes (see Bakhtin 1981: 84) that are conceptualized as otherness to Western modernity. Such timeplaces include, in addition to the 'authenticity' and 'innocence' of childhood, the medieval age in Europe or the present-day Orient, where 'ageless' and 'profound' traditions are felt to speak for a kind of social well-being that Westerners have lost due to their modernization. Not all of this discourse on non-modern virtuousness is mere Romantic escapism or condescending rhetoric to the noble non-Westener. As has been pointed out by Eric Hobsbawm, it has played a notable role in the formation of Western social criticism (Hobsbawm 1982: 3).

## Tradition as Modernity's Otherness

Both instead of and in addition to antiquity and classicism, it became common during the 19th and 20th centuries to characterize that which modernity is distinguished from as 'tradition' and 'traditionality'. This temporal categorization has contributed to the common practice of conceptualizing tradition and modernity as oppositions. In other words, directly related to the processes of modernization and the idea of cultural evolution in it, tradition and modernity have been constructed as dichotomous categories. Tradition is placed in the cultural otherness of modernity and on a unilinear continuum in which modernity succeeds and replaces chronologically – and even destroys – that which is traditional.

According to Diarmuid Ó Giolláin, the dichotomy between modernity and tradition has a historical foundation in the change in meaning of the word 'modern'. Ó Giolláin writes that in the course of the 19th and 20th centuries, the word modern "took on the connotation of 'improved' from the older – though surviving – connotation of 'belonging to the present', as opposed to 'ancient'. 'Modernization' originally referred to the alteration of buildings and of spelling, but it came to mean something undoubtedly desirable. (…) A key implication of modernization is that tradition prevents societies from achieving progress. Hence to be modern is to turn one's back on tradition, to live in the present and be orientated only towards the future." (Ó Giolláin 2000: 12–13.) For this reason, according to Ó Giolláin, "The modern age is inherently destructive of traditions" (Ó Giolláin 2000: 12).

The dichotomy of modernity and tradition constructs a historical narrative according to which social life and societies are first based on tradition, signifying thus static cultural continuity and conservatism, while modernity follows tradition, signifying cultural change and the end of tradition. Tradition here is a metaphor for permanence and stability (see e.g. Eisenstadt 1974: 2; Finnegan 1991: 107), while modern is a metaphor for change and innovation (see e.g. Calinescu 1987: 3). But in addition to exemplifying a metaphorical relationship, the synonymization of change and modernity makes all changes agents in the eradication of tradition, which then makes 'tradition' a denomination for pre-change.

The dichotomy of tradition and modernity is a modern theoretical axiom on social change, according to which modernization stands for the decrease and eventual disappearance of tradition. The dichotomy is built upon a theory that has become so influential that it can be argued to direct cognitive patterns in conceptualizing and discussing modernity – as well as tradition and traditionality. As put by Harold Rosenberg, "The famous 'modern break with tradition' has lasted long enough to have produced its own tradition" (Rosenberg 1959: 9).

More and more criticism in anthropology and sociology has been targeted at this dichotomy. Paul Gilroy wants to rethink "the concept of tradition so that it can no longer function as modernity's polar opposite" (Gilroy 1995: 188). Arjun Appadurai writes that "One of the most problematic legacies of grand Western social science (Auguste Comte, Karl Marx, Ferdinand Toennies, Max Weber, Émile Durkheim) is that it has steadily reinforced the sense of some single moment – call it the modern moment – that by its appearance creates a dramatic and unprecedented break between past and present" (Appadurai 1996: 2–3). John B. Thompson writes in a similar manner that the notion that tradition disappears in the face of modernity has come to be regarded as "one of the most powerful legacies of classical social thought" (Thompson 1996: 91). Because of this legacy, 'tradition' continues to denote, in sociological discourse all that is regarded as conservative, static and undynamic. In these conceptualizations, change takes place only in the modern, and in fact, change denotes and is indicative of modernity, while tradition denotes the lack of change and the lack of modernity, even resistance to change. Recent discussions on detraditionalization and post-traditionality have offered renewed insights into the idea of a fundamental rupture as well as the dichotomous relationship between tradition and modernity (see e.g. Giddens 1994). To what extent these provide a dramatic departure from the sociological legacy remains to be debated (see e.g. Thompson 1996: 89–90; Siikala 2000: 64–68; Bauman & Briggs 2003: 306–307).

As a social theory, the dichotomy of tradition and modernity has been used to designate two different types of societies and communities, traditional and modern, which are regarded as mutually exclusive and standing in historically succeeding positions to each other. In sociology and anthropology, some of the major ways of discussing the historical process from premodernity to modernity have been the polarization of *Gemeinschaft* and *Gesellschaft* (Ferdinand Tönnies), mechanical and organic solidarity (Émile Durkheim), traditional and rational hegemony (Max Weber), and small tradition and great tradition (Robert Redfield). Similar polarizations include simple and complex societies, folk culture and official culture, and folk culture and mass culture. In folklore studies, it has not been uncommon to operate with the temporal opposition of 'in the olden times' and 'nowadays'. The former implies the presence of tradition, and the latter, the lack of it.

The difference between these polarities is not only temporal but also concerns the nature of social organization. For Tönnies, *Gemeinschaft* stands for intimacy, close personal knowledge, and stability, while *Gesellschaft* is a society characterized by ego-focused and specialized relationships. For Durkheim, mechanical solidarity refers to a society founded upon likeness, with no tolerance for difference, while organic solidarity stands for a society founded upon the integration of difference into a collaborative and harmonious whole (see e.g. Cohen 1985: 22). A common view running through these various approaches is that of individuals' social lives becoming more and more specialized, not only in their labor but also in all of their social relations (Cohen 1985: 22; see also Collins 1994). Modernization, therefore, is a process of individualization and specialization.

In the Weberian perspective, which is based on the binary opposition between reason and tradition, modernity stands for rationality, in terms of overcoming superstition, while tradition denotes lack of such rationality. In the spirit of the Enlightenment, modernization denotes the opposite of 'traditional religious authority' and the subsequent increase of individual rational reflection – even though for Weber the development would eventually result in an increase of bureaucratization. In all of these dichotomizations, that which precedes the modern is conceptualized as traditional. Traditional societies lack the propensities of modern societies.

## Tradition as Model and Pattern

Tradition is not, however, always conceptualized as being in opposition to modernity or denoting resistance to it. As an act of interpretation, as discussed by Richard Handler and Jocelyn Linnekin, tradition as a model of the past is inseparable from the interpretation of tradition in the present. "To do something because it is traditional is already to reinterpret, and hence to change it." (Handler & Linnekin 1984: 281.) Indeed, as processes of change, appropriation, and interpretation, and as authoritative relationships created between the present and the past, traditions appear as rhetorical constructions that denote an active and political process of creating historical meaning. Thus, instead of traditions being 'handed down' from the past to the present, from one generation to the next in the manner of inherited property, they are 'lifted up', as it were, in a process of traditionalization (see Hymes 1975: 353–354). As is pointed out by Linnekin, "the content of the past is modified and redefined according to a modern significance" (Linnekin 1983: 241). It is worth noting, though, that the perspective that puts emphasis on political agency in the present continues to construct tradition as past authority, in the Weberian sense, and thus signify both modernness and opposition to the modern.

As far as human cognitive ability for individual reflection and social access to political agency is concerned, the categorical distinction drawn between modern and traditional societies has been severely criticized in recent years. At the same time it has also become clear that modernist theories of the traditional society and its alleged communal and communitarian orientation have ignored or played down the explicit policies, ideologies and discursive practices with which modern societies have been directed towards communal orientation, conventionality, normative control, as well as towards cultural, political and racial homogeneity. In fact, the idea of racial homogeneity gained popularity in both laypeople's views and medical science in the late 19th century and in the early 20th as *modern progress* (see Mattila 1999).

Tradition is un-oppositional to modernity also when used as a metaphor for cultural continuity, as an indication of the presence of history in the present. Even though tradition and history have in afore-mentioned discourses been treated as binary oppositions, and Eric Hobsbawm in his seminal book (1983) tried to show that traditions do not qualify as history, it has become common, especially in the current heritage industry boom, to use tradition and history as nearly synonymous concepts. An interest in tradition means interest in history. Tradition is seen as a historical resource in the making of the present.

When tradition and history are treated as being closely related, they occupy a similar position vis-à-vis modernity. In heritage discourses they are given a positive function in the service of the modern; the presence of their representations suggests a sense of cultural continuity over the general sense of rupture. This is a positively charged quality as it enables the use of traditions as statements in identity politics; traditions can be said, for example, to symbolize the inner cohesion of a given group and the continuation of its existence as a recognized social entity. However, such continuity may also receive a negative charge when tradition stands for persisting attitudes or practices that appear to be difficult to eradicate – when, for example, tradition as a continued cultural practice is in conflict with the law.

Tradition as history may mean two mutually opposite things. In addition to pastness as past history, tradition and traditionality can refer to pastness in the present, the continuation of the past in models and patterns of speech, thought, belief, cultural practice, etc. Most apparently, such continuations are interpretations of and arguments for continuity, as that which is called a tradition to be continued is a symbolic construction. In scholarship, as discussed by E. A. Tiryakian – albeit with regard to sociology – traditions stand for "models of social reality that provide normative and cognitive orientations having heuristic significance in the devising of research and the interpretation of established data" (Tiryakian 2001: 15825). From this perspective, tradition is equated with the notion of the scholarly paradigm and its institutionalizations. It is worth noting that when conceptualized as models and patterns and as symbolic constructions of cultural continuity, whether literary or mass mediated, traditions exist just as well in modernity as in non-modernity. "All societies, all institutions except for some brief char-ismatic moments when 'all things are born new' are marked to some extent by tradition." (Tiryakian 2001: 15824.) Indeed, modern societies can be said to be full of – even based on or legitimated by – traditions in the sense of following established collective models and cognitive patterns of repetition. Such traditionality can be argued to have as much centrality in the minds of modern people as it has had in so-called traditional societies.

This view corresponds to what Paul Heelas has called the coexistence the-sis between detraditionalization, tradition-maintenance, retraditionalization, and the construction of new traditions: "Most comprehensibly formulated, coexistence theory holds that people – whether 'premodern' / 'traditional', 'modern' or even 'postmodern' / 'post-traditional' – *always* live in terms of those typically conflicting demands associated, on the one hand, with voices of authority emanating from realms transcending the self *qua* self, and on the other, with those voices emanating from the desires, expectations, and com-petitive or idiosyncratic aspirations of the individual." (Heelas 1996: 7.)

From this one can conclude that tradition and modernity must not be seen as oppositional, since modernity contains traditionality. Yet, the dichotomiza-tion of tradition and modern cannot escape its temporal dimension, because the traditions to be followed or no longer followed may be very different. The use of 'tradition' to designate societies and sociocultural formations that no longer exist is consonant with the tendency to call traditional that, which is not up-to-date or most recent. While 'modern' stands for novel-ties and innovation, 'tradition', as distinct from the 'modern', refers to that which is regarded as belonging to the past or representing past ways, styles or techniques. Even though recent scholarship has argued against the classic idea of dichotomizing traditional and modern, the dichotomy persists as a cognitive model parallel to such other fundamental dichotomies as old and new, right and left, warm and cold, north and south, east and west, raw and cooked, etc. Tradition is a temporal concept, its referential meaning being constituted as distinct from modern. It emerges from the comparison and the making of a distinction.

Everyday language will suffice here as evidence, and we can take any modern innovation, such as the development of digital cameras, as a case in point. Making print-outs from negatives used to be the standard way in which photographs were produced, but digitalization and the technical ease of transferring camera shots directly to the personal computer for editing and viewing have made paper print-outs a 'traditional' format. This type of novelty production is appropriated into a discursive practice that generates traditional-ity. Thus, by representing, manifesting and arguing for modernity, novelties create traditions. Similarly, a microwave oven is a modern oven, while an electric oven, which used to be considered modern before the microwave oven was invented, is nowadays called a traditional oven. A wood-burning oven is not only considered traditional but even primitive, and as such, it is subject to either rejection or exoticization. When exoticized in modern use, for example in retro fashion, it may even become 'postmodern'.

Again, in scholarship we talk about modern methodology in relation to those methods that used to be dominant but are either no longer employed or are used by a decreasing minority; the old methods are called traditional methods. As an analogy to this usage, societies that are non-present are traditional for the very reason that they are not modern, that is, in the present. Accordingly, the former socialist countries of Eastern Europe may now appear as 'traditional societies'. In the same way, people whose life is not characterized by the most recent technological innovations and most modern social institutions, live a traditional way of life – not necessarily because their life would be founded upon long established and unquestioned traditions, but because of not being characterized by the most modern elements. Such qualifications and predications are based on the use of 'traditional' and 'modern' as temporal qualifiers, as synonyms to 'old' and 'new'. It is only by extension – by a social theory – that 'traditional' is also conceptualized as denoting stability and lack of change in society or continuity and legitimacy,

A case in point about the idea of tradition as legitimacy is provided by John Keane with his commentary on the fate of civil society in Eastern European countries under Communism. Keane writes that "one-party systems can function only by frustrating or extirpating this region's old traditions of civil society" (Keane 1988: 2). Slightly later in his article he refers to the same processes as "besieged democratic traditions" (op. cit.: 4). 'Tradition' does not only refer to the political institutions and practices that used to characterize and lay the democratic foundation for the civil society in these countries, but it also makes a reference to their pastness, that they no longer exist (or rather, did not exist at the time of writing). Keane elucidates his own political commentary by employing the term 'tradition' or 'old traditions' for the pre-Communist political institutions. This is to valorize the legitimacy of these institutions and thus comment critically on their extermination.

The use of tradition and modern both as temporal qualifiers and as qualifiers of way of life and social structuration is highly relevant in relation to the rather common idea that in modernity, traditions disappear and die. Traditions in this rhetoric usually refer to particular social practices, which are conceptualized as social organisms having a life and a death. This metaphorical usage, which has been prevalent for example among folklore scholars, may undermine the use of the concept as an analytical tool. Yet, at the same time it reveals something fundamental about the complicated concept of tradition.

It is worth noting that when we call traditional that which has been surpassed by something new, we are naming traditional that which *is* disappearing, for the very reason that it has been surpassed by something new and modern. In other words, instead of traditions necessarily disappearing, that which disappears or falls out of use is named traditional. Change itself is conceptualized through a distinction or conflict between tradition and modernity, and that which yields to change is categorized as tradition. This rhetorical practice tends to create an impression that traditions are constantly vanishing, as things constantly change and fall into oblivion in the ephemerality of human life and social communication. As all things pass, phenomena that were once considered traditions to be followed disappear into history, as they fall out of use. However, if 'tradition' denotes a model and a pattern, it is a contradiction in terms to talk about traditions vanishing, since that which has vanished is no longer a tradition – in the sense of a model for social action or practice. It has stopped being a tradition, and therefore it cannot be documented as one. Attempts at their documentation produce representations that are *reports* of bygone traditions rather than representations of practices or thoughts that would continue to be circulated and transmitted and in that way indicate the continuation of a tradition. Most commonly, such report-type representations are produced in ethnography and folklore collecting, often with the politically charged motivation of constructing heritage for a given social or political group.

Thus, interestingly enough, in our modern language, or in our language of modernity, 'tradition' is a term that refers to both that which continues to exist and that which no longer exists. Social phenomena are called traditional when they exist as socially constituted models and patterns, as their existence signifies continuity and for that reason, also stability. Yet, they are called traditional also when they no longer function as models and patterns but have been surpassed by something new and modern. Indeed, in addition to the fact that we make constant observations of how social life is transient and once-established ways yield to changes and new formations, it is our use of language to predicate time with the qualifiers of 'modern' and 'traditional' that creates and reaffirms the idea of traditions as constantly yielding and being on the verge of extinction. In such an experience, we also determine whether this yielding of elements in social life is charged with positive or negative value, and we construct ideological discourses on whether that which yields 'deserves' to do so or not.

This calls attention to the temporality of modernity and thus demands a slight re-evaluation of the critical stance against the modern–tradition dichotomy. There are good reasons why it has become common in recent decades to attribute reflexive agency to the processes of traditionalization, and some of this criticism has been justly targeted at questioning the classic scheme of modern versus tradition. Gisela Welz, for example, writes that tradition is no longer seen as "a mindless reproduction of past habits, but instead a response to contemporary challenges", and she suggests that "being modern means to be self-reflexive about tradition" (Welz 2000: 10–11). Still, the emphasis given to reflexive agency in the conceptualization of tradition in the present cannot escape its temporal dimension, which, by definition, reproduces the distinction that it purports to negate. This makes tradition versus modernity a tricky dichotomy. There is no categorical opposition when tradition refers to cognitive models of repetition, but there is one when the two terms denote a temporal difference, as well as a difference in value. The categorical opposition can be easily observed in the heritage-making processes that employ the language of tradition versus modernity by presenting heritage and tradition as synonymous. The cultural representations that are selected for making heritage-political claims are commonly called traditions, with a special emphasis on their character as cultural properties; that is, representations with an ownership label.

# 3. Folklore in Modernism

## Promodern and Antimodern

When the dichotomization of tradition and modernity is employed as a social theory, tradition has been used in two kinds of ideological and value-laden statements about modernity: one that can be called 'promodern' and the other 'antimodern'. It has been customary to regard these as bipolar oppositions, but I would rather regard them as two expressions of one and the same project of modernism, that is, of the construction of difference and otherness between the modern and the non-modern. They are thus two versions of the same narrative of modernization.

To be promodern is to favor modernness, modernism and modernization; to take a positive and optimistic attitude towards modernity and the innovations brought along with it. From the promodern perspective, to be modern is to be progressive. The promodern orientation may contain, for example, a belief that modernity brings blessings to the humankind through technological, economic, social, and moral development. Such an idea – sometimes presented with a heroic narrative ethos – finds its purest expression in the project of the Enlightenment, established originally by Montesquieu, Voltaire, Immanuel Kant, David Hume, among others, in the eighteenth century.

Based on a universalistic idea of reason and rationality, and the belief in its unlimited increase and a steady evolution of science and technology, Enlightenment ideology argued for an irreversible force of civilization that was expected to bring about continuous improvement for all mankind. This was supposed to happen by emancipating people with critical rationalism from normativeness and the alleged restraints of traditionality, especially from 'traditional religious authority', and by liberating them from irrational beliefs and behavior.

To be traditional is to be non-modern, but since non-modernity is here a linguistic construction only, to be traditional is to be modern in a different way than in explicit promodernism. In traditionalism, one orients towards the past in the making of the modern, with a preference for older ways, beliefs, values and technologies. From the promodern perspective, to be traditional is to be regressive.

Traditionalism also denotes a critical, skeptical, pessimistic or disapproving attitude towards changes that (are made to) represent modernization. Such changes are caused by industrialization, technologization, bureaucratization, standardization, urbanization, social fragmentation, individualization, commercialization, etc. One of the core tenets in traditionalism – often manifested in a narrative ethos of loss and decadence – is the notion that modernization has destroyed or threatens to destroy traditions as representations of community and collective identifications, regarded by many as key elements in human spirituality and social well-being, its core meanings and its cultural heritage.

Traditionalism can present itself in antimodernism, which means resistance to modernization or a refusal to modernize. Well-known examples of antimodernism are such religious groups as the Old Order Amish and the Old-Believers. The Amish are a group of Mennonites and Anabaptists who wish to separate themselves from the rest of the world and resort to self-sufficiency, declining to adopt such modern conveniences as electricity. The Old-Believers refuse to recognize the reforms introduced in the seventeenth century by Patriarch Nikon (1605–1681) to the liturgical texts and practices of the Russian Orthodox Church (see e.g. Čistov 1976: 224–225; Pentikäinen 1999a). Paradoxically, as pointed out by K. V. Čistov, the Old-Believers, despite their conservatism, enhanced the spread of modern literacy, as they needed to be able to read and copy old, pre-Nikon liturgical texts without the help of priests and other Church officials.

Yet another example of antimodernism is provided by Luddism, which has its historical origin in a revolt in 1811 against English textile factories when these started to replace craftsmen with machines. According to the Internet pages of the School of Education at the University of Colorado at Denver, "Today's Luddites continue to raise moral and ethical arguments against the excesses of modern technology to the extent that our inventions and our technical systems have evolved to control us rather than to serve us and to the extent that such leviathans can threaten our essential humanity" (Luddism 2002). As this quote, at least partially, exemplifies, the antimodern orientation is based on a notion that modernization causes alienation from a number of social values ranging from work, nature and the sacred to humanity, collectivity, community, localness and traditionality. This alienation, then, results in a lack of authenticity in the rationalistic, secularist, technological and commercial culture of the industrialized, mass-mediated and allegedly 'de-vernacularized', 'de-localized' and 'detraditionalized' Western modernity.

The making of rural life as a pastoral idyll from an urban perspective represents yet another example of antimodernism. In American transcendentalism, which paralleled early 19th-century Herderian nationalism in Europe, the rural folk were regarded as "emblems of spiritual truth" (Bustin 1988: 2). In a manner familiar from the Cartesian dualism of spirit and matter, which implies that the excess of one means the lack of the other, antimodernism conveys the idea that modernization through technologization brings about materialism, which then alienates people from spiritualism. Thus, the less modernized, the more spiritual people are, and vice versa.

Antimodernism is not, however, mere criticism of modern developments. In addition, it participates in the conceptualization of spatial relations (also on a global scale) by constructing non-modern othernesses that are seen to (still) possess that which modernity is felt to destroy. While the modern self is seen as being subject to fragmentation and detraditionalization, attention is directed to sites where the positively valued aspects of community making apparently continue to exist. Elements of culture, philosophy and social values originating from these sites are then appropriated as novelties in the making of a 'better' modernity and modern selfhood. This is a form of edification that makes antimodernism, too, orientate towards the future. When antimodernism finds expression in the making of the allegedly non-modern a source for spiritual, moral, mystical, exotic, or nostalgic compensation for the alleged lack of tradition and authenticity in the experience of the modern, it is fundamentally a modern project.

This is one of the reasons why the bipolar opposition of promodern and antimodern as well as that of tradition and modernity must be regarded as conceptual and rhetorical constructions. *Per se*, they exemplify a major characteristic in modernism to construct reality into one-dimensional and seemingly separate categories and domains of thought. Indeed, Randall Collins argues that modernism arises from a propensity of the West to categorize its social conflicts and its trajectories of historical change in terms of a single continuum. "In politics", Collins writes, "we attempt to array our factions along the spectrum from 'Right' to 'Left'; in religion we label 'traditionalists' and 'liberal reformers', just as in arguments over cultural styles we generally distinguish 'conservatives' and 'progressives' " (Collins 1992: 171). Collins points out how such polarizations as 'liberal' progressive, leftist modernist, on the one hand, and 'conservative' traditionalist, rightist anti-modernist on the other, are one-dimensional distinctions and ideological myths imposed upon a multidimensional and a more complex organizational reality (Collins 1992: 172).

Thus, the stereotypical linking of tradition and conservatism, on the one hand, and modernism and progressiveness on the other, hardly qualifies for an operational social classification except in particular historically specific contexts. Such links are prescriptions instead of descriptions. That which is regarded as promodernist can appear antimodernist as well, and that which is progressive in a particular setting can from another viewpoint seem quite conservative. This applies especially well to the use of traditions as historical styles in the making of the present and its collective symbolism. It also applies, for example, to musical and visual arts, including those verbally artistic expressions that folklorists call folklore. An artistically progressive and innovative approach to past models and styles can create either progressive or conservative political statements, depending on a variety of factors. Manifestations of 'counter culture' or 'going native', and preference for 'soft technology' and 'recycling' against 'hard technology' or 'technocracy', are at the same time antimodernist and promodernist, conservative and progressive. Nationalism is a modern ideology, but nationalists are often traditionalists. Thus, the promodernist and antimodernist perspectives on modernity are in a dialectical rather than in a categorically oppositional relationship to one another.

## Modernity's Paradox

Modernity, as sensed and described by Charles Baudelaire, is an experience of life as transient, fleeting and ephemeral (see Calinescu 1987: 4–5, 48; Harvey 1989: 10; Baudelaire 1989; cf. Wallgren 1989: 37). In addition to creating a continuous desire for novelties, especially for new technological innovations, such an experience has also given rise to discourse on the loss of that which recedes in time beyond recovery. One aspect of this discourse on loss is that the ephemerality of the present creates a longing for the eternal and the immutable. Tradition, and folklore as its synonym in folkloristic discourse, serves as a metaphor for that which is solid, fixed, and crystallized. It may provide a psychological anchor in the experience of ephemerality, as it manifests permanence that lasts through time.

In recent decades, the biological metaphor of root has been adopted and employed for the same purpose. It denotes spatio-temporal continuation in social life and a sense of belonging that is founded upon biologically determined genealogies, family histories or the presence of preferred references to the past. Traditions and roots are thus synonymous when placed as opposites to the continuous and rapid cultural and social changes, which are felt to be the trademark of modernity and 'the modern lifestyle'. Tradition, folklore, and roots are, in this sense, discursive responses to the experienced ephemerality of modernity.

When 'tradition', associated and synonymized with 'root', connotes with permanence and timelessness, any change is potentially felt as a loss and a threat to the sense of cultural continuation. Change, from this perspective, comes to mean a rupture in what is conceptualized either as a static system or a 'smooth' and anticipated development in time and history. It therefore receives a negative charge. As an idea of an irreversible process, change – in addition to producing novelties – creates a discourse on loss. The sense of the loss of cultural traditions, folk traditions or roots finds a parallel in the more and more concerned discourses on the irreversible loss of natural resources, making the discourse on the loss of culture and cultural diversity a metadiscourse on eco-catastrophes and the loss of biodiversity (see e.g. Ó Giolláin 2003: 42–45).

Writing is a practice with which people prevent spoken words from vanishing into thin air – provided that the written text can be preserved. Language is thus a means to produce both ephemerality and a sense of permanence, but paradoxically, languages are themselves subject to disappearance. Indeed, languages are often likened to endangered species and their loss is paralleled to the decline of cultural and biological diversity. Payal Sampat at the Worldwatch Institute highlighted this connection in her article 'Last Words: The Dying of Languages' (Sampat 2001), which was publicized as reporting that out of the world's 6,800 languages, 3,400 to 6,120 may be extinct by the year 2100. When the Tokyo-based English-language newspaper *Japan Times* reported on the contents of this article, the heading dramatized the loss: "World's 6,800 languages are dying as we speak" (*Japan Times*, June 21, 2001: 7).

The modern awareness and sense of loss is closely related to what has been called the modern sense of alienation. Yet, instead of a psychological state of estrangement, alienation here denotes a sense of lack in direct, unmediated experience and control of meaning. This is how alienation is present in Karl Marx's highly influential economic theory, in which it stands for the lack of directness and control in the relationship between the product and its producer, between the commodity and its manufacturer, in the capitalist society (e.g. McLellan 1982: 37–38). Rather similar are Henri Lefèbvre's Marxist ideas on the commodity as an agent of capitalist domination and colonialism in the modern everyday (e.g. Lefèbvre 1991), as well as Jean Baudrillard's views on mass consumption as disciplined waste that ultimately destroys the individual, social relations and the environment (Baudrillard 1975). This sense of alienation is also referred to when modern 'neo-liberalist' society is said to be manipulated by invisible 'market forces' over which individuals as producers and consumers have no control. Alienation denotes here the loss of an allegedly once-possessed political influence and cognitive control.

Because of the sense of loss and alienation caused by drastic social changes, perpetual technological innovations, increase in the mediated forms of production and consumption as well as politics and policy making, modernization, while creating a sense of progress and representing the progress of science and technology, is at the same time embedded with critical discourses about itself and its own project. This criticism is not a total rejection of the modern but, rather, an expression of the dilemma in which, as phrased by David Harvey, one has to destroy in order to create (see Harvey 1989: 16–17). Modernity is, therefore, a fundamentally paradoxical experience. James Clifford describes this by saying that "modern ethnographic histories are perhaps condemned to oscillate between two metanarratives: one of homogenization, the other of emergence; one of loss, the other of invention. In most specific conjunctures both narratives are relevant, each undermining the other's claim to tell 'the whole story,' each denying to the other a privileged, Hegelian vision. Everywhere in the world distinctions are being destroyed *and* created." (Clifford 1988a: 17.)

Many others have pointed to the same paradoxical or contradictory nature of modernity. Marshall Berman has noted how being modern is to be "both revolutionary and conservative: alive to new possibilities for experience and adventure, frightened by the nihilistic depths to which so many modern adventures lead, longing to create and to hold on to something real as everything melts. We might even say that to be fully modern is to be anti-modern: from Marx's and Dostoyevski's time to our own, it has been impossible to grasp and embrace the modern world's potentialities without loathing and fighting against some of its most palpable realities." (Berman 1982: 13.)

Thus, according to Calinescu, there are two conflicting and interdependent modernities: one socially progressive, rationalistic, competitive, and technological, the other culturally critical and self-critical, bent on demystifying the basic values of the first (Calinescu 1987: 265). One aspect of people's intrinsically contradictory way of experiencing modernity is the sense that "modern civilization has brought about a loss of something precious, the dissolution of a great integrative paradigm, the fragmentation of what once was a mighty unity" (Calinescu 1987: 265). For this reason, it is part of being modern to lament, in an antimodernist stance, the loss of an imagined traditional order, a 'lost community' and 'true values', and then project this onto sites or times that are made representations and ruins of such an order.

Modernity is also paradoxical in its diffusion, as those who escape modernity in their search of non-modern authenticity and lost communities inescapably take modernity with them. When modernity's otherness is constructed through modern criticism, the sites of such otherness grow distant as they are approached. Claude Lévi-Strauss claims that anthropology is the study of a society that sets itself to destroy precisely those things that give it most flavor. Accordingly, he has suggested that 'entropology', not anthropology, "should be the word for the discipline that devotes itself to the study of this process of disintegration in its most highly evolved forms" (Lévi-Strauss 1967: 397). Discussing the theme of the 'vanishing primitive' as a narrative structure, James Clifford quotes Adolph Bastian as saying "For us, primitive societies [*Naturvölker*] are ephemeral. At the very instant they become known to us they are doomed." Similarly, Clifford quotes Bronislaw Malinowski as saying "Ethnology is in the sadly ludicrous, not to say tragic position, that at the very moment when it begins to put its workshop in order, to forge its proper tools, to start ready for work on its appointed task, the material of its study melts away with hopeless rapidity." (Clifford 1986: 112.)

The feeling of the object disappearing just as it becomes an object is closely related to the touristic experience of looking for 'authentic' places where no (other) tourist has entered before (see MacCannell 1989). Paradoxically, authenticity is lost upon the visit by the first tourist. There may be a parallel to this in the way in which male humans yearn for 'authenticity' and 'purity' in females – as spaces where no man has entered before. In an analogy to ethnography, one yearns for a virgin land in order to be the first to take its virginity. (For a discussion on the way male folklorists have described their encounters with female performers in sexual terms, see Kodish 1987.)

## Sociology as the Science of the Modern

Both of the two seemingly oppositional modernist projects are represented in the academic categorization of scholarly disciplines, which is, of course, itself a product of modernity and modernism. The two projects are different in their ways of commenting on the processes of modernization, since they conceptualize and judge tradition and change in seemingly opposite ways and have a seemingly different approach to the 'irrationalities' of the premodern. While the promodern project distances itself from non-modernity by rejecting it or by calling for its rejection, the antimodern one similarly establishes distance by exoticizing non-modernity and by transforming it into critical representations through a modern and modernist gaze.

The promodern direction has found its academic foundation mainly in the discipline of sociology, which is not only called the science of the modern but is regarded as having its matrix in the very process of the Enlightenment. According to Stuart Hall, it was in the discourses of the Enlightenment that 'the social' emerged as a separate and distinct form of reality, which could be analyzed independently of the 'other-worldly' or supernatural – that is, 'rationally' (Hall 1992: 2; see also Hall 2000a: 4). Focusing on the social organization of modern societies and providing an explanation for "the course of the capitalist modernization of traditional societies" (Habermas 1984: 5), sociology has been founded upon a narrative of a unilinear movement from traditional to modern, and from community to society. This is also a narrative of progress, according to which a specialized, modern society is better able to develop continuously and deal with new problems and social forces than what is called a traditional society (Eisenstadt 1974: 2).

As such a narrative of progress, the evolution from tradition to modernity has in the main been discussed in sociological research as a process of emancipation and detraditionalization. A good example of this is the book entitled *Detraditionalization* (Heelas, Lash & Morris 1996), which is "designed to contribute to the growing debate concerning the extent to which our age has moved beyond tradition" (Heelas 1996: 1). Based on Durkheimian and Weberian perspectives, traditionality in this discourse stands for the foundation for intellectual authority and normative community bonds – especially those established by the medieval and early modern Christian Church – that block individual expression and choice, innovation and rational reflection. Accordingly, traditional societies are regarded as being "informed by belief in established, timeless orders" (Heelas 1996: 3). By contrast, modernity stands for self-conscious and reflexive action and for liberation from traditional authority, including freedom of speech and thought. Thus, tradition receives negatively charged attributes, while modernity is pregnant with positively charged ones. Tradition is seen to dominate so-called traditional societies which, because of their traditionality, are regarded as having been marked by collective control, unreflexive authority and hierarchies, normative worldview, static social structure, lack of creativity and lack of rationality.

In an apparent West-centric bias, modern sociology, by claiming rationality to the moderns, has constructed the non-modern cultural other as something fundamentally irrational. Since this irrationality is associated with collective control, mechanical solidarity, and unreflecting conventionality, becoming modern means to become a free and self-reflective individual (see e.g. Jallinoja 1991: 34–42; Giddens 1994). Modernism in sociological theories thus rejects and opposes tradition, connoting social bonds with the negatively charged concept of traditionality.

It is worthy of noting that in many sociological treatises of the modern/traditional relationship, tradition is not a canon, a taxonomy or a list of any particular social behaviors or cultural practices, but it stands for that which is not modern, whatever is regarded as modern. Like our everyday use of 'traditional', as an opposition to that which is most recent and 'just now', 'traditional' in sociological parlance has no referential meaning except in contrast to modernity and the social changes identified within it. As such, 'tradition' is a synonym for the non- or premodern. Tradition stands for that which the modern surpasses, and therefore it denotes the social and cultural domain that modernity is separated and distinguished from.

Still, the concept of tradition does point in certain directions, as it locates the lack of the modern in a number of settings. Such temporal and spatial settings include medieval and early modern church authority, religion as the dominant source of ideas, peasant irrationality, absolutist political power and established systems of control (see e.g. Hamilton 2000: 30). In Weberian sociology, tradition makes a general reference to 'the old rule' or the past authority of gerontocracy, patriarchalism and patrimonialism (see Weber 1964: 341–358). It thus argues for restrictions and conventionality in the past and individual freedom in the present. As modernization is positively charged, to be modern is to be progressive and open to new ideas and values, while to resist new things and perspectives is to be old-fashioned, conservative and traditional. Tradition is a mode and a motive for being in the world. As put by Harriet Bradley, "Traditional motives are based on respect for custom and acceptance of long-standing forms of behaviour, often backed by religious or superstitious beliefs. People do things 'because they've always been done that way'." (Bradley 2000: 132.)

Since tradition has not been sociology's research object, very little analytical attention has been paid to traditionality as a domain of social practice and cognitive processing. Attention has also escaped traditionality as containing active processes of interpretation, reflective argumentation and political agency. Instead, traditionality has been seen as the very opposite of such things. Tradition and modernity appear to follow a sequential order, in which tradition ends where modernity – including and indicating reflective and political action – begins. Since sociology has been regarded as a science of the modern, the points of rupture between the past and the present, between tradition and modernity, have marked the beginning of the sociologist's research territory.

Yet, even though the tradition/modernity opposition continues to make the sociologist promodern, not all sociologists have subscribed to the notion of modernity as an enduring story of success. Modernization may be viewed as a narrative of progress, especially that of rationality, but at the same time there have been scholars that are more sensitive to the destructive elements in modernity. A well-known example is Max Weber, for whom modernity stands for rationalism and liberation of people "from the garden of enchantment in which magic and primitive gods had ruled their lives" (Turner 1984: 65). Yet, the totality of rationalization in Weber's scenario for the future of modern societies leads to bureaucratization and the loss of humanity. Rationality and reason, in other words, would not bring "a Realm of Freedom but the domination of impersonal economic forces and bureaucratically organized administrations, not a Kingdom of God on Earth but an 'iron cage' in which we were henceforth condemned to live" (McCarthy 1985: 176; see also Haferkamp 1987; Bernstein 1991: 4).

## The Paradigm of Loss in Folklore Studies

While in sociology 'tradition' has stood for a lack of perceived historical change in social structure and worldview, in anthropology, ethnology and folklore scholarship the same concept has meant a form of social and cultural order based on oral communication. Tradition has here been a descriptive term for the culture of non- or pre-literate societies, in which knowledge, rules and social organization are preserved in memory and communicated by word of mouth (Ben-Amos 1984: 100–101). Such oral societies tend to be presented, especially by folklorists, as collectivities that lack all aspects of internal social hierarchization. Modern societies, in contrast, are typically characterized as being based on individualization, structural specialization, social mobilization, literacy, high levels of urbanization, and exposure to mass media (e.g. Eisenstadt 1974: 1–2). All these elements have been interpreted to indicate the lack of tradition in modernity both in the sociological and folkloristic sense.

From this perspective, folklore scholarship has to a large extent subscribed to the same modern–traditional schema as the sociologist, but from a different interest position. Both the folklorist and the sociologist construct and represent their object of study within a general discourse of change and a grand narrative from tradition to modernity. Yet, one of the central ways in which the discourse on change is put forward in folklore studies is the conceptualization of the object of study within a discourse on modernity as loss. Loss of culture, loss of tradition, loss of identity, loss of traditional values, loss of morality, and loss of exceptionally valued folklore genres.

Like the sociologist, such a discourse positions the folklorist on a threshold. This is a crisis position both in the sense of an emergency situation as well as a turning point (from the Greek 'krinein', to separate; *Webster's* 1984: s.v. 'crisis'; cf. Anttonen 1992: 25). The present of the researcher is the very moment of 'just now' and of change. While the sociologist mainly looks towards modernity as a landscape of novelties, the folklorist looks towards tradition as a landscape that appears to be closing in on the very spot where the researcher is standing (see also Knuuttila 1994: 18–20). According to Barbara Kirshenblatt-Gimblett, "Ours is a discipline predicated on a vanishing subject. The time of our operation is the eleventh hour. Before the eleventh hour there is life, after the eleventh hour death." (Kirshenblatt-Gimblett 1996: 249; see also Kirshenblatt-Gimblett 1998a: 300.)

Yet, not all folklore studies have been predicated with such a devolutionistic approach. As pointed out by William Wilson (1976: 70–74), the historic-geographic method, as originally designed and formulated in the 1870s by Julius Krohn in Finland, was not based on the idea of a continuous degeneration of folklore. On the contrary, Krohn was an evolutionist who believed that Finnish-language folk poetry gradually developed from primal motifs and small poetic units into larger entities in the course of time and the geographic dissemination of folk poems. His son Kaarle Krohn, however, eventually rejected such evolutionism. Krohnian and post-Krohnian folklore studies came to be characterized by a quest for the pure, original form or the abstracted 'normal form', which could be considered, at least in principle, the historical origin for all available versions and variants.

Accordingly, the evolutionism of Julius Krohn turned out to be a passing note within the longer history of folklore studies. The survival theory of the Grimm brothers, as well as that of the British evolutionist anthropologists, served as the foundation for an emergent paradigm based on the modern discourse on loss and cultural impoverishment. Folklore, with tradition as its claimed synonym, became for both 19th and 20th century scholars a continuous near-death experience, as the research object was perpetually talked about in terms of living and dying. Alan Dundes has described this as the devolutionistic premise in folklore theory, according to which folklore not only deteriorates in time but the universe of folklore is being run down because of change and progress (see Dundes 1969). Since such a devolutionary process is attributed to social, economic and technological changes, this is a theory of modernization.

Because of its alleged lack of traditionality, modernity in this paradigm is seen as fake, artificial, superficial and trivial. The dichotomy of modernity and tradition thus authenticates tradition as a cultural other and sees deliberate making – that is, faking – of tradition as taking place only in the modern. This bias constructs folklore into a travel account from authenticity to inauthenticity, from the discovery of its original, 'living' and pure state to a condition marked by political, scholarly, and commercial intervention, appropriation and abuse – something negative that has been termed fakelore or folklorism (see Bendix 1992, 1997).

Modernity is also seen as an agent causing standardization. While in the 'folk culture' of premodernity cultural expressions were allegedly spontaneous and transmitted spontaneously, in a modern society they are regarded as rule-governed and channeled into the regulated activities of associations and semi-official activity groups. The premodern social groupings have thus been regarded as real, genuine, and authentic communities, while the modern ones are considered both artificial and superficial (see e.g. Kuusi 1974).

Yet, in addition to the social changes brought about by modernization, folklore has generated its discourse on loss through an interest in the study of immigration and the changes in traditions due to people changing location and place of residence. Roger Abrahams points to such discourse on the loss of traditions in conjunction of Englishmen and other Europeans migrating to America (Abrahams 1992b: 65). Until recent decades, immigrant folklore to a great extent meant research on the 'loss of traditions' when people migrate, with the research focus set on comparing what kind of folklore people had possessed in their places of origin and what they no longer mastered in their places of immigration (see e.g. Dorson 1959: 135–136). More recent folkloristic research on the making and display of ethnicity in multicultural situations, initiated among others by Barbara Kirshenblatt-Gimblett (1978),

tends to emphasize migration as a source for creativity in tradition and traditionality, instead of regarding it as a loss.

Folklore research as discourse on decadence is not a lone rival to the
promodernist discourse of sociology. It is part of a set of academic fields
– all born in modernity – that have participated in the modern discourse on
cultural loss by documenting, describing and putting on display representations of past ways of life and cultural knowledge. Some of these, especially
the various branches of the discipline of history, are felt to be neutral to the
processes of modernization. For this reason, cultural or art historical interest
in the past – which mostly concerns the culture of the educated upper classes,
the political elites, artists and the intelligentsia – tends to be regarded as
representing an 'innocent', that is, a non-argumentative, interest in history.
Recent historical scholarship has, however, questioned this notion.

Folklore studies, ethnology and cultural anthropology have tended to
be 'pro-traditional'. Focusing on the uneducated lower classes within the
confines of the scholar's own national sphere, or peoples and communities
on allegedly lower levels of civilization outside the Western world, these
disciplines have justified their own existence and manner of representation by
attaching special value to that which is regarded as being marginalized and
falling into oblivion because of (Western) modernization. In the 19th century,
according to Peter Burke, "students of what they called 'folklore' were often
conservatives, who saw themselves as defending traditional values against
the assaults of modernization" (Burke 1992: 293). Ernst Dick has traced
this trait in the discipline back to Herder, being in tune with "Herder's love
for the simple people, his interest in earlier traditions, and his bias against
modern civilization" (Dick 1989: 16).

But in addition to being a disposition towards modernity, traditionalism
and antimodernism have certain methodological consequences. On the one
hand, the discipline continues its association with the past, and guides its
practitioners "to search for people who continue to practice certain arts and
crafts in the old ways" (Abrahams 1993a: 7). The folk are, in other words, to
be found "in the old-fashioned peoples allegedly living by an earlier mode
of social organization" (Abrahams 1993a: 4). On the other hand, nostalgia
is generated for an 'older sense of community' or a *Gemeinschaft*, in which
communication has allegedly been unmediated and people have experienced
each other directly, 'immediately'. As put by Richard Bauman, "There's more
than a touch of the nostalgic romantic in most of us, and we're still under-
standably attracted to the old stuff" (Bauman 1983: 154). Calling attention
to folklore as antiquity, Roger Abrahams points to the "strange status" of
the "scarce remains of past cultures (...) as dislocated remnants that carried
with them a certain mystery and power" (Abrahams 1993a: 3). Indeed, it is
this mystery and power of the old and the exotic – the antique as a souvenir
from unvisitable places – that often entices people to folklore studies.

'Face-to-face' is a metaphor often used by people in general and folklorists in particular to describe direct, unmediated interactions, and it is in such
communicative and interactive situations that folklore by many folklorists
is thought to abound. According to Abrahams, "we maintain the impression

that folklore is best found at the center of the household operation or in some other place commonly characterized by good and friendly talk" (Abrahams 1993a: 24). Such a characterization bears witness to the fact that even though folklore has often been conceptualized as a scholarly taxonomy, even a canonized body of texts, it at the same time continues to be referred to as a chronotope of ideal communication and unmediated interaction. Recently, Diarmuid Ó Giolláin has described this sense in the discipline and its object by saying that "Folklore escapes clear definition, but its aura gives it an immediate emotional resonance" (Ó Giolláin 2000: 2). As such, it functions as an unspecified qualitative opposite to that which is regarded as modern (cf. Benjamin 1992).

### The Collector's Gaze

Especially in its early stages the folklore discipline was characterized by a gaze away from modernity into the cultures of the lower classes, the *vulgus in populo*, the uncivilized, the illiterate, the non-Whites and the 'ethnics', which all became the designated reference point for the concept of folk in folklore (see e.g. Newell 1888; Dundes 1966, 1977). The dichotomy of tradition and modernity and the paradigm of loss have continued to model both the methodology and the rhetoric of the discipline into two interrelated projects: a gaze into the margins of modernity in search for authenticity (see Bendix 1997), and a mission to collect folklore in a manner that has been termed 'eleventh-hour ethnography' (Kirshenblatt-Gimblett 1996), 'saving from the fire' (Abrahams 1993a), or 'salvage or redemptive ethnography' (Clifford 1986: 112–113).

As far as the English-speaking world is concerned, the folkloristic mission to collect was chartered in England in 1846 by William Thoms, who coined the term 'folk-lore' to refer to "a slowly but surely disappearing knowledge" (Ben-Amos 1984: 104). Since Thoms characterized his coinage as denoting "the manners, customs, observances, superstitions, ballads, proverbs, etc., of the olden time" (Thoms 1965: 5), the notion of folklore as a vanishing substance was inscribed in the original formulation of the concept. William Wells Newell presented this in the American context in the 1880s, establishing the American Folklore Society "to encourage the collection of the fast-vanishing remains of folk-lore in America" (Newell 1888). The mission to collect has continued to characterize the discipline especially in those countries in which the folklore archive is a central institution. Its vibrancy in the 1990s can be seen, for example, in the statement by Lauri Honko, who, with reference to the Unesco Recommendation for the Safeguarding of Folklore and Traditional Culture, encouraged "us all [to] go wherever valuable traditions are in danger of passing away without a single act of documentation" (Honko 1992: 4).

Such documentation can be justified with a number of good reasons. One of them is the fact that the accumulated collections provide indispensable means for historical research and cultural analysis. Yet, this is not merely a pragmatic question. As James Clifford has pointed out, "The other is lost, in disintegrating time and space, but saved in the text" (Clifford 1986: 112). More recently, Richard Bauman and Charles Briggs have rather sardonically asked, with reference to the Unesco Recommendation, how "these fragile oral traditions, nested protectively in communities" are to be safeguarded "against the juggernaut of industrialized culture" (Bauman & Briggs: 308). Their 'answer' to the question is this:

> The solution: more intervention by experts, enabled by [Unesco] Member States: encouragement of scientific, universalizing, rationalized tasks and tools (national inventories, global registers, coordinated classification systems, standard typologies, harmonized collecting and archiving methods), establishment of an institutional infrastructure for such expert tasks (national archives, documentation centers, libraries, museums, seminars, congresses), and support for the specialists who do the safeguarding work (training courses, full-time jobs for folklorists). (Bauman & Briggs 2003: 308.)

The political value of the created text rests on the transformation of social practice and performance into a representation, which is then appropriated into discourses on both heritage and its technical production. The archive paradigm in folklore studies, which is stronger in some countries than in others, implies a political standpoint according to which cultural identity is best protected and argued for by depositing representations of both vibrant and receding practices in the archive and then selecting material for public presentations, for example in the form of museum displays or books targeted at the consuming and reading public. Folklore speaks – for example the language of nationalism – through collections.

When conceptualized as a vanishing object, folklore calls for immediate documentation. As an object to be documented in ethnographic practice, folkloric communication becomes a collectible, an item that can and should be carried away and included in classification systems designed for such collectibles. As pointed out by Dan Ben-Amos, most definitions of folklore have conceived of it as a collection of things. "These could be either narratives, melodies, beliefs, or material objects. All of them are completed products or formulated ideas; it is possible to collect them." (Ben-Amos 1972: 9.)

Creating collections is not an innocent form of representation. Instead, it is an activity pertaining to the politics of culture and history and contributing to the discourses on difference and the political construction of continuities and discontinuities. Collections depoliticize the communication from which 'folklore' as entextualized artifacts is extracted. At the same time these artifacts are transformed into mimetic representations that create their own politics. When conceptualized as collections of items brought back from modernity's otherness, folklore may speak for the politically correct way of constructing local or national heritage. Yet, such collections may also carry on the rhetoric of confirming the political distinction drawn between the moderns and the non-moderns, the educated and the folk, the civilized and the exoticized others, the West and the rest.

Collections both display and generate power. As put by Clifford, ethnography's disappearing object is "a rhetorical construct legitimating a representational practice" (Clifford 1986: 112). This practice, as discussed by Abrahams, dramatizes the power of the collector. In such practice, the rarity of the disappearing object legitimates its status as a representation of difference (Abrahams 1993a: 18) – and as discussed by Foster, as an exotic object of art (Foster 1982: 30).

Archives and museums are useful modern innovations for the presentation and representation of history and culture, but they are not innocent depositories of collectibles. Instead of providing unmediated material for research and learning about other times and places, the collecting as well as the display of that which has been collected is always embedded in its own rhetorics and politics in terms of who is represented, how, for whom, and for what purposes (see e.g. Clifford 1988b, 1988c; Lönnqvist 1989: 29–31; Kirshenblatt-Gimblett 1991 and other articles in Karp and Lavine 1991; Kirshenblatt-Gimblett 1992, 1998b; Stewart 1993; Kurki 2002). In addition to providing systematic access to systematized information, archives and museums give meaning and value to their possessions by the very act of making them part of collections and entities constructed both aesthetically as well as in view of their purpose in the representation of culture. Such collections do not only create rationalized models and filters for subsequent collecting (see Frykman 1979: 235–236), for the selection of that which 'deserves' to be collected. In addition to this, they also speak of the esteem for large quantities and belief in their power and adequacy in metonymic representation.

Archived materials – or any other ethnographic materials, for that matter – are never transparent in their ways of mediating and representing the cultural contexts from which they were extracted. They can purport to provide future generations with "a chance to get a reliable picture of the traditional ways of life in eras past" (Honko 1991: 29), but the reliability of the picture is always a question of interpretation and authorization, which the archive and the museum through their own institutional power tend to make invisible. Barbara Kirshenblatt-Gimblett makes the essential point by saying that "lists and collections obscure the hand that shapes the representation. They create the illusion of genuine, which is to say, unmediated, folklore." (Kirshenblatt-Gimblett 1988: 145; see also Briggs 1986: 22.)

James Clifford has called the collecting of folklore "rule-governed, meaningful desire" (Clifford 1988c: 218). Since one cannot possibly document everything that falls into oblivion, one must "select, order, classify in hierarchies – to make 'good' collections" (loc. cit.). Such systems speak for rational, "rule-governed possession" based on the aesthetics of taxonomy, instead of a 'fetishistic' fixation on single objects (Clifford 1988c: 219; see also Stewart 1993). Speaking for rational possession, such systems also constitute disciplinary discourses. As put by Barbara Kirshenblatt-Gimblett, "Objects become ethnographic by virtue of being defined, segmented, detached, and carried away by ethnographers" (Kirshenblatt-Gimblett 1991: 387; also Kirshenblatt-Gimblett 1998: 17–18). This means that disciplines make their objects and in the process make themselves. Indeed, as the gaze creates its object, that which is regarded as folklore becomes a representation of such a category within a particular discursive practice constructing the discipline of folklore.

## Folklore as Literary Text

Folklore in the sense of oral tradition has most commonly become accessible in collections through the means of writing. Throughout the history of the discipline, the documentation of oral tradition has meant by definition its transformation into a written format, and it is only during the most recent decades that writing as a form of representation has come to be discussed by folklorists. As documents of orality that the folklorist purports to save from oblivion, folklore recordings are fragments that are entextualized and transformed into literary imitations of their orality. As such they are arti-factualized. Yet, unlike in *belles lettres*, the author of the folklore text has been regarded as a mere transcriber, which tends to conceal the subject and subjectivity of the authoring and, therefore, the authorization of the text as a folklore document.

The documents of orality are mimetic representations of the very communicative contexts from which they are extracted, of that which cannot be carried away (Kirshenblatt-Gimblett 1991: 389; see also Bauman & Briggs 1990: 72–78). As such, they are transformed into metonymic representations of the cultures and communities in which they were originally produced. As pointed out by Susan Stewart, the separation, manipulation and appropriation is founded upon particular means of making literary artifacts, the value and aesthetic qualities of which are historically specific and ideologically motivated (Stewart 1991: 6–7). Yet, in addition to aesthetic qualities, such metonymic representations have to do with territorial identifications such as the construction of national and regional cultures and the incorporation of particular areas and populations into particular political and ideological entities.

When materials recorded from oral communication, such as songs, proverbs and narratives, receive their value as printed, metonymic representations of, for example, the nation and its cultural heritage, folklore as a document of orality is in a fundamental way conceptualized as – and entextualized into – literature. This has been quite paradigmatic in folkloristic discourse since its emergence as a discipline. When coining the word 'folk-lore' to replace 'popular antiquities' and 'popular literature', William Thoms conceptualized the collecting, organizing, and publishing of antiquities as part and servant of the country's *literary culture* (see Thoms 1965: 5). The same applies to the act of collecting and publishing folklore in Finland; the *Kalevala* epic was received as the first important work in Finnish *literature* and continues to be valued as such (see e.g. Honko 1980a: 2, 1980b, 1987b: 130–133; Karkama 2001; Anttonen 2002, 2004a). For Matti Kuusi, folklore is *unwritten literature* (see Kuusi 1963).

As a form of literature, folklore is by implication old and ancient, because in the historical sequence of orality and literacy, it has to predate written literature. It is also regarded as more authentic than written literature, which, by definition, is an individual, and therefore, modern (and in its idiosyncrasy, a non-traditional) product of human creativity. Susan Stewart has argued that folkloristic genres, such as the epic, fable, proverb, fairy tale, and ballad, are artifacts constructed by a literary culture. As such, they are projections of authenticity onto oral forms that are thus 'antiqued', distressed, made old. Stewart emphasizes that "when oral forms are transformed into 'evidence' and 'artifacts,' they acquire all the characteristics of fragmentation, symbolic meaning, and literariness that are most valued by the literary culture" (Stewart 1991: 7).

The practice of 'making old' is a rhetorical means to embed the collected materials and the cultural forms they represent with the value and prestige of age. In discourses in which history carries authority, age is the most advantageous property that the folklore materials can have in the argumentative contexts into which they are incorporated. Age matters when folklore is presented as a testimony of national culture, the political claims made in its name or as symbols for an ethnic group aspiring for linguistic and/or cultural rights and/or political sovereignty. It embodies the idea according to which the essence of the power of tradition is to legitimate the present act with a historical precedence. For this reason, that which is claimed traditional is most prestigious when claimed to be old. Proverbs, for example, tend to be rhetorically charged with the claim that they are 'ancient wisdom'. In 19th-century Finland, the oral verse found from among the illiterate and preindustrial segments of the population was conceptualized as 'ancient' poetry, even though no ancient document was available, as the earliest recording dates from the 16th century. It is indeed the politicization of age that Hobsbawm attacked with his criticism of the invention of tradition (see Hobsbawm & Ranger 1983).

In addition to its position as part of a collection, the argumentative value and force in that which is regarded as folklore or tradition has derived from its conceptualization as an antiquity. An antiquity is an object that receives its value from being a rarity that comes from a distant timespace and carries, as it were, time and history within itself. In England in the 18th and 19th centuries, that which is now called folklore was called 'popular antiquities' to denote cultural forms and expressions regarded as being relics, remnants and curiosities of older times, that is, deriving from premodernity. In this coinage, 'popular' refers to cultural, spatial and class-based otherness, while 'antiquity' refers to its value as a rare representation of temporal otherness.

Roger Abrahams has called antiquated documents of cultural otherness "ruins in the landscape" (Abrahams 1993a: 10–11). In a similar manner, Nicole Belmont has argued that folklore scholarship is founded upon such temporal distancing in which oral traditions are made representations of ancient times, and referred to with the metaphors of monument and ruin (Belmont 1986: 25–26, cited in Tarkka 1989: 249). Such ruins are not mere glimpses of the past. They are monuments that both prescribe and legitimate a particular way of writing and representing history. According to Abrahams, they endow a piece of land with ancient meanings and thus sacralize the landscape and its control as claimed territory (see Abrahams 1993a: 10–11, 17). According to

Bendix, "collecting reifies the communicative processes that are folklore and renders them into a desirable relic" (Bendix 2002: 113). Despite the terminological shift made by the antiquarian William Thoms in 1846 (see Thoms 1965), 'folklore' in folkloristic research has continued its earlier semantic meaning as an antiquity. This, then, has emphasized the idea of folklore as a thing of the past, despite many present-day folklorists' efforts and arguments to the contrary. By definition, antiquity is an item of non-modernity, temporally opposite to or distant from modernity.

The same applies to the idea of folklore as classic. Conceptualized through the temporal qualifiers of modern and its opposites, that which is traditional can also be seen as 'antique' and 'classic'. Retaining its sense as 'popular antiquity', folklore stands for that which in human cultural production and communication not only threatens to vanish due to such 'alien factors' as modernization, but appears to remain – or rather, gain – in value and create a sense of historical permanence and continuity in the transitory nature of human existence, the fleetingness of time, and the falling into oblivion of both natural and human-made products. Those that remain or seem to remain are classics. They are timeless by enduring time and persisting through it. Folklore is also conceptualized as a 'classic' in the sense of 'first class', as the term was understood in the first centuries A. D. in Rome (Calinescu 1987: 14). The search for and display of gems of folk expression and artistry ('classics' among the *populus vulgus*) have characterized the discipline especially through its devolutionistic premise, dominant in the early 20th century. When made objects of nostalgia, the classics become qualitative souvenirs from places unvisited and unvisitable.

A similar type of distance between the modern and the present is created through the continuing and even increasing tendency to synonymize 'folklore' with 'tradition'. Considering the fact that the concept of tradition has, to a great extent, surpassed 'ancient' and 'classical' as the designated term to denote the temporal opposition to 'modern', the synonymization of 'folklore' and 'tradition' cannot escape from making 'folklore' and 'modern' contradictions in a temporal sense. From this perspective, any argument for the occurrence of 'folklore' in the modern is an issue of 'still'. Indeed, any such occurrence is by definition an argument.

Turning instances of orality into antiquities is to embed the documents with power not only to represent but also to transform. As an antiquity, a text is extracted from those communicative and rhetorical contexts in which it has become an object of interest and value for the collector/scholar. As a consequence, it is drawn into another communicative and rhetorical context in which it receives its status as a representation of not only the communicative and rhetorical context from which it was extracted from (as mimesis) but of particular past ways of experiencing life and spatiotemporal otherness in general (as metonymy). In other words, folklore as circulating discourse is transformed into folklore as the collective representation of a 'folk'. As such, its argumentative value depends on how it fulfills the rhetorical purposes set for the contexts into which it has been integrated – in the discourses into which it has been recontextualized.

56

The conceptualization of tradition as selected artifacts has gone hand in hand with the process of folklorization. This is to say that the collecting and study of folklore does not 'find' or 'discover' folklore, as if this were an objectively existing natural object, independent of its role and position as an object for the folklorist's gaze. Instead, the gaze that looks for folklore, whether regarded as vanishing or as vibrant, incorporates particular cultural phenomena into the discourse on folklore and the folklore taxonomy designed within this discourse. In this discourse the term 'folklore' stands metacommunicatively for particular types of acts and utterances in a set of classifications. It also serves as a metaphor for cultural continuity and socially constructed models in verbal artistry and poetic expression, and in symbols of collectivity and traditionality. The folkloristic gaze, in other words, does not only find historicity and collectivity in human communication and social life; it makes it folklore, that is, folklorizes it.

This does not mean that the phenomena regarded as folklore do not ontologically exist. Rather, it means that particular, selected elements in human culture and communication receive their epistemic meaning and value as objects of this selection through their inclusion and appropriation in the scholarly category of folklore. In other words, the process of folklorization, the collecting and naming of cultural phenomena as folklore and putting them on display as collections of such, is to incorporate particular elements and processes of communication, for example, particular generic expressions of verbal artistry, into a particular type of social knowledge, which is then given epistemic power to legitimate the very practice of representation.

To folklorize is to detrivialize. That which gets to be selected and objectified by the folklorist as a representation of cultural otherness is trivial to the scholar when it lies outside its role as an object for the folklorizing gaze. It is thus detrivialized as the folklorist recontextualizes it into new discourses by objectifying it, collecting it, classifying it and putting it on display. Folklore taxonomy, folklore collection and folklore presentation are discourses of detrivialization. The detrivialization is especially conspicuous when folklore as representation is made by its very presence to comment on modernity and its otherness in a discourse on difference. In addition, as fragments and extracts from the ephemerality of human life and interpersonal communication, folklore recordings also function as means to detrivialize the ephemeral and create a sense of permanence (cf. Kirshenblatt-Gimblett 1991: 391). As such, folklore functions like a photograph that captures the passing of time, finitude and death (cf. Turner 1987: 150). In its own permanent, 'saved-from-oblivion' form, it detrivializes the moment of capture, and transforms it into a recognizable and recollectable moment that at the same time comments on the act of representation. It does this by representing that which signifies absence, adding thus to its value as a token of rarity, age, and class.

## The Search for a Lost Community

Representing a conception common at the time, Richard Bauman wrote in 1983 that it is "one of the great ironies of our intellectual history as folklorists (...) that the discipline of folklore emerged just at the time that traditional folk society, as ideally conceived, was recognized as a declining way of life under the impact of technological and economic change" (Bauman 1983: 153). Since then, there has been an increase in arguments that the discipline did not emerge 'ironically' at such an eleventh hour, but instead, the discursive practice of studying and collecting that which is called folklore has been a particular response to the advent of modernity and the effects of modernization (see e.g. Abrahams 1988, 1992a, 1993a; Becker 1988; Bustin 1988; Bauman 1989). Instead of ironically coinciding with modernization, the essence of folkloric practice lies in its argumentative relationship to modernity and modernization.

According to Roger Abrahams, the response of the emerging American folklore scholarship to modernization was a counter voice to the praise of progress, and as such, it was part of a larger intellectual movement that expressed mistrust in modernity. Like the many European forms of antimodernism, Abrahams writes, American intellectuals "looked to the past and to an older sense of community and tradition in order to understand their growing sense of alienation and loss" (Abrahams 1988: 61). These "thoughtful Americans" looked to earlier epochs (e.g. the Middle Ages), 'simpler' societies (e.g. the American Indians), and to childhood as "times and cultures exhibiting more energy and imagination and encouraging a wider range of vigorous experiences" (Abrahams 1988: 62). Abrahams's account of the antimodernist basis of folklore scholarship, which Dillon Bustin also connects with the romanticism of Henry David Thoreau and other transcendentalists (see Bustin 1988), gives testimony to the notion that that which came to be collected and studied as folklore was regarded as providing modernity (at least the alienated upper class intellectuals in the American context) with regenerative power and moral nourishment found among the illiterate and exotic other.

For this reason we can argue that folklore scholarship, when conceptualized as a moral or a national project, did not emerge from a realization that folklore as *the* cultural heritage and embodiment of moral or symbolic properties in peasant culture was just about to vanish due to modernization. On the contrary, that which was perceived as vanishing came to be valorized, politically established as cultural heritage in a national arena and/or regarded as an embodiment of preferred moral properties. Consequently, that which was initially marginal and trivial for those in the political and intellectual centers of modernity was brought into their symbolic discourses in the center by collecting specimens of marginal cultural forms and attaching to them special, partly nostalgic and partly moral use value, both as a commentary against certain processes of modernization and in the service of certain others. As a metaphor for a 'lost community', the past, as it was interpreted to be represented in folklore, provided a means to criticize particular modern changes and innovations which were felt to be lacking in collectivity or moral property or were felt to cause such a lack. Yet, paradoxically, such discourse at the same time produced more of the very modernity that was seen to produce loss.

Folkloristic discourse on the vanishing object follows the traditionalist perspective according to which modernity generates inauthenticity and a sense of loss of directness and unmediatedness in production, consumption, and communication. Yet, folklore research is not mere nostalgia undermining its own emancipative power. On the contrary, as pointed out by Bryan Turner about nostalgia, by converting the past into a Utopian homestead, it may lay the foundations for a radical critique of the modern as a departure from authenticity (Turner 1987: 154).

This especially applies to American folklore scholarship, which not only in its formative, post-transcendentalist stages but especially in its late 20th-century developments is to a great extent constructed as a project of edification that purports to fight and undo what are regarded as the alienating and "disruptive forces of modernity'" (Bauman 1983). Here folklore, as denoting 'face-to-face' interaction and direct, unmediated experience, is conceptualized as a trajectory against modern alienation. The same applies, according to Hermann Bausinger, to Germany, where folklore and folklife have been "anti-modernist constructions based on a regressive ideology (…) compensating for the alienation of modern life" (Bausinger 1990: xi). 'Folk', 'folkness', and 'folk society' as modernity's constructed othernesses are projected as resources for sites and states in the experience of directness, unmediatedness, and intimacy.

Based on the notion that modern society is socially distant and differentiated, the nostalgic projection becomes a form of social commentary that uses the concepts of 'folk' and 'folk community' for the representation and defense of the ordinary, the intimate, and the local, which are regarded as some of the crucial building blocks of identity making in modern society – as much as in a traditional society. Unlike Herderian and Hegelian nationalism in Europe, which valorizes folklore as a representation of national symbolism and ancestry, the American transcendentally oriented appropriation of nostalgia for a 'lost community' looks for alternative ways of making and experiencing modernity. Steven Zeitlin has, accordingly, called folklore studies a discipline of advocates, in which the goal is "fostering webs of cultural meaning, linking past and present through tradition and creativity, encouraging the process whereby human beings, as Dell Hymes (1975: 369) puts it, shape deeply felt values into meaningful forms" (Zeitlin 2000: 5).

The search for alternative ways to experiencing modernity is a continuous cultural flow between centers and peripheries. The present is actively made and created by bringing culture from that which is conceptualized as marginal and otherness to that which is conceptualized as a center in one's experience of modernity (cf. Hannerz 1991). For the folklorist, this is an issue of bringing culture from among the 'folk' to the 'non-folk' with the intention of making the 'non-folk' more 'folk'. As put by Dillon Bustin, the purpose is "to find in folk culture the inspiration for improved community life" (Bustin 1988: 5). As such, folklore scholarship comes close, as also noted by Zeitlin (2000: 14), to the classic definition of a revitalization movement (see e.g. Wallace 1956: 265), but its philosophical foundation as socio-political activity is different. It is noteworthy that both the folk and folklore are qualitative categories.

Jane Becker describes the folklorists' moral agenda as follows: "Living in a world of sophisticated technology, politics, and bureaucracy, we still seek to give meaning to our lives and perhaps seek an alternative model of living by maintaining and reviving folk traditions. Using interpretations of traditional culture, we continue to search for ways to identify ourselves as groups and as members of particular communities." (Becker 1988: 55.) Thus, possibly because many prominent folklorists in the United States started out as folk song revivalists (see Jackson 1985; Kirshenblatt-Gimblett 1988: 141), the idea of 'reviving' social and community life has become one of the essential motivational forces in folkloristic activity, especially in the 'folkloristic community work' of public sector folklore (see e.g. Baron & Spitzer 1992; Kirshenblatt-Gimblett 2000). This is a form of practical training and political participation which for many of its protagonists means the appropriation of the qualities attributed to a folk society as arguments in the making of modern national, ethnic and residential communities. Becker writes that Americans "seek connections with a perceived simpler, more natural, preindustrial past. In this search, we have consistently turned to idealized concepts of 'folk' to define and sustain notions of community amid rapid and disruptive change." (Becker 1988: 19.)

Perhaps more than for anybody else in the American context, folklore is for Henry Glassie a moral philosophy, its virtue being "that it is charged with values, saturated with opinions about how one ought to live in the world" (Glassie 1983: 127). With reference to Dan Ben-Amos's definition of folklore as artistic communication in small groups (see Ben-Amos 1972), Glassie points to what he regards as the key moral propositions of folklore: First, folklore is artistic, aesthetic and created by someone who is committed to its creation, and therefore folklore stands against both triviality and alienation, "that which prevents people from preserving active control over their own creative energies". Second, folklore is communication, and thus it brings people together and stands against radical individualism and solipsism. Third, folklore is artistic communication in small groups, and thus it "engenders personally involved connections among people who exist in on-going associations". And since shared values, according to Glassie, hold people together in groups, they have a shared sense of morality, and thus, folklore also stands against amorality (Glassie 1983: 131). Interestingly enough, that which the founders of American folklore scholarship, according to Abrahams, felt they were being alienated from, due to the vanishing of that which is called folklore, Henry Glassie finds residing in that which *he* designates as folklore. Folklore for him stands for – and stands up for – everything that is good, positive and edifying, and therefore, is opposed to the negative aspects of modernity.

In Glassie's moral philosophy, the negative aspects of modernity constantly threaten folklore. "If modernity brings exploitation through alienation, cheapness through triviality, moral failure through radical individualism, desperation through the destruction of small-group orientation, then folklore fights back. If modernity brings standardization, mass production, then folklore results from nonstandardization, from variation. If modernity means constantly changing fashions, folklore means stable traditions. The purpose of fashion is to create class disjunction; the purpose of folklore is egalitarian integration of the little community" (Glassie 1983: 136.)

Even though Glassie's perspective is antimodern, it is not non-modern. On the contrary, its antimodernism finds expression in the making of the non-modern a source of 'spiritual' compensation for the alleged lack of tradition or authenticity in the experience of the modern. As such, his perspective is an inseparable part of modernity and its continuous reconstitution. The same applies to other things folkloric – whether considered 'fakelore' or 'real folklore' – in which people find regenerative power and creative force. The moral antimodernism of such perspectives is essentially a modern trajectory.

## Folklore in the Modern

Most folklorists today will argue that the dichotomy of tradition and modernity no longer applies. Indeed, the general trend in folklore studies during the last four or five decades has been, to borrow a phrase from Seppo Knuuttila, "a return to the present" (Knuuttila 1989). This means that originally past-oriented research has gradually been adjusted to find its study objects closer to the scholars' own present. Accordingly, folklore is no longer regarded merely as a thing of the vanishing agricultural past but is also found to exist in modern industrialized society. In fact, according to Ilana Harlow, "Current folklore theory affirms that folklore is not threatened by modernity – that it is a creative response to contemporary conditions" (Harlow 1998: 232). Similar views continue to proliferate.

This perspective was emphatically put forward by Alan Dundes in the mid-1960s, when he launched his famous redefinition of 'the folk' to refer to "any group of people whatsoever who share at least one common factor" (Dundes 1965: 2). In support of his reformulation of the key concept of the discipline, Dundes argued that "If modern folklorists accepted the nineteenth century definition of folk as illiterate, rural, backward peasant, then it might well be that the study of the lore of such folk might be a strictly salvage operation and that the discipline of folkloristics would in time follow the folk itself into oblivion" (Dundes 1977: 22). Thus, in fitting in a number of present-day phenomena under the heading of folklore and in disassociating 'the folk' from the uncivilized and the illiterate, Dundes's reformulation aimed at deruralizing and modernizing not only the concept of folklore but also the discipline of folklore. This would also mean taking distance from 19th-century Herderian nationalism as the ideological foundation of the discipline.

Dundes's reformulation was, thus, an issue of the folklorists becoming modern. With his explicitly "modern conception of the folk" (Dundes 1977: 24), Dundes indicated that in order to be *modern* – instead of being traditional – the folklorist is not to accept the traditional definition of folklore that associates it with the past and vanishing rural culture. In other words, a *modern* folklorist "sees members of modern societies as members of many different folk groups" (Dundes 1977: 24). A modern folklorist regards folklore as thriving in modernity. In addition, as pointed out by Dorothy Noyes, the terminological shift to the sociological concept of the group was intended to overcome the "classist, racist, and antimodern connotations of *folk*" (Noyes 1995: 452).

The subsequently common and often replicated idea of folklore thriving in modernity is not merely a rhetorical catchphrase to convince folklorists that they continue to have something to study in modernity. It is also supposed to provide a new answer to the old question of how folklore is transmitted and disseminated; how it is 'living'. Dundes's formulation of the folk argues for a close interrelationship between the existence of folklore and the groupness of a group. Indeed, in modern folklore scholarship, groupness came to be seen as the fundamental soil for folklore to emerge and to persist – in variations. As a product of a group, folklore came to be seen as signaling its identity. This sociological approach is continued in Dan Ben-Amos's definition of folklore as artistic communication in small groups (see Ben-Amos 1972) as well as in Henry Glassie's wordings about folklore and tradition: "Folk and lore link people and expression in a functional circle. Epic and nation, myth and society, custom and community – all conjoin communications and groups. The group exists because its members create communications that call it together and bring it to order." (Glassie 1995: 400.)

Lauri Honko presented in Finland similar conceptions as Dundes did in the United States, and at the same time. Honko's basic tenet was that instead of merely existing and traveling, folklore does something: it functions socially. This functional orientation correlated with the contemporaneous methodological trend of putting the 'folk' back into 'folklore'; that is, to set the scholarly focus on singers and narrators and other individual performers that in addition to standing out as individuals would still be recognized as being members of a given social group. The folk of 'folklore' came thus to be perceived as individuals in their role as members in a folk group; in other words, as individual tradition bearers who are members of a tradition-bearing community. For Honko in his modern sociological thinking, folklore became a "natural, even a vital element of the life of every member group. The members of the group may not all know each other, but they are more or less familiar with the group's common fund of tradition, its values, norms and symbols." (Honko 1991: 25.) Honko even stated that "Familiarity with this collective tradition is the true criterion for membership" and that folklore is the factor holding the group together (Honko 1991: 25–26). Here, the social basis of folklore becomes an even stronger determinant of the category than textual corpuses and related taxonomies. Folklore study is, thus, a kind of sociology of circulating texts but with a much stronger focus on the group in which a given text allegedly circulates than the circulation itself.

Many scholars came to share the view of folklore thriving in modernity and contributing to group making in society. This trend was also seen as an indication of the field of folklore being finally detached from antimodernism, romanticism and Herderian nationalism. Ruth Finnegan wrote in the early 1990s that "it has become increasingly acceptable to study new and changing institutions rather than just those that could be deemed 'old,' to consider urban as well as rural environments (there is now, for example, the emerging branch of study known as 'urban folklore'), and to include the interaction between oral and written forms as potentially equally as interesting as these separate modes of human communication once believed to be 'pure' and 'authentic'." (Finnegan 1991: 110.)

Because of the rather general acceptance of Dundes's formulation, as well as of similar developments in some countries even prior to the international distribution of Dundes's ideas, the concept of folklore has gradually expanded to denote many sorts of traditional culture and expressive forms which do not necessarily have anything to do with peasant traditions, lower or vulgar classes of society, illiterateness, orality, collectivity, or anything else that used to be regarded as the basic characteristics, qualifications, and requirements of 'traditional' folklore. In this sense, the concepts of 'folk' and 'folklore' have not only been modernized but they have also been democratized – as democracy is a true modern value and political idea. As a consequence, just about anything can now be folklore and anybody can be folk (see also Dorson 1978: 267; Abrahams 1992a: 44).[2]

To be sure, the process of modernization, deruralization, denationalization, contemporarization and democratization of folk and folklore began before Dundes formulated it into a definition. In the 1950s in Germany, Hermann Bausinger studied structures of everyday narrative and the 'folk culture' of the technological world (see Bausinger 1990). In Finland, Matti Kuusi declared in his inaugural lecture in 1959, upon attaining the distinguished academic position of Professor, that the *Schlager*, the pop song, is the folk song of today (Kuusi 1959; see also Pöysä 1994: 227–228). He was willing to include even the university auditorium in the list of sites in which modern folklore could be found. In the United States in the early 1960s, Roger Abrahams took a step into the urban world and wrote his dissertation on street corner music in a big city ghetto (Abrahams 1964). Ever since these landmarks, folklore research has continued its move not only from the countryside towards the city, but also from non-modernity to modernity.

This development has been characterized by an increasing acceptance of modernness in those social processes that are regarded as folkloric, although it required an eventual 'postmodern' perspective to accept the multitude of modern, and especially commercial, phenomena as part of the proper field of folkloristic topics. For example, instead of seeing the upper classes of society or popular, mass-mediated culture as 'the enemies of folklore' in the classical Dorsonian way (see e.g. Dorson 1950; cf. Ben-Amos 1984: 110), there has been a growing interest in finding, collecting, studying, and publishing 'modern forms of folklore'. In the 1970s and 1980s, these comprised, for example, jokes and urban legends, which do not circulate in oral communication only but are also found in modern mass media – often published and/or edited by folklorists.

Such perspectives have provided the folklorist with a multitude of reasons to continue pursuing the discipline, instead of letting it fall into oblivion with those folklore genres that are deemed classic and representative of premodern times. Indeed, the 'return to modernity' (to paraphrase Seppo Knuuttila) has resulted in a growing tendency to study tradition not only in historical and rural settings but also in contemporary contexts. These have provided the discipline with new 'frontiers', such as the urban one in the 1980s (see Kirshenblatt-Gimblett 1983), and more recently, the personal one, comprising personal narratives, family histories, life stories, letters and diaries and the sociology of the everyday.

The folklorist's return to modernity has in many regards followed the sociological paradigm that was firmly established in the discipline in the 1960s. This paradigm was especially conspicuous in the 1970s and 1980s, when the popular trend, for example in the Nordic countries, was to study folklore as a manifestation of local, regional and national identities. According to Lauri Honko, a leading figure in this trend, collective identity was the key to study folklore and its variation, and the study of folklore and its variation was instrumental in studying collective identity (Honko 1982: 16; see also Honko 1988). Such a perspective makes a direct link between the circulation of folklore and the cultural identity of a social group. According to this logic, folklore does not only stand for a positively evaluated element in bringing cohesion between people, but serves to indicate of the cohesiveness of any group that has folklore. Honko continued the functionalistic premise of the sociological paradigm to his final works (see Honko 1999).

As far as folklore methodology and taxonomy is concerned, the folklorists' return to modernity has often meant a search for *functional equivalents* between traditional and modern societies. According to Knuuttila, folklorists continue to be traditionalists when they look for the old in the new. By this Knuuttila means that only those modern-day phenomena are selected as objects of research and scholarly attention which can be derived phenomenologically or analogically from the products of preindustrial folk culture (Knuuttila 1994: 20–21). Those that are claimed to be items of modern folklore represent new forms of folklore because they are seen to contain elements that are familiar to the folklorist from the old forms of folklore.

It is worthy of note that such a perspective makes the earlier conceptions of folklore frames of reference against which the 'folkloreness' and authenticity of modern phenomena is evaluated. Selected present-day and especially urban phenomena are claimed as legitimate folkloristic study objects on the basis of their correlation with earlier, agrarian traditions. These can range from a variety of professional practices and their recollections to text messages sent with mobile phones. This has at least two consequences. First, the observed similarities yield easily to arguments for cultural continuity and the continuation of traditions. Second, as pointed out by Knuuttila, the past determines the present and the present is described in light of the past (Knuuttila 1994: 20).

Even though research conducted from such premises can produce invaluable insights and information about given modern phenomena, the said perspective does a great deal more than just continue the dichotomy between modern and traditional. Despite their explicit statement to deny the idea of 'fakelore', folklorists authenticate the earlier, that is, the traditional, forms of society and the communicative means and forms employed in them. These are still employed by scholars as cognitive models in the conceptualization of folklore, even though the expansion of the folklore taxonomy would make it appear otherwise. The folklore of the so-called premodern folk society continues to be used as a basic conceptual framework, which makes the traditional phenomena in the present appear as folklore in 'modern forms' and 'modern embodiments'.

Indeed, in a manner reminiscent of Matti Kuusi's 1959 statement about the *Schlager* being the folk song of today, Dan Ben-Amos writes: "the mass media provides the modern world with the equivalent of folk tradition" (Ben-Amos 1984: 110). Similarly, Henry Glassie states that "the culture of commerce in its production, say, of automobiles and office buildings is not the antagonist of folk art but its embodiment in new forms" (Glassie 1988: 221). Here modernity is seen as an agent that has transformed folklore – and the observation is embedded with optimism and confidence in modernity.

Such constructions as those denoting the 'renewal', 'revival' or 'revitalization' of tradition also make the given modern phenomena equivalents in transformation. The emphasis is on the link that the present-day practices supposedly make with their claimed predecessors. But in addition to indicating mere continuation, they are supposed to appear as intentionally made replications. For this reason, the allegedly present forms of folklore are not that far from being regarded as survivals or remains, except that they are attributed more agency in social meaning than what survivals or remains might have. As such, they continue to be seen as copies that authenticate their origins. At the same time, they also continue to represent what Raymond Williams has called the residual elements of culture (Williams 1977: 121–127).

The essentialized status of traditional folklore can also be seen in the tendency by folklorists to argue that the traditional genres of traditional societies are still the proper research object of folklore studies, its symbolic center and core materials (see Anttonen 1994b). Each national tradition of folklore studies embraces their own nationalized set of 'classic genres'. A somewhat related issue is the motivation by folklorists to travel to far-away places to look for authenticity that is allegedly missing or scarce in modern Western folklore. Lauri Honko explicated this rather clearly by stating that the material available for folklorists in the Third World countries "is many times more interesting, at times almost unique, than the materials at the disposal of the folklorists in the West" (Honko 1992: 4). Modernity, from this perspective, is seen to produce only second-rate folklore.

The critical comments about folklorists favoring inherited biases in their search for functional equivalents apply to my own thinking as well. In some of my earlier articles and essays from the 1980s (Anttonen 1982a, 1982b, 1985) I discussed traditions in modernity in accordance with the devolutionistic master narrative that constructs the history of traditionality as a unilinear process from the 'original spontaneity of folk culture' to standardized mass culture. However, instead of categorically regarding mass-mediated culture as a destroyer of traditionality, I was looking for such 'new traditions' in modernity that would correspond to the old ones in unofficialness and in spontaneity, in a manner reminiscent of Robert Redfield's oppositional pair 'great tradition' and 'small tradition'. I placed the qualities of unofficialness and spontaneity in contrast to the official or authorized forms of distributing knowledge and power in society.

I obviously continued the practice of defining the categories of the folk and folklore in qualitative terms. The 'folk' was politically progressive, as it was seen to stand both for modernity's otherness and for democracy and democratic aspirations. I found 'real traditionality' and folklore production in movements for alternative life-styles, counter culture, and the international networks of consuming those musical genres whose performers do not receive funding from government-subsidized institutions. As regards the regenerative power embedded in such phenomena, my interest and viewpoints even retrospectively make sense. If tradition denotes cultural models and patterns, I was not mistaken in seeing traditionality in the making in these phenomena. Yet, I was obviously also projecting onto these social processes my own (and to some extent collectively shared) idea of authenticity, spontaneity and 'direct', unmediated experience. For the legitimization of this projection, I used the term 'tradition', which to me appeared prestigious. At the same time, this was a move to deny 'real' traditionality in those spheres of action that looked politically conservative to me.

## Folklore as Contestation

The continued dichotomizing of tradition and modernity in modern culture springs from the continued use of traditional and modern as temporal qualifiers. The linguistic opposition constructs the dichotomy in the reality to which the signs of 'traditional' and 'modern' refer. As traditionality denotes both a continuous model and that which is no longer used as a model, the use of the term tradition for continuing social processes inescapably constructs a polarization with the present.

The dichotomization is also intentional, because it is pregnant with ideological purposes. For example, the differentiation of the traditional from the modern may work for a statement in support – in the confirmation of the legitimacy – of traditional institutions, practices, ways of life, values, as well as for the conservation of traditional material objects. When 'modern' stands for bourgeois hegemony, unwanted foreign influence, or cultural imperialism, to speak of the traditional is to take an explicitly political stand for those opposing that which is claimed as modern. In fact, to a noticeable extent, folklore scholarship has in many institutional settings since the 1970s been characterized by a humanistic mission to speak for the underdog, the subaltern, the under- and misrepresented populations, and their political rights to continue cultural practices that have become – or are intentionally constructed as – symbolic of their cultural uniqueness and/or their aspirations for political independence. Roger Abrahams, among others, emphasizes the viability of studying folklore "in terms of its contestive motives and its deployment for purposes of resistance to dominant cultural practices" (Abrahams 1992a: 35). In their recently published study on modernist ideologies on language in works of philosophy, political theory, anthropology and folklore, Richard Bauman and Charles Briggs make it clear in the outset that, having set out to locate "ideological charters for persistent practices of oppression" and "structures of inequality and domination", they are looking for "new modes of thinking and acts of political resistance" (Bauman & Briggs 2003: viii–x).

Such a political agenda in folklore studies derives at least partially from the Marxist perspectives of Antonio Gramsci and Luigi Lombardi-Satriani, who equate folk culture with the subordinate class and interpret folklore as "a specific culture that derives from the lower classes with the function to oppose the hegemonic culture, the latter being a product of the dominant class" (Lombardi-Satriani 1974: 103; see also Cirese 1982; Lears 1985). This perspective, by definition, emphasizes the idea of folklore as an oppositional and subversive force. It also exemplifies the trend to define folklore on the basis of a political function.

The dichotomizing of folklore and modernity has characterized both the Marxist approach as well the edification approach that has developed in American folklore scholarship, partially in the tradition of William James's pragmatism and the older tradition of transcendentalism. But in addition to the ideological framework, folklore and modernity play opposite roles in the narrativization of modernity as the diffusion of innovations.

Charging tradition negatively and modern positively characterized the acculturation and innovation theories that became fashionable in the 1950s and 1960s. These theories would predicate those people that adopt innovations with positive qualifications, while those that oppose or reject innovations and remain with the customary are negatively qualified (Sarmela 1979: 20). Those who embraced innovations were considered 'modern', while those who opposed them were regarded as 'traditional' and 'conservative'. With reference to this tendency, Seppo Knuuttila has pointed out that arguments that circulate in favor of innovations tend to be taken as representing rationality, while those against the innovations are retrospectively formulated into humorous anecdotes (see Knuuttila 1989: 93–94; Knuuttila 1994: 41). Thus, being 'traditional' in a context in which the 'victorious' side signifies modernity is both documented and ridiculed with folklore that dramatizes the said opposition.

Folklore and narrativity are here associated with acts and arguments that stand for traditionality and as such, for opposition to change and innovation. Instead of the breakthrough of novelties, the domain of folklore attracts narration about the people, objects and ideas located in modernity's otherness. Resistance to technological innovations is one such field of topics. A related example is provided by jokes that men tell about women's ineptitude when it comes to handling a car and especially in parallel parking. Such jokes suggest that women depend on the cultural knowledge and the logics of rationality that men choose or do not choose to provide them with (see Anttonen 1998:

387). This does not only position women in a domain likened to premodern orality, in opposition to the technologically adept men of modernity; it also reproduces folklore as discourse that locates its objects and topics in modernity's otherness.

# 4. Postmodernization in the Making

## From Promodern to Antimodern

In the 1980s and 1990s, the traditionally promodern discourse of sociology started to foreground some of the discipline's antimodernist legacies. While in classical sociology modernization was viewed as a narrative of progress, especially of increasing rationality, there were now a growing number of sociologists who became sensitive to the more destructive elements in modernity. In what was labeled postmodern theorizing, modern society came to be regarded as an organization that not only limits the freedom of individual subjects but also, as Marx had argued, alienates people from the value of their social and economic action. Modernity was thus criticized for having reduced individuals to anonymous masses, and modern technology came to be regarded as having made society a "cold press-button society" (Mongardini 1992: 59).

Similarly, modernity came to stand for self-preservation and the repression of man's 'inner nature' and his "anarchic impulses of happiness" (Wellmer 1985: 11). From this perspective, postmodernism came as a "liberation from the rational mind" and a counter-act for the alienation allegedly caused by capitalism. Postmodernism thus stood for a "rediscovery of spirituality" and a "rediscovery of the aesthetic justification for life" (Mongardini 1992: 61). In a manner not so different from what has been regarded as antimodernism, postmodernism offered a framework for expressing the feeling that modernity had foregrounded material values at the expense of spiritual ones. Indeed, in the critique and rejection of the belief in unlimited growth in both material wealth and moral enlightenment, postmodernist arguments followed a long line of social criticism and cultural pessimism. Yet, while antimodernism would denote a turn against modern developments, postmodernism would denote a turn against modern establishments.

One of the most famous early manifestations of such perspectives – in addition to the work by Friedrich Nietzsche – was *Untergang des Abendlandes* (The Decline of the West, 1918) by Oswald Spengler (1959). Cultural pessimism emerged from observations that the development of a modern society and the 'disruption of traditional frameworks' – be they family, community, or political mechanisms – may lead more often to disintegration, delinquency, and chaos than to a new viable modern order (Eisenstadt 1974: 2; see also Freud 1962).

Critical perspectives on modernity emphasized that instead of progress, wealth and happiness, humankind has been cursed with wars, discrimination, cruelty, poverty, assembly line factory work, excessive consumption, culture industry, waste and environmental problems, ecological catastrophes, etc. Here many were reminded of Max Weber's pessimistic vision of the loss of meaning in life as a consequence of the triumph of rationality and scientific reasoning. For modernists and postmodernists alike, modernity – and post-modernity as accelerated modernity – came to stand for individualization and detraditionalization, which may bring emancipation and individual freedom, but which, at the same time, deprive people of their communities and 'true', normative, collective, humanistic and spiritual values.

Accordingly, for the postmodernist Jean Baudrillard, mass consumption became disciplined waste that is ultimately destructive of the individual, so-cial relations and the environment (Baudrillard 1975). Baudrillard perceived modern (and postmodern) culture to be in a crisis and loss of authenticity, in which the distinction between the real and the illusory disappears into a sequence of simulations and simulacra (Baudrillard 1983a). The represen-tations are more real than the things represented, which eventually leads to the end of true social relations and thus, to the end of the social (Baudrillard 1983b). Similarly, Mike Featherstone saw the simulational world as being devoid of all meaning, thus creating a "hyperspace in which we live beyond normativity and classification in an aesthetic hallucination of reality" (Feath-erstone 1989: 151–152; cf. Eco 1986). Scott Lash characterized modernity as the fragmentation and differentiation of social institutions, both horizontally and vertically (Lash 1990).

Such social and cultural criticism may have been a project for social re-form but it has not always been that distinct from antimodernist statements that may undermine emancipative aspirations with nostalgia. While cultural criticism can lead to a theoretical understanding of modernity and capitalism (see e.g. Haug 1980; Marcus & Fischer 1986), or the contestation of West-ern hegemony by non-Western societies and aboriginal ethnic groups (see e.g. Friedman 1992a), it can also lead to cultural pessimism, which can then turn to romanticism and construct idealizations in cultural otherness, in that which is placed in the category of the pre- and non-modern. Folklore and folk societies may become their projected representations. Indeed, both in the name of antimodernism and postmodernism, modernization can come to be seen as an evil that allegedly destroyed the paradise of the 'traditional society'. Consequently, we may again start looking for and discovering 'noble savages' who seem to possess the quality of life that modern people appear to have lost. Or, we may argue that such present-day social problems and issues as crime, drug abuse, alcoholism, teenage pregnancy, pornography, divorce, rootlessness, terrorism, etc., are consequences of a breakdown of community traditions, values and public morality due to modernization. The call for traditions as positive social forces (and authority), both in collective identification and moral behavior, often find substance in such experiences.

Yet, in addition to serving as a binding force, the call for tradition may also lead to political fundamentalism.


## From Antimodern to Promodern

As I have indicated above, the dualistic categorization of academic disciplines into promodern and antimodern as regards their position and stance to modernity is not completely valid, even though such ideal conceptualizations do exist. Anthropologists, ethnologists and folklorists do not always differ from sociologists in their social theories and perspectives on modernity and modernization, whether these are promodern or antimodern. Since its emergence, folklore scholarship, for example, has been antimodernist and traditionalist, orienting towards the past and that which is regarded as vanishing in modernization. Yet, at the same time, it has in fundamental ways been promodern and employed its 'non-modern' research materials for the making of modernity and for supporting modernization processes, especially those of nationalization and the project of enlightenment. Moreover, folklorists have been quick to utilize the latest developments in modern technology for the documentation of vanishing lore.

Antimodernism and promodernism are positions and perspectives that are historically specific and subject to change. In the course of the 1980s and 1990s, new trends emerged in folklore scholarship that indicated a growing interest in adopting a more accepting attitude towards modernity, especially towards those features that are regarded as some of modernity's most characteristic traits, namely commercialism and the commodification of culture. Scholars started to question the classic mass-culture critique and the modernist dichotomy of folk culture and mass culture, which, as Ben-Amos points out, attributes the positive value of genuineness to folk culture and regards mass culture as corruptive, "shallow and manipulative" (Ben-Amos 1984: 111). Decades earlier, perspectives that Ben-Amos was referring to used to be shared by folklorists and media scholars alike. A quote from Dwight MacDonald provides a good example:

> Folk Art grew from below, it was a spontaneous, autochthonous expression of the people, shaped by themselves, pretty much without the benefit of High Culture, to suit their own needs. Mass Culture is imposed from above. It is fabricated by technicians hired by businessmen; its audience are passive consumers, their participation limited to the choice between buying and not buying. (MacDonald 1957: 60.)

Such a dichotomous viewpoint might make it anomalous to argue that expressions of folk culture would thrive in modern, technological societies. Indeed, as is pointed out by Dorothy Noyes, such a view presupposes that "The handmade would vanish in the face of the machine, and the products of the machine could express nothing but the machine" (Noyes 1991: 58).

In order to promote the idea that folklore is not only a thing of the non-mass-mediated past, many folklorists started to change their perspective on the nature of mass-mediated communication. If folklore is to be 'found' (or 'discovered') in the age of technology, it cannot be something that stands in opposition to mass communication and lives outside of it. On the contrary, it must be something that lives within the culture of technology. This argument came up strongly in the work of Hermann Bausinger as early as the late 1950s. When his book was translated into English in 1990, its main argument came to coincide with current debates on a more relaxed approach to commercialism among folklorists. While the modernist dichotomy between folk culture and mass culture could still find support from such Frankfurt School critical theorists as T. W. Adorno and his critical writings on culture industry (Adorno 1991; yet, see Bernstein 1991), the idea of folklore thriving in the age of technology was seen to require correlations instead of oppositions between mass-mediated communication and that which is called folklore.

Accordingly, modern and 'postmodern' folklorists started to look for symbolic dimensions in the mass media, and to respond to the progressive potentials of technological innovation as well as commodification. Here such media scholars as John Fiske gained importance as sources for folklorists to draw upon (see e.g. Fiske 1987, 1989). Indicating an accepting attitude towards commodification, Dan Ben-Amos called for "a post-modernistic folklore in which tradition is not only made self-conscious but often put up for sale" (Ben-Amos 1990: ix). While modernist folklore made great efforts to distinguish fakelore from folklore, postmodernist folklore, according to Ben-Amos, "has acquired new symbolic significances in which the spurious obtains a new genuineness in its new contexts" (Ben-Amos 1990: ix).

In addition to arousing discussion on what 'postmodern folklore' in a 'postmodern age' might look like (see e.g. Bacchilega 1988; Workman 1989; Warshaver 1990), the debate on folklore's relation to mass-mediated and commoditized technology kindled new perspectives on the relationship between vernacular processes and the mass media. John Dorst, for example, asked whether we are "in the historical moment that marks, not the end of folk culture or the end of the vernacular mode of production, but the end of that discursive practice which sustains the distinction between the vernacular, the folk, the marginal, and so on, on the one hand, and the dominant, the mainstream, the official, the mass, on the other" (Dorst 1990: 189). In the name of postmodernity, Dorst called for new possibilities, new concepts, and new understanding of the relationship between the "vernacular spheres of experience" and consumer culture. Emphasizing that these are not straightforward antagonists, as was previously thought, Dorst urged the folklorists to pay attention to a given process that takes place under the conditions of postmodernity and advanced consumer capitalism. He called this process the "vernacularization of the commodity" (Dorst 1988: 218–219).

By 'vernacularization of the commodity' Dorst means the process in which the commodities that are produced in present-day capitalism are localized in meaning and use, and through this localization and vernacularization they become, according to Dorst, items of 'folk expression'. It is noteworthy that Barbara Kirshenblatt-Gimblett discussed the same phenomenon some years earlier in terms of 'customizing mass culture'. This concept stands for "the ways in which users modify mass-produced objects to suit their needs, interests, and values, and naturalize mass culture items into new systems of meaning and activity" (Kirshenblatt-Gimblett 1983: 215).

The perspectives that foreground the dynamics and emergent qualities in technological communication do not yield easily to the traditional dichotomization of folk culture and mass culture, unless folk culture is made to signify all that is dynamic and personally meaningful in mass-mediated communication, that is, all that the folklorist would regard as valuable and interesting. Indeed, be it in the name of postmodernity or something else, it is worth considering how the dichotomy of folk / non-folk as well as that of mass culture / folk culture may construct separate communicative realms, and background or even obscure the processes in which people in today's societies participate in multiple discourses through different communicative channels, face-to-face, and the various forms of electronic communication and mass media. The methodological danger in the conceptualization of the production of 'local' meanings as a 'folk culture' is in the potential that it might be just another rhetorical move to construct the object of folkloristic research through the traditionalist analogy.

To be sure, the dialectics of vernacular and mass-mediated processes have their own traditional and traditionalizing forms. There is, for example, traditionality in mass-mediated products themselves, as they follow or contest particular genres of expression and style. There is also traditionality in the relationship between the mass media and the consumer. This includes the ways in which mass mediated products are made meaningful both personally and collectively – as discussed by both Dorst and Kirshenblatt-Gimblett. The desire for consuming mass-produced and mass-mediated novelties is not merely a question of trends and fashions but serves to indicate of the continuous making of traditions, both in terms of creating collectivity and making social distinctions.

Some of these processes, as pointed out by Roger Abrahams, can be discerned "in the conservationist mood that seeks to resist consumption and to privilege recycling, remodeling, renovating, repairing, restoring, customizing, and humanizing mass-produced objects and environments" (Abrahams 1993a: 6). Yet, as this and the above-mentioned perspectives tend to be sensitive only to the vernacularized *use* of mass-products by the consumer, a 'postmodern' perspective on the folklore of vernacularization would also have to acknowledge the value of things that are 'from elsewhere' and stay that way. Adding to the complexity, mass production may also 'learn' to promote elements of vernacularization as a marketing strategy for selected target groups. Accordingly, when 'traditional meanings' emerge in the processes and practices of customization, tradition-producing agency is not only to be found among the 'postmodern equivalent of the folk', that is, the consumers of late capitalism, but also among the designers.

Not all folklore theorists have welcomed postmodernism in all of its manifestations. Henry Glassie, as discussed above, chooses not to position folklore on the margins of modernity, but instead, locates his moral agenda in folklore research in an established modernist tradition. In this tradition, in order to make a comment on the politics and aesthetics of the present and the modern, one symbolically turns away from the modern, towards a cultural other in the premodern. As is pointed out by John Dorst, Glassie "enjoins folklorists to find common cause with those great modernist figures in the arts (Yeats, Joyce, Kandinsky, etc.) who turned to the folk for aesthetic renewal and critical perspective" (Dorst 1988: 217). Glassie's open criticism of the postmodernist movement in fine arts, as well as his call for an elimination of the term postmodernism (Glassie 1988: 222–223) is shared by Dorst, who, although encouraging folklorists to enter the discussion on postmodernity, opposed *postmodernism* and its critique of modernism. In fact, Dorst says: "Folklorists have much to gain in seeing themselves as participants in the ongoing modernist project. The apparent claim of the postmodernists that this project is at an end needs to be dismissed." (Dorst 1988: 217.)

Such standpoints in favor of the modernist tradition in the objectification of the cultural other must be viewed in light of the general debate on postmodernism and its political agendas. Although both Glassie and Dorst made references to postmodernism as a discourse on art, their standpoint parallels the reactions against those postmodernist arguments that call for the end of all master narratives, including the moral ones. For example, in its moral project for social reform, modern folklore scholarship finds a common cause in the position taken by Jürgen Habermas in relation to the postmodernists, especially the French post-structuralists, as well as to the older critical theorists of the Frankfurt School, such as Theodor W. Adorno, Max Horkheimer and Walter Benjamin. Rather than rejecting the Enlightenment project, Habermas wishes to complete it, and he stands up for a critical social theory that is meant to be a contribution in the transformation towards a rational society. In this society, "human beings exercise fully their capacity for self-conscious control over social processes, and in [it] there is an absence of dominative power relationships and ideological consciousness" (quoted in Keat 1981: 3; see also Rorty 1985: 171; McLennan 2000: 642–644; Habermas 1981, 1989).

The postmodernist Jean-François Lyotard criticized Habermas for subscribing to a metanarrative of emancipation (Lyotard 1984: 60), while Habermas criticized the French postmodernists for neo-conservatism, that is, for being indifferent to the problems of contemporary society. Following Habermas, Richard Rorty criticized Michel Foucault for being "a dispassionate observer of the present social order, rather than its concerned critic" (Rorty 1985: 172). Postmodernist thinkers such as Foucault and Lyotard, according to Rorty, in their fear of being caught up in a metanarrative about the human subject, refrain from identifying themselves with the culture of the generation to which they belong or with any social reform (Rorty 1985: 172).

Similarly, Jacques Derrida came to be criticized for being a hermeneutic whose deconstruction of metaphysics has no theoretical-practical point; thus, for lack of any practical usefulness, it is pure intellectualism. Therefore, according to Madison, "the activity itself becomes purely and simply *destructive*, a kind of theoretical vandalism" (Madison 1988: 110). Indeed, when postmodernism represents "general dissatisfaction with contemporary society in which everything is regarded as false", it is not surprising, according to Randall Collins, that late 20th century intellectuals turned their philosophical admiration "to those existentialists who were most politically conservative and most anti-modernist, Nietzsche and Heidegger" (Collins 1992: 182).

So, when folklorists such as Glassie and Dorst in the late 1980s disassociated themselves from antimodernist postmodernism, they associated themselves with antimodernist modernism, which, paradoxically, is quite promodern in its antimodernism. They welcomed postmodernity as far as it served to widen the scope of folkloristic research to include those modern and postmodern cultural processes that were earlier excluded from the folklore taxonomy. Yet, postmodernism continued to be regarded as a threat to the discipline when it was felt to question the modernist practice of constructing modernity in the manner established by modern artists in their search for authenticity and inspiration in cultural otherness. The folklorist continued to liken himself to the modern artist and the ethnographer, instead of the modern consumer.

# Part 2
## Tradition, Modernity and the Nation-State

# 5. Folklore as Nationalized Antiquities

All cultural research and representation focus on that which is regarded as having value among those who engage in such activity. This means that scholarly practice is always value-laden and therefore also value promoting and argumentative by nature. By presenting and representing that which is regarded as carrying value, or by contesting given values as well as practices that signal these values, research makes statements not only about that which it presents and represents but also about itself and the society in which it is practiced. As knowledge is not objective but receives its epistemic authority in rhetorical contexts, all research is based on an interrelationship between the epistemic and the pragmatic.

This tenet also applies to information about past or present culture and cultural practice. It is never studied or collected for its own sake, because no such 'own' sake or intrinsic value exists. The obtaining and collecting of that which is regarded as valuable cultural information becomes meaningful only in particular argumentative contexts, both among those who collect and those who are positioned as sources of such collecting. The same point has been made, among many others, by Virginia Dominguez, who writes that objects of ethnography are collected and the people who produce them are examined "not because of their intrinsic value but because of their perceived contribution to our understanding of our own historical trajectory" (Dominguez 1986: 548). The motivation to 'discover' and cast a particular discovering gaze lies not in the object itself but in its value for the one who discovers it, gazes at it, and puts it on display.

Discussing the scenario of the global homogenization of culture, Ulf Hannerz has pointed out how such a vision is directly linked to a line of domestic cultural critique. Those who are "grieving for the vanishing Other" are doing it in order to bring in "fuel from the periphery for local debates at the center" (Hannerz 1991: 109). In fact, all anthropology, in addition to being, in the main, research on non-Western cultural forms, or just because of it, is fundamentally a commentary on the Western societies in which the research is practiced. (See e.g. Lévi-Strauss 1967: 381–392; Marcus & Fischer 1986.) Thus, what is categorized as cultural otherness has an ideological, political and practical meaning to those who are making such a categorization. When the peripheral is objectified for its value in the redefinition of the center, a gaze from the center to the periphery comments on the conditions in which it is cast. It receives its meaning in relation to these. Phenomenologically speaking, the object of the gaze cannot be perceived independently of the motivations, politics, and rhetorics of the gaze that makes it its object.

Intertwined with economic and political goals, the common Western interest in non-Western cultural formations continues to be based on an exoticizing curiosity and on a discourse on difference, which places the exoticized in a particular argumentative position vis-à-vis those who exoticize the observed or constructed differences. Such exoticization has also been present in the antiquarian and nostalgic interest in the marginal cultures of Western history and modernity – an interest that has especially characterized folklore research. This has, however, never been a mere disinterested expression of value or longing for otherness and for what is lost due to changes in culture and modernization. On the contrary, the value and emotion charged in folkloristic activity, in collecting, archiving, indexing and studying traditions of, for example, the nationally significant cultural other – spatially and/or temporally defined – is always a comment on modernity, on one's own society, and its politics of culture.

Indeed, the rhetorical context of social relevance can be regarded as one of the continuous 'shadow dialogues' in which the ethnographer, as discussed by Vincent Crapanzano, is engaged in his or her dialogic encounter with the informant (see Crapanzano 1990, 1992). The meaning of the information and representations produced in these encounters is estimated, and therefore also anticipated by the ethnographer, in the context of negotiating social values and constructing both cultural selfhood and cultural otherness in the societies in which the ethnographic representations are brought into public and scholarly discussion and put on display.

As I have discussed in the earlier chapters, folkloristic activity in modern society has to a great extent subscribed to a modernist paradigm of cultural loss. In this paradigm, one mourns over that which changes and is lost when cultures become modern. In accordance with the dichotomization of the modern and the traditional, modernization is conceptualized as the loss of tradition. Yet, instead of merely indicating regret or melancholy for the vanishing, or longing for what has already been lost or become distant, the modern sense of loss has been a projection of the deprived and alienated self. In the sense of nostalgia as homesickness, one has longed for the metaphorical home of the constructed and imagined space and time prior to a given change, which thus becomes a chronotope of tradition. In accordance with an antimodernist theory of modernization, which has argued for the loss of *Gemeinschaft* in the course of modernization, one has felt nostalgia for the 'home' of the lost community of unmediated communication and its allegedly moral contents that are perceived as having been destroyed by modernization, technologization, media-mediation and by the fragmentation of traditional social organization.

Inscribed into one of the most commonly held theories of modernization, such a feeling of deprivation and alienation has called for a variety of strategies to deal with the alleged loss of culture and value in modernity. The folkloristic activity of collecting and salvaging vanishing lore is one of these. In addition to receiving its moral justification from 'saving' culture for posterity at the eleventh hour, its agenda is based on the estimation of the value that the salvaged material is regarded as carrying and creating for those who participate in this activity, as well as those for whom the material is put on display as representations of culture, history and heritage.

Thus, as a provider of a picture of the past, that which is regarded as folklore has an explicit role to play in the making of the present. In other words, the practical value of collecting and archiving folklore lies in the use that it is regarded as having in the making of modernity and in the general debate and competition over collective and normative values in it. This makes folklore scholarship not only fundamentally modern, but utterly political and rhetorical, as the discipline is continuously making statements through the selection of collectibles, through the ways of collecting, and through the ways of displaying that which has been collected, both in research publications and in archives and museums.

Without questioning the cultural historical value of such collections, or the many possibilities that they offer and open up for historical research, I believe that it is of utmost importance that the collected materials be viewed as representations created in particular rhetorical contexts, employing particular strategies in the making of the present, and that their nature as such be integrated into both their analysis and the estimation of their political significance.

## Nationalism as Territorial Symbolism and Control

Contributing to the line of thinking whereby folklore scholarship always serves some pragmatic purpose and political agenda, Roger Abrahams points out that the discipline was originally formulated by antiquarian scholars who saw "the possibility of obtaining political and social advancement" in the study of antiquities (Abrahams 1993a: 3). In addition to the antiquarians receiving public recognition for their interests in the constitution of the public sphere in society, Abrahams describes the selection of certain territories and ethnicities into the scope of a particular collecting enterprise as a hegemonic move to assert political control over these areas. Antiquities, writes Abrahams, endow a piece of land with ancient meanings and thus sacralize the landscape and legitimate its control.

Such thinking is evident in William Camden's historical survey of British topography, the collection of antiquities entitled *Britannia* of 1586, and the questionnaires sent out by King Philip II in 1575 and 1578 in New Castile to survey information on local saints, legends and shrines (Abrahams 1993a: 16–17). These and similar actions elsewhere in Europe provided an apt model for the Swedish king Gustav II Adolf, who in 1630 issued a decree that led to the establishing of a Council on Antiquities in 1666. This decree was a call "to search for and collect all kinds of ancient relics and objects to glorify the fatherland" (Ben-Amos 1989, viii–ix; see also Sarajas

1982: 23–24, 222; Honko 1987a: 67–68; Honko 1987b: 127–128; Stewart 1993: 140–141). The political context for this was Sweden's competition over control of the Baltic Sea region with Denmark, where a similar call for 'ancient testimonies' had been made earlier. As concluded by Abrahams, "These monarchs were expanding their domains at the same time as they consolidated and sacralized their home realms" (Abrahams 1993a: 17). In this they used, says Abrahams, "the devices of organized authority made possible by the development of a bureaucratic governmental structure, and of print technology and its attendant techniques of reporting and organizing information" (Abrahams 1993a: 17).

The quest for domination over land by monarchs with the help of historical information and reports of ancients beliefs and narratives anticipates the methods used in nationalism for the creation of national cultures, national consciousness and national symbolism. As Benedict Anderson has argued, the making of modern nations as cultural units, as 'imagined communities', became possible only through printing technology and print-capitalism, which created unified fields of exchange and communication above spoken vernaculars (Anderson 1983: 47). Publishing and distributing written texts, that is, literature, in a print-language that was standardized from a multiplicity of vernaculars in a particular territorial unit, created a nationally defined public sphere and laid the basis for a national consciousness.

Such literature mainly consists of *belles lettres* and literary representations of folk poetry, such as the *Kalevala* epic in Finland, compiled by the medical doctor Elias Lönnrot in the early 1830s and published, in its first edition, in 1835. Yet, it also includes the questionnaires used by royal, state and church authorities to gather information about their subjects. One descendant genre in this is the printed questionnaires that ethnologists and folklorists in the Nordic countries continue to use for collecting material in both nationally and regionally significant museums and archives, and for surveying past and present customs, practices and beliefs. Indeed, as modern citizens have learned to be enlisted in the national population register and fill out tax and health reports (cf. Frykman & Löfgren 1985; Löfgren 1993b), people have also learned to fill out questionnaires concerning old, receding and residual ways of life and other topics of cultural historical interest that museums, archives, governmental or academic institutions devoted to the preservation of national heritage choose to inquire about. People have also learned to use their written reports strategically for their individual motivations and goals in the representation of past forms of life and specimens of human culture. As part of the nationalizing project especially in the Nordic countries, such questionnaires are not entirely innocent means of finding information; they function to produce territoriality by mapping territories and both consolidating and monitoring territorial and national identification (see also Häkli 1994, 2000).

In the 19th-century nation-building processes, the collecting of information about that which was regarded as premodern became a legitimate activity in the making of the modern, especially in the definition of the national territory and in the writing and representation of its history. Intellectuals in many countries followed the ideas presented by the German philosopher J. G. Herder about national cultures being manifested in the oral traditions of the lower classes. Accordingly, in and around Finland, the collecting of traditional verbal artistry of the marginally located illiterates, for example in the villages and forests of Eastern Finland, Karelia and Ingria, was laden with national political interests and goals. The human sources of folklore collectibles were expected not only to identify with Finnish nationalism but also to provide materials for the symbolic construction of Finnishness.

Similar processes of symbolic appropriation took place during World War II, when Finland had occupied parts of Eastern Karelia across the Soviet border. Scholars were sent out to collect information about local, Finnish-language folk culture, in order to preserve it in museums and archives as well as to create a national consciousness among the local population (see Laine 1993; Pimiä 2003). The collecting activity had the argumentative purpose of encouraging local people to identify with the Finnish nation-state across the political boundary. In a manner reminiscent of the methods employed by the early modern rulers, as discussed by Abrahams, the collecting of cultural products adopted into the concept of folklore functioned as a direct attempt to integrate territories into particular cultural and administrative spheres, and to legitimate their control with that which is conceptualized by the collector as 'tradition'. In Eastern Karelia, this was part of the project of creating Finland's *Lebensraum* (see Pimiä 2003: 77–78).

Yet, it is also worthy of note that the collecting of traditional verbal art in Eastern Karelia during the Second World War was not the only means used in the pursuit to legitimate the inclusion of these territories in the Finnish state. More weight was placed on geography and botany to provide 'natural' grounds to the argument for 'natural' borders (see Laine 1993). This followed the nationalistic idea supported particularly by Enlightenment philosophers in 18th-century France, according to whom "mountains and rivers as such, devoid of any historical determination, formed the limits of polities" (Østergaard 1991: 14).

## An Issue of Power and Loyalty

The making of modern nation-states and their unified national cultures has taken place in accordance with the modern political ideology of nationalism. In addition to print-capitalism, it has required the employment of mass literacy, mass schooling and mass symbolism. In pursuit of political sovereignty in a particular territory, nationalism legitimates states as administrative organizations with the idea that their inhabitants, raised in the name of democracy from subjects to citizens, 'belong together' by, for example, sharing a common origin and history in culture and language (cf. Latin *natio* 'birth'). Such a collective foundation is then expected to yield legitimacy to the state institution and its power over the territory. In this light, nationalism is a theory of political legitimacy based on the idea of congruence between the political and the national units (Gellner 1983: 1; Hobsbawm 1990: 9;

Hobsbawm 1992). For Herder, who coined the term nationalism, the only rational form of state is based on a *Volk,* 'people', which he used in a rather metaphysical sense to describe a collection of special qualities and virtues that make each state an identifiable culture (Birch 1989: 17–18; see also Wilson 1973; Dick 1989).

Nationalism is intrinsically about power and control over a territory and the people living within its confines, excluding from power and political decision making those who are regarded as outsiders. It encourages a given population to identify with a given nation and discourages separatism as well as mixing of those who 'belong' and those who 'do not belong' in the congruence of culture, history, language, religion, economy, citizenship rights and political structure. Territorial protectionism, ethnocentrism and racism have, of course, a history extending far beyond the birth of nationalism, but in modernity such distinction making is often channeled into the ideology of nationalism.

As Benedict Anderson points out, nation-ness has become a norm in modern political discourse, "the most universally legitimate value in the political life of our time" (Anderson 1983: 12). Accordingly, nation is regarded and institutionalized as the highest status that a population group can reach, and nations form alliances and political institutions (such as the United Nations or the European Union) into which only nations are accepted as members. Moreover, every individual, in order to enjoy full status as a sovereign individual, is expected to be a member of some nation. Having a nation and national membership has come to be regarded as an inherent attribute of humanity (Gellner 1983: 6; see also Østergaard 1991: 22).

Indeed, the ideology of nationalism must be considered a far more important watershed between modernity and premodernity as historical periods than, for example, technologization, industrialization, secularization, etc. These have no doubt caused a number of drastic changes in social structures, worldviews and ways of life, but they have not changed individual and collective identifications as much as the creation and symbolic representation of membership in nations and nationhood. As Eric Hobsbawm says, "the modern nation, either as a state or as a body of people aspiring to form such a state, differs in size, scale and nature from the actual communities with which human beings have identified over most of history, and makes quite different demands on them" (Hobsbawm 1990: 46).

According to Roland Robertson, the ideal of nationalism triumphed during the period from 1750 to 1920, involving "the attempt to overcome local ethnocultural diversity and to produce standardized citizens whose loyalties to the nation would be unchallenged by extra-societal allegiances" (Robertson 1990: 49). Such an expectation of loyalty characterizes all national projects, and accordingly, the transnational networks of, for example, the Jews have generated suspicions about the extent of their identification with the nation-state and their patriotism, instead of qualifying them with the positively charged label of cosmopolitan (Gidlund & Sörlin 1993: 72–73).

Today such expectations of loyalty mainly concern immigrants and 'guest-workers' and, to a lesser degree, refugees and asylum seekers. Their presence in nationalized territories finds support as a token of modern multiculturalism. Yet, at the same time, much public attention is focused on phenomena apparently indicating their lack of adaptation and integration into the national culture of their host country. The concepts of modernity and tradition are often used to explain – and reconfirm – the differences in culture, values and social practices between the host country and the origin of the incomers. The failure to adapt and integrate, which may be exemplified with the continuation of kinship-centered and male-controlled marriage networks between the country of immigration and the country of origin, is in popular, media-mediated discourse often taken to indicate the incomers' lack of modernity. The idea of traditionality as lack of modernity manifests itself here in the tendency to view the so-called traditional societies as organized around kin relations and lineages, which would constitute a dramatic difference from the modern society (see During 1994: 48).

## The Local and the Translocal

Even before present-day multiculturalism, nation-building processes have been characterized by the dialectics of the local and the translocal. One of the reasons for this is that "language myths are extraordinarily resilient, emerging in near-identical form in one *ethnie* after another, generation after generation" (Law 1998: 173). Nation building is embedded with a unifying goal to create an entity from among the manifold local and regional cultures and languages within the borders of the state, but as Ulf Hannerz and Orvar Löfgren emphasize, the nationalization of local culture is itself a transnational project, taking place in different nations in more or less similar ways (Hannerz & Löfgren 1992). Thus, the definition of national selfhood, although based on local and historically specific strategies, is not independent of similar processes elsewhere, but in a particular historical setting both represents and participates in a global discourse on the construction of the national (see also Friedman 1988 and 1992b; Löfgren 1989). Such processes are based on what Löfgren calls the cultural grammar of nationhood, an established set of symbols that are used transnationally for the making of a nation (Löfgren 1989: 8–9, 21–22; see also Löfgren 1991: 101; Löfgren 1993a, 1993b).[3]

Since a national entity requires the homogenization of regional differences within its territory, the nation is a semi-artificial construct, a standardized idiom formulated out of a multiplicity of actually spoken idioms (Hobsbawm 1990: 54). Such standardization then sets the framework for the making of distinctions between the local and the translocal, including the regional within the national. When creating local identities in competition with other local identities elsewhere in the nation, nationally and internationally standardized models are employed to make a particular local distinct from other locals and to argue for that which is regarded as giving it competitive advantage (Hannerz & Löfgren 1992). Thus, in addition to manifesting a local identity, the similarity of the model as well as the contents put on display contribute to the construction of a national culture.

Yet, instead of being a compilation of diverse elements, the arbitrariness of a national identity is naturalized with an aura of factuality making it appear real and unquestionable, 'natural' (LiPuma & Meltzoff 1990: 89). The naturalness of the constructed entity is created with a variety of political mythologies and strategies of representation that set the nation into a narrative (see Bhabha 1994: 139–170), conveying for example a finalistic idea about the nation-state as a natural end-goal for the history of any people (Sörlin 1992: 48). Such a project typically includes the nationalization of the nation's history and even prehistory; the production of a historical metanarrative about earlier cultural forms in a particular territory leading, as it were, to the making of the national unit. This supports Anders Linde-Laursen's point, according to which nationalism not only uses folklore but *is* folklore – national identity being an established narrative tradition about its population, politics, economy, and history, and having hegemony over other, alternative formulations (Linde-Laursen 1991: 16).

In addition to narrative and mythological constructions, the cultural and historical belonging of a nationalized population has also been created through the present-day meaning of the word 'ethnicity'. *Ethnos* in Greek originally referred to 'the primitive Other', such as heathens (e.g. Rasila 1986: 9–10; Viljanen 1994: 143), on the basis of which, until recently, only minorities – not the majority of the population and their dominant culture – were regarded as being 'ethnic'. Recently, however, the concept has become rather prestigious in the argumentation for the cultural integrity of any linguistic, religious or other social group. In their politics of exclusion, based on 'ethnic nationalism', many nation-states today define the marriage of the political and the national in such a way that those members that differ 'ethnically' from the majority are regarded as inadequate representatives of the national. Yet, also in separatist projects nationalistic aspirations are often founded on ethnic grounds, as groups that define their selfhood as ethnically constituted aspire for a nation of their own. Such emancipative aspirations are rhetorically supported with the authority placed on history and historically founded 'ethnic identity'. In this 'ethnic historiography', ethnic groups have come to be viewed as locales of traditions and traditional culture. Accordingly, cultural traditions have become some of the most powerful means in representing intragroup historical continuity and integrity, and therefore also their 'heritage', which is then used as legitimization in their claim for political sovereignty.

When nations are constructed on 'ethnic grounds', ethnicity is founded on the one hand upon a testimony of a traditional, locally grounded culture and its history. Yet, on the other hand, the cultural logic of an 'ethnic' testimony is founded upon a modern, translocal and transnational discourse in which elements from a traditional and locally grounded culture are appropriated into the construction of such a testimony. The presentation of an ethnic identity is, therefore, a process of making distinctions that are not only ethnographic but also politically desirable. Ethnic formations are constructed in a process that can be called the ethnicization of culture. In this interpretative and argumentative process, cultures and local specificities come to be viewed as distinct through 'an ethnicizing gaze' that makes the observed distinctions 'ethnically' relevant.

## A Discipline with a National Agenda

As antiquities retained among the lower classes of society, folklore has been conceptualized as products of cultural otherness founded upon a class distinction. As has been pointed out by, for example, Roger Abrahams and Bengt Holbek, the 19th-century interest in folk culture and especially the cultural ways of the rural population was directly related to the question of the redistribution of power between the bourgeois middle-class and the aristocracy (Holbek 1981: 133; Abrahams 1993a: 3–4, 9–10). In order to fight the absolute monarchy and the political power of the elite, and in order to manipulate the lower classes into the hegemonic control of the middle-class, the bourgeoisie spoke in the name of the people, and in a nationalistic enlightenment project transformed the rural populations into enlightened citizens and made them aware of being nationals. Thus, instead of 'the nation awakens', as the common metaphoric phrase goes, premodern forms of society have become modern by way of nationalizing the rural populations and by drawing peasants and other subjects of the state into nationhood and constructing their collective identification on the basis of their membership in the nation-state (see e.g. Weber 1976; Tilly 1990; Østergaard 1991).

Holbek describes folklore's role in this as follows: "It is the middle-class's enthusiastic rediscovery of 'the folk' which raised the traditional songs and narratives to a status of 'national' treasures, in spite of the fact that very few of them are specific to any ethnic group and in spite of the fact that the impoverished persons who entertained themselves with this sort of thing had scarcely anything that could be called a national consciousness." (Holbek 1981: 134–135.) Here Holbek makes an important point about the recognition of identities. Nationalistically minded folklorists have tended to collect, index and display materials that have received their meanings as nationally significant symbols not from their performers but from the people who collect and display them. Consequently, Lauri Honko has advised folklorists not to do this. "Describing group identities means selecting symbols and metaphors. It is of crucial importance that we as researchers do not make these selections, and that our verbalisations of identity feeling are governed by selections made by members of the group to be studied." (Honko 1988: 8.)

Holbek's point is in line with the arguments made by Julius Krohn and other early diffusionists about the non-national character of folklore (see e.g. Hautala 1954: 190–191). Thus, folklore's relation to nation and nationalism is here a question of whether the cognizance of particular folkloric items correlates with national borders. To claim nationalistic significance for material that, according to Holbek, does not correspond to the national boundaries in its area of appearance, is "misuse of folklore", which "is still promulgated by less-informed writers and propagandists", but which "has gradually been abandoned within professional circles in the course of this century" (Holbek

1992: 5–6). Here Holbek appears to be guided by the notion that professional folklorists in the 20th century no longer hold on to the tenets of Herderian nationalism. The same view is also evident in the statement made by Lauri Honko, according to whom it was the scientific task of the new discipline of folkloristics, during the second half of the 19th century, to place the national folk tradition in its 'right perspective', since much of what is assumed to be national has in reality been borrowed from other cultures (Honko 1980a: 2). The awareness of the fact that culture does not always correlate with the nation is regarded as a proof against the premises of Herderian romantic nationalism in modern folklore study.

However, whether the use of folkloristic material for territorial claims is 'misuse' or not cannot be judged solely on the basis of the material's correlation – or lack of it – with given territorial boundaries. Holbek's point undermines the power of symbolism and metonymy, which do not require such exact correlations. Symbolism and metonymy are argumentative relations. With its historical background in the legitimization and sacralization of territories with antiquities, and in the related Herderian idea of the nation as being embodied and voiced in traditional culture, especially in the poetry of the folk, folklore scholarship has contributed to nationalist symbolism and metonymy by providing 'ancient testimonies' of history in the national language for the legitimization of the political state as a national unit. By transforming tradition into heritage, and by metonymizing tradition in the course of its representation, folklore scholarship has created 'national texts' that are authored by 'the folk' and speak in the voice of 'the nation'.

This is not a coincidental historical development but a scholarly practice. Oral traditions do not become nationally significant and symbolic merely by existing somewhere, but through their transformation into literature and literary collections, through their adaptation and entextualization into material objects of display preserved in sites that are nationalistically relevant and significant, such as archives, museums, and universities. Folklorists have contributed to the making of modernity and its nationalization by collecting traditional cultural expressions on the margins of modernity, from among 'the folk', and by bringing these to the symbolic centers of society, institutions of history and ethnography in national capitals, sites that have obtained prominent roles in the representation of the nation's history and culture. Even though engaging mainly with texts instead of material objects, folklorists have been active in what can be described as the monumentalization of the patrimony. "In order for traditions today to serve to legitimize those who constructed or appropriated them, they must be staged." (García Canclini 1995: 109.) This staging, while it has served national interests and employed nationalized raw materials, has been transnational in nature, based on models of representation that circulate internationally. The imaging of the local follows transnational models of imaging the local.

The nationalization of history, and antiquities as its representations, is embedded in the very name of the folklore discipline, which was coined by the English antiquarian William Thoms in 1846. Influenced by German Romantic nationalism, Thoms suggested replacing the Latinate term 'popular antiquities' with a word of Anglo-Saxon origin (Thoms 1965; see also Dorson 1968: 75–90; Bustin 1988: 2; Abrahams 1993a: 9). Yet, despite the terminological rejection of antiquities in the name, folklore studies in Thoms's England continued to have an antiquarian stance, and, in the spirit of the emerging evolutionary anthropology, it focused on survivals and historical reconstructions (Wilson 1973: 819). Roger Abrahams emphasizes that the antiquarian interest in English folklore research was nationalistically charged, and the choice of the new term was directly linked to this. Says Abrahams:

> Thoms suggested a terminological shift from popular antiquities to anglicize the project [of collecting, organizing, and publishing], giving it a particularly British nationalist cast in an effort to bring his countrymen into line with other national literatures that he had discovered in his antiquarian compendia of the 'lays and legends' of other European polities. (Abrahams 1993a: 9.)

As an Anglo-Saxon compound, Abrahams points out, 'folklore' communicates the message that "aspects of a British national character might be revealed by deploying this new term in discussing old matters and archaic gestures" (Abrahams 1993a: 9). Antiquarian study, nationalistically and patriotically named as folklore, was therefore pursued "in the service of the British Union, and by extension, of the imperial crown" (Abrahams 1993a: 16).[4]

Close connections with folklore research and nationalism can be found in most European countries. In Germany, when the nobility and the Enlightenment ideologists looked to France for cultural inspiration, the doctrines of popular sovereignty and individual rights put up by the French Revolution were felt by the German elite to threaten their political system, which was still based on feudalism. In this situation, the German elite found political support in Herder's metaphysical idea, according to which the traditional ways and songs of the lower classes of society represent and manifest the 'soul' of the nation to which the lower classes are regarded as belonging. The German elite found refuge "in the historic past and a belief that Germany could only be saved if it trusted to tradition and the law of historic continuity rather than to rational experiments" (Aris 1965: 219, cited in Fox 1987: 566; see also Wilson 1973; Bendix 1992). Thus, particular cultural items or phenomena were defined as traditional for particular political purposes: first, to oppose particular currents of ideology (German Romanticism against the rationalism and cosmopolitanism of French Enlightenment), and second, to legitimate a particular territory as a nation and a particular form of administration to control it.

Similarly, in studying the making of Greek national identity, Michael Herzfeld writes how there is always argument on how and by whom the past is represented. The competing images of 'Greekness' are ideological formulations, constructions of history and culture, which are chosen on the basis of what is regarded as relevant in the attempt to define cultural continuity. The discipline of folklore was created in the process of obtaining historical justification for identification with a nation, "providing intellectual reinforcement for the political process of nation building that was already well under way" (Herzfeld 1982: 4). Aiming to show that "the peasants, the largest demographic element, retained clear traces of their ancient heritage" (Herzfeld 1982: 7), 19th-century Greek folklorists claimed for their independent Greek nation direct descent in the Hellenic tradition and a corresponding role in European civilization.

Indeed, born out of a political interest in legitimating states with oral history, folklore scholarship has been fundamentally nationalistic in its argumentative position towards the society in which it is practiced. Yet, according to Seppo Knuuttila, because of their privileged position in the academic representation of the national culture, folklorists have actively warded off any reflection upon the ideological nature of both their research object and their own research in the constitution of knowledge through cultural representation (Knuuttila 1993: 68–69; see also Alsmark 1982; Fernandez 1985; Löfgren 1989; Abrahams 1993a; Eriksen 1993). The political premises of folklore studies come forward in the often-circulated slogan "Anthropology is born of colonialism, folklore is born of nationalism" (Köngäs-Maranda 1982: 53), or "What colonialism is to the history of anthropology, nationalism is to the study of folklore" (Kirshenblatt-Gimblett 1988: 143). Still, one can encounter a rather condescending tendency to locate the nationalism of folklore only "in smaller European nations", while "the absence of nationalism as a component of folklore" would be "unique to the American configuration of folklore" (Ben-Amos 1998: 259).

William Wilson describes folklore's national agenda as follows:

> A driving force behind the development of folklore studies, nationalistic studies were in the beginning intimately associated with the efforts of zealous scholar-patriots who collected and studied the lore of the common folk, not just to satisfy their intellectual curiosity or enlarge their understanding of human behavior, but primarily to lay the foundations on which their emergent nation-states would one day rest. In this movement, the nationalistic attempt to redraw political boundaries to fit the contours of ethnic bodies merged with the romantic emphasis on feeling and intuition, on nature, and on the past as the source of inspiration for the present. (Wilson 1998: 441.)

The close link between folklore studies and nation making has not only been taken for granted but it has been seen as constituting one of the cornerstones for the discipline and its identity. In 1979 Brynjulf Alver made the following identity-political statement on folklore and national identity: "It is of course self-evident that folklore and folk poetry in particular must serve the cause of the national ideologies. It is a heritage that we must take with us when we claim that ethno-folkloristic studies are of importance since they serve to strengthen national identity and to give people a sense of historical perspective." (Alver 1979: 4; see also Alver 1980: 15.) Alver follows here the discipline's Herderian legacy in linking folklore studies with "the struggle for cultural and political independence". His argument also points to a preference for viewing the nation as an ideal community, with folklore as a token and carrier of communal identity within the ideal community.

Still, around the same period, folklorists adopted a viewpoint according to which the discipline is no longer nationalistic, since folklorists have active international contacts and their discipline is international in character. The presupposition here is that international and national are mutually exclusive, and that international activity does not make any nationalistic claims. Similarly, nationalism is understood to denote clannishness, which international cooperation allegedly has replaced (see e.g. Honko 1980a: 3). A counter-argument to this idea would refer to the transnational character of making nationalist claims and the production of nationalist symbols. Even ultra-nationalist political groups (often in the right wing) are in close contact and cooperation with similar groups in other countries.

Recent discussions concerning scholarly agency and the politics and poetics of scholarly practices and cultural representation have called attention to other aspects in the political advocacy of folklore. Without necessarily questioning the argumentative or subversive potentiality of folklore representations in the aspiration for cultural or political independence by an ethnic group or a stateless nation, scholars have become aware of the processes of cultural homogenization and the suppression of diversity that nation-making processes also have entailed. If folklore speaks for the nation, it speaks for a particular political construct. As such, instead of automatically signaling a morally justified political development, it might also speak against political, ethnic, linguistic or religious diversity in the name of the nation's inner unity and cohesion. Abrahams makes a point to this effect:

> The recent history of much of Eastern Europe shows that one people's nationalism can be transformed into the means by which other peoples are disenfranchised. This process can result in the wholesale displacement, or even murder, of the group denied national status. (Abrahams 1993a: 5.)

It remains to be debated whether the juxtaposition of the anthropology/colonialism relationship with folklore/nationalism relationship provides a parallel to the less studied relationship between postcolonial anthropology and postnational folklore studies. In any case, 'postmodern' reflexivity on the discipline's representational practices, textualization, epistemology and ideology should not automatically be dismissed as a political argument *against* nationalism. The contribution of folklore research in the making of nation-states and national cultures is not an issue that should be categorically judged as being morally right or wrong, even though folklore scholarship can be characterized as a moral project within the production of modernity. If folklorists choose to be nationalists for patriotic reasons, their argumentative position may be critically assessed with another one that questions patriotism and nationalism as political premises in scholarship, but neither position *per se* is more scientific than the other. Having a nationalistic bias is a political choice, and therefore our judgment of it cannot be independent of our own argumentative positions in relation to the means, goals and identity constructions involved.

## Promodernist Antimodernists

When nationalizing individual and local communication and transforming it into objects of display with nationalistic claims, folklore scholarship has operated in what appears to be a paradox in relation to one of its founding arguments about modernity and modernization. Traditionally, folkloristic activity has legitimated the collecting of cultural forms and expressions with the claim that this material is on the verge of extinction because of modernization. Yet, that which is collected and documented is transformed into literature and then used for a variety of political statements, including the nationalistic one, in the modernization of society. That which is called folklore is made to serve and speak for the very process that is argued to be the cause for folklore's alleged extinction.

In a similar paradox, folklore scholarship stands in a close argumentative relation to the very enlightenment project that has aimed at uprooting the culture that folklorists originally set out to study and preserve in text. The scholarly interest as well as the romanticizing and exoticizing gaze into the folk beliefs and myths of primitive and premodern societies have coexisted with the enlightened scholar's efforts to spread literacy, Western aesthetics, state control, nationalistic sentiments, Christianity, and a rational worldview among those regarded as being empowered by irrational beliefs and customs (see also Knuuttila 1989: 94–95).

Such ambivalence or dualism has characterized much of earlier folklore collecting. A case in point is Jaako Länkelä in 19th-century Finland, a collector responsible for making some of the largest and most significant collections of oral verse from Ingria, partially across the Russian border. He describes his informants as preservers of barbarian remains from ancient superstitions. Emphasizing that his motivation is that of an observer, without having any intention to disparage the "national value of the people", he depicts the culture of his informants as being at the dawn of civilization, and looks forward to seeing the effects of the school system in uprooting "darkness from the minds of the people" (Länkelä 1865; my translation; see also Ilomäki 1992: 105–106).

Instead of nostalgia for an 'authentic' culture destroyed by enlightenment, such a statement exemplifies the societal position that folklorists and folklore collectors take between tradition and modernity. There may be a preference for the antimodernist rhetoric of traditions disappearing due to the spread of modernity and literacy, but when folklore studies is conceptualized as a discipline that has science, enlightenment, patriotism and nationalization as its argumentative premises and pragmatic goals, the folklorist does not stand for the salvation and preservation of traditions in locations where these are found. If the folk have been considered uneducated, unenlightened and irrational, as was the case especially in the 19th century, the preservation of their folklore, lifestyle or cultural integrity has not been the objective for the modern, enlightened ethnographer. Documentation, the act of representation, overrides preservation, the act of political partisanship.

In a seeming paradox, the modern discipline of folklore has nostalgized the traditional culture that yields to modernization, but at the same time has celebrated the modern progress of science and nation making and thus enhanced the modernization that causes the traditional culture to yield. Folkloristic activity has conceptualized its study objects with the rhetorical imagery of life and death, but at the same time it has selected symbolic representations and transformed them into commodities of higher literary quality, in order for them to serve the creation and consolidation of national identification and nationalistic sentiments. Death to the tradition means life to the nation. Making the representations of tradition into national monuments and their historical ruins, folkloristic activity has enhanced not only the diffusion of modern methods of collecting, documentation and display, but also the modern political culture of representational government that draws a significant share of its legitimacy from historical symbolism and collective identification.

The apparent paradox disappears, however, when we consider the representations of tradition as a form of modern possessions. As I will discuss in later chapters, the construction of historical symbolism with folklore has entailed that the ancient or premodern traditionality that the scholar has discovered, together with the making of antiquities as its representations, serve to indicate a historical process and thus, the nationalized population's ability to progress and modernize. Selected products of cultural practice are collected and put on display as traditions that speak for 'collective roots' and 'heritage'. But these are not to be continued as cultural practices, because their continuation would speak of a lack in people's capacity to modernize. For this reason, traditions as social practices are made into representations that are to be possessed, for example, in collections. Possessing traditions that speak for bygone antiquity and history serves as evidence of progress and modernity.

Indeed, the conception of folklore as an antiquity, the related idea of the past as a lost community and folklore as its ruins, has provided a powerful means for providing symbolic legitimation for the establishment of new collectivities such as nations. For this reason, the emergence of folklore scholarship is just as much related to the symbolic processes in the making of a nation-state and the writing of its unwritten history, as to an antimodernist moral project against the allegedly alienating forces of modernity. Therefore, premodern and preindustrial life as a more or less harmonious 'folk society' or a site of cultural authenticity with direct, unmediated interaction has not been something that some intellectuals – alienated or not alienated – have tried to 'save' from falling into oblivion at the eleventh hour. Instead, this is an image constructed and continuously reconstructed by such modern discourses as folklore scholarship to make modernity's otherness, which then acquires political use and value in the making of that very modernity which is regarded as having destroyed that which the image depicts.

As already noted, an important element in the modern and modernist traditionalism of folkloristic activity is its character as a moral project. Serving nationalistic aspirations and promoting enlightenment are regarded as making a positive and optimistic statement about modernity and the process of modernization, which may otherwise be considered to alienate people from the traditional and the historical. Thus, in addition to being a political attempt to claim or obtain legislative and juridical authority for a particular ethnic group or other community, nationalism is an issue of morality. In other words, the antimodernist statement about modernity and the nostalgic gaze on the vanishing are essentially moral statements. They are not merely laments over lost treasures but an attempt to bring alternative values, meanings and technologies to the fore, to make a comment on the present and to participate in its constitution. Thus, instead of regarding the apparent paradoxes in the discourse on folklore as weaknesses, they can, on the contrary, be considered the strength of folkloristic arguments in the politics of culture. The power and mystery of antiquity, that which is claimed to be on the verge of disappearance, and that which is claimed as tradition and a manifestation of historical continuity, can provide a politically effective means in the making of claims in local, regional, and national identifications and the advancement of rights for particular populations and social groups.

As discussed above, the traditional folkloristic strategy is to folklorize cultural practices deemed traditional, make them collectibles, and put them in large quantities in storage or on display in archives and museums to represent the national culture metonymically and to make a symbolic claim for the preservation of the nation's cultural heritage. According to such an 'archive strategy', cultural identity is best protected and argued for by depositing textual representations of it in the archive and then producing selected and edited materials in books for the consuming and reading public – as commodities of tradition in which authenticity is claimed as a guarantee of quality. Such an archive strategy can be compared and discussed in relation to alternative ways in making representations of traditional culture speak out on cultural rights and political claims. Without questioning the symbolic or moral value of the archive or its practical use in documenting and accessing information, it must be acknowledged – in addition to the epistemological questions of representation – that in many societies and postcolonial arenas today, building a national tradition archive may not be the most effective means in fighting cultural hegemony. In a context where the museum has served the staging of power, archives may also come to stand for such hegemony (see García Canclini 1995: 135–144).

# 6. Tradition and Political Identity

The development of ethnically integrated nation-states and the near-global distribution of the ideology of nationalism are some of the most important political processes of modern times and aspects of modernism. Today this development has reached a reflexive turning point in which nationalism as a model for economic, political and territorial identification has in a number of arenas been questioned. Many of the old nation-states are going through processes of transformation and redefinition in terms of economic and information systems, cultural and ethnic foundations, political loyalties, and geographical boundaries.

Some of the major factors in this development are the increasing internationalization of capital and the formulation of a world system of production and consumption that transcends the territories of the nation-states and national economies. Local, regional and national economies, cultures, political structures and spaces of identification are no longer – if they ever were – isolated units but integrated parts in a global system of relations. (See e.g. Featherstone 1990; King 1991; Friedman 1994a.) As a consequence, "The very concepts of homogenous national cultures, the consensual or contiguous transmission of historical traditions, or 'organic' ethnic communities – *as the grounds of cultural compararativism* – are in a profound process of redefinition" (Bhabha 1994: 5).

This development is also characterized by new technological forms of information transmission, such as satellites, cables and computer networks, which produce new transnational and postnational geographies and deprive the national media of their role in integrating populations into national units of audience. Consequently, collective identities are in many symbolic ways deterritorialized as alternative networks of communication and identification and information systems have become available through the transnationalization and globalization of culture, economy and the media (see e.g. Morley & Robins 1995; Castells 1996; Elkins 1997; García Canclini 2001).

Moreover, the increasing flow of people of various origins, cultural and religious backgrounds and political loyalties across ethnic, religious, political, economic, and geographical borders have changed cultural landscapes and turned ethnically more or less homogeneous nation-states, some more and some less, into multiethnic and multicultural societies. Even more than the emerging new economic networks across old state boundaries, voluntary and involuntary migration and the growing number of refugees and other displaced and diasporic people have brought new, both powerful and problematic, dimensions to the making of state-based, national, regional, local, and ethnic identities. This also applies to those territories that are not directly affected by new political borders (see e.g. Bendix & Klein 1993; Abrahams 2000; Klein 1997, 2000).

In Europe, the general discussion about recent changes in the global economic, political and cultural map has primarily concerned Europe itself. Throughout the 1990s, the major element in this was the simultaneous integration and disintegration of Europe, which took place politically, economically and culturally. The still on-going economic integration – the making of a European ecumene[5] – has been composed and executed first and foremost by the European Union (EU), formerly known as the European Economic Community (EEC) and the European Community (EC). Some of the major goals of this centrally governed organization of member states are the partial and/or gradual disintegration of many national institutions and the integration of large parts of Europe into a common market free of customs regulations, protectionist legislation and different currencies. After the signing of the Maastricht Treaty in 1992 and its coming into effect in 1993 – which also marked the beginning of the Union as it now exists – the EU has gained more and more political meaning and power. Ever since then, one of the most heated issues in its development has been the extent to which national democracies and national economies – the cornerstones of nation-states – should yield to a postnational economic and political federation, a European federal state.

In contrast, since the late 1980s Eastern Europe was characterized by a geopolitical disintegration, which in major ways shook up the whole of Europe politically and culturally. The 50-year political and military status quo established after World War II and manifested in many practical and ideological ways in the division of Europe into two blocs and an 'Iron Curtain' in between, was shattered into pieces when, first, the symbol of the division, the Berlin Wall, came down in November 1989, and second, the other half of the Cold War, the Soviet Union, was, as a result of domestic intrigues, wiped off both the political and the geographical map in December 1991. In related turmoils, the Soviet satellite states in Eastern Europe gained sovereignty, the two Germanys were reunited, the Baltic states regained their independence, Belarus and the Ukraine disconnected their nation-state ties with the Russians, the Czechs disbanded with the Slovaks, and Yugoslavia dissolved into a brutal ethnic war.

In a seeming contradiction, the Western European countries took steps towards integration in the name of supranationalism, postnationalism, federalism, confederalism or, in more familiar terms, post-industrial capitalism and economic pragmatism stripped of national loyalties, while Eastern European countries, including Russia and the other countries that arose into sovereignty from the ruins of the Soviet Union, discarded the Soviet-based state-nationalism and took steps towards ethno-nationalism and ethnic separatism – in addition to discarding socialism and beginning to integrate into the Western European economic networks. After the initial euphoria of the nationalist and separatist revolution in the East, many of these countries mapped themselves geopolitically in Central Europe or 'the Europe Between' and started to search for security guarantees in the West, in membership in the European Union and/or NATO.

As regards the major cultural and political identifications in Europe today, one of the most significant outgrowths of the European economic and political integration has been the heated debate concerning the future of the nation-state and the ideology of nationalism. The increasing internationalization of economic and information networks has given many people a reason to declare the end of nationalism, to be replaced by, among other things, federalism, pan-Europeanism, cosmopolitanism or neo-regionalism. Eric Hobsbawm concluded his seminal book on nationalism – written just before the great turmoils – with the notion that because of "the supranational restructuring of the globe", the phenomenon of nationalism is "past its peak" (Hobsbawm 1990: 182–183). More emphatically, in building a stronger economic entity, the European Union has tended to consider the old national boundaries not only artificial but also necessary to be nullified, as nationalism is viewed as a 'disintegrative force' and national cultures and national economies are regarded as 'selfish' and considered to block the realization of 'common European interests' – that is, the development of the European Union as envisaged in the Maastricht Treaty.

Much of the logic and motivation behind this reasoning has been credited to the aftermath of the Second World War and the political will to avoid the kind of nationalistic developments that led to it. Yet, the increase in the value of 'common European interests' must also be attributed to the post-war political situation in which the major European countries were forced to rearrange the colonialist structures of their respective national economies. The integration of European economies and political structures has thus paralleled the disintegration of colonial economies and politics both in the West-and-the-rest relations and within Europe itself.

To some extent the disintegration of Western European nationalism started to provide a potentially liberating effect – in terms of culture, tradition, economy and political rights – for those regions or ethnic, linguistic or religious minorities that have had to yield to the assimilatory policies of nationalism and nation-states (Smith 1990: 175). The aspirations for a 'Europe of the Regions', an idea that Europe should be constituted on the basis of regions, cities and other economic and administrative units smaller than the state, emerged to carry rather similar denationalizing overtones (see e.g. Gidlund & Sörlin 1993; Harvie 1994; Cronberg 2000).

Regionalism may, however, also encourage nationalism, and at the same time as many in the name of economic, political and cultural integration have called for the death of nationalism, for many others the dimension of the national has only become stronger and politically more powerful as the integration proceeds – and especially as the intentions to develop the European Union towards a federation have become clearer. At least two interrelated phenomena may be discerned here: one concerns the popular opposition to giving up established or newly defined national symbols, and the other, the increased consumption value of the national and its territorial foundation.

Functions and symbols of sovereign nation-states, such as the national parliament, started to attain new meanings and an increase of value in the context of opposing the plans to centralize more and more political power in the headquarters of the Union in Brussels. Many came to fear that the strengthening of the Union's power would cause the Member States to lose not only much of their independent legislative force but also their independence as sovereign states. This would then undermine the traditional political congruence between the state and the nation. It would threaten the foundation of the national as a cultural unit, as some of the most central national symbols of the state would disappear.

The federalist process in which the Union pushed for the Economic and Monetary Union (EMU) caused similar reactions. Part of the common monetary policy, national money (or more precisely, state-based currency) in each Member State was, and still is, to retreat and make way for the euro, the common European currency. Although a national currency has not always been listed in the cultural inventories of national symbols, it certainly became one when it was time to make the dramatic change. A country's own currency came to carry value as a symbol of national independence regardless of whether the country's national economy was independent in reality or not. In order to calm down popular opposition to the federal currency, the European Union had to make a compromise between the federalists and the nationalists by allowing the Member States print their respective national symbols on the flip side of the euro coin.

Second, although the idea of economic and political integration across nation-states and national economies is gaining more and more ground and spreading, for example, from Europe to South America, South-East Asia and elsewhere, there are many global institutions which foreground and celebrate nation-states as political-symbolic constructions instead of obscuring or dissolving them. Indeed, the breakdown of the primariness of the national economy and the relativization of its boundaries has not shown to be as fatal to the ideology of nationalism as has been thought. In fact, even though – or probably just because – the media are becoming more and more delocalized and postnational – that is, independent of national loyalties – some of their most popular products, especially international sport competitions, explicitly foreground and encourage national frames of reference and national identification and that way discourage the fragmentation – or rather, the de-nationalization – of identities. Rather paradoxically, the deterritorialized media help create communities with a sense of place.

One reason for this tendency must be economic, as national identification has to a great extent become a form of collective, media-mediated consumption with a large market for products appealing to national feelings. Another, interrelated reason is social. Despite the internationalization, postnationalization and pluralization of identities, the social expectation to anchor oneself to a place, a particular locale and a social world, has not significantly decreased.

This can be regarded as one of the foundations for the continuing value of national identification – especially of the identification with the national territory – as one of the major dimensions of social identification. As observed by Ulf Hannerz, transnational personal ties and other linkages "tend not to coalesce into any single conspicuous alternative to the nation" (Hannerz 1993: 386).

Indeed, national symbols are today in greater demand than ever before, just as much in the West as in the East, as nation-states compete against each other in an ever-growing number of internationally integrated and standardized arenas. National distinctions continue to be created on the basis of uniqueness in character and mentality, but to an increasing extent nations are also imagined by raising individuals and teams – especially in sports but also in business – to the status of national heroes as they win in arenas of internationally integrated activities. Both the international arenas and nationally adopted international currents, instead of replacing national identifications, tend to foreground nations, nationalism and national frames of references (see e.g. Blain et al. 1993).

Related to these processes is the growing impact of tribalism in global economic networks (see e.g. Kotkin 1993) or social networks (Maffesoli 1996), and the resurgence of religious nationalism in state politics (see e.g. Westerlund 1996). Of great importance here is also the wide-spread popular movement of nationalistic violence, which, on the one hand, is indicative of the ideological, psychological and emotional opposition to mixing – that is, sharing identity space with – those who 'belong' and those who 'do not belong' in the nationalist congruence of culture, history, religion, economy, and political structure. Although channeled in modernity into the ideology of nationalism, such opposition has a long history in territorial protectionism, patriotism, xenophobia, racism and other community-making ideologies. On the other hand, the publicly and privately conducted acts of nationalist discrimination are indicative of the reluctance to share state-based economic, social and territorial benefits and resources with the growing number of incoming 'non-members' of the state, non-Western immigrants and refugees.

## *Towards a European Consciousness and a European Identity*

In addition to creating many new common European policies, practices and arenas of interaction, European integration has encouraged the Europeification of domestic policies and administration and has greatly Europeanized the popular consciousness. The many changes in boundaries have reshaped the sense of place and belonging and helped to build a new type of European consciousness. This is evident in, for example, the way in which Europe became a popular frame of reference, making the idea and concept of Europe a topic of constant discussion and definition. Probably more than in actual economic or political terms, Europe has 'come together' in talk and narration about Europe.[6]

When concerned with identifications, such interest is both politically motivated and has political ramifications. Instead of being purely a geographical unit, Europe is defined both qualitatively and politically, and this is manifested, among other things, in the way in which Europe and the European Union are used as synonyms. This contains, on the one hand, the expansionist idea that the European Union is 'truly' European only when the Eastern European countries have become members – which places Germany and its re-established capital of Berlin right in the center. On the other hand, in countries applying for membership in the Union, people have tended to talk about 'going to Europe' or 'taking the Europe train', which implies that they would be in Europe – politically, that is – only as members of the European Union. A related issue here is the fact that as a consequence of the gradual expansion of the Union, new boundaries have been erected to areas where there used to be almost none. This especially concerns the former Eastern European countries and their gradual 'Europeanization'.

European consciousness is not the same thing as European identity. In fact, it has repeatedly been commented on how the problem with the centrally governed European Union is, as well as with the European integration, that there is no such thing as a collective European identity. The European Union may wish to present itself as a federation, a united states of Europe, and as such a conglomeration comparable to a nation, but it lacks the means to create 'national European' identification among the various state populations. In terms of identification, there is hardly anything more than the shared value of economic, political and cultural cooperation between the Member States. This creates a European consciousness but not a European identity. Applying the concept used by Eric Hobsbawm (1972: 392, 404), Ninian Smart (1983) and others, the EU lacks the civic religion of nationalism, a set of motivations developed in the national citizens that gives them "a primary and overriding sense of obligation" towards the territorial state "and eliminates the various other obligations that they feel towards other groups and centres within or without the territory" (Alapuro 1982: 114). Europe, and especially the European Union, lacks a cultural and political identity that would produce loyalty and allegiance (see also Shore 2001).

One of the reasons for this, and indeed, one of the major problems of the Union and causes of skepticism towards it, is that it is viewed as being led bureaucratically by an elitist group of politicians. The rationale of economic integration does not seem to convince people of the importance of political integration, if the citizens of the Member States feel that they lack adequate political weight in the system. According to one EU critic, it is a historical paradox that the undemocratic EU would not be accepted as member in the EU (Wallgren 1997).

To replace national identification with European identification, both the European Union as a top-down organization and many ideologically and politically oriented bottom-up discourses offer European-ness or Europeanism as an alternative collective identification. Instead of concerning European consciousness only, European-ness or Europeanism is meant to be an identity in the sense that it is constituted in relation to cultural and political otherness. In other words, it is expected to comment on being European through an argumentative distinction made in relation to people and sociopolitical systems elsewhere, and create loyalty and allegiance that way.

Indeed, Europe is not defined only on the basis of its 'intrinsic ingredients', as such 'intrinsic-ness' is always an ideological construction that naturalizes certain elements and categorizes certain others as foreign or marginal. Especially since the Age of Discovery, Europe and European-ness have been defined and conceptualized against, for example, the other continents as well as such symbolic systems and constructions as Islam and the Orient. Today Europe may be constructed, for example, as a political-economic unit that draws its identity from competition in global business, trade and policy-making force against the two other economic super-powers of the world, the USA and Japan.

The idea of Europe may also be a cultural landscape constituted by an image of the 'European past' and based on the myth that the core of Europe lies in its Hellenic heritage. As discussed by Michael Herzfeld, Jonathan Friedman and others, throughout European development after the Renaissance, Greece was incorporated into an emergent European identity as a legitimate ancestor and the Greeks were considered primordial Europeans. Greece stood for Science, Progress, Democracy and Commerce, that is, the signs of modernity, which at the same time signaled the opposite of everything Oriental (see Friedman 1994b: 120; Herzfeld 1982).

In addition to the origins, the heritage of Antiquity has also been interpreted as providing Europe with a 'spiritual' instead of an 'economic' identity space. Making Europe a landscape of literary civilization and sophistication can provide an alternative to the equation of European-ness and the European Union, or it can be directed, for example, to oppose the expansion of American popular and media culture. In a somewhat similar manner, being European might also be argued to mean being Christian – whether Catholic, Protestant or Orthodox – which then may be used to construct a landscape of Europe based on a fear of the expansion of Islam, especially Islamic fundamentalism. These issues have recently been heavily debated in conjunction with the global threat of terrorism, the EU Constitution and Turkey's possible EU membership.

Indeed, fear is one of the driving forces in the development of the European integration, as the more or less independent nation-states choose not to depend only on national defense but look for security guarantees from each other. This applies to most of Europe but is most conspicuous in the Eastern European countries, which have been eager to become members in the European Union and/or NATO. Moreover, it is no longer a secret that even though Finland's application for membership in the European Union was officially defended with economic arguments only, the wish for security guarantees was the main political motive. Security is also the major issue today as the Finns debate on the possibility of applying for membership in NATO. The issue of security brings geopolitics to the fore and makes the extent to which identities – political and cultural – are constituted on the basis of geopolitical interests and evaluations a core issue.

## Cultural Identity as Political Identity

In addition to much talk on the economic, political and legal aspects of the European integration, as well as on European consciousness and common European identity, the recent changes in Europe have given new stimulus to academic studies and discussions concerning such 'cultural' issues as cultural identity, ethnicity and ethnic identity, nationalism, national identity and national mentality, local identity, regional identity, multiculturalism, ethnic pluralism, immigrant identity, gender identity, etc. In fact, cultural identity has in recent years become a key interest in many social scientific and humanistic fields, including sociology, history, anthropology, linguistics, ethnology and folkloristics. Such interest is not only coeval with the processes of integration and disintegration in Europe, but constitutes intertextual links with these on both academic and practical levels.

The drastic changes in the European geographical and economic landscape have also brought the concept of boundary to the front line of scholarly discussion. The decades of frozen stand-still in Europe after World War II made boundaries look fixed and objective, and played at least a partial role in inviting scholars to hold on to the study of social phenomena as subjects of diffusion and objects of cartographic mapping on the one hand, and to the study of isolated ethnic groups and the perseverance of their oral and material traditions on the other. Gradually, especially in the 1970s and 1980s, new epistemological perspectives started to emerge in both the social sciences and the humanities which, at least to some extent, directed methodological, theoretical and philosophical interests both to boundaries and to the cognitive processes of category formation. These emphasized the spatiality, territoriality and temporality of social processes, and questioned the idea of cultures and ethnicities as holistic and objectivist systems. The purity of forms – both academic ones and those constructed by academics in their research – gave way to disciplinary, cultural and cognitive hybridity (see García Canclini 1995; Kapchan & Strong 1999).

Although the beginning of the re-evaluation of cultural boundaries as not fixed but flexible, blurred and hybrid, temporally precedes the reshuffling of territorial and cultural boundaries in Europe, the dramatic political changes in the late 1980s and early 1990s no doubt increased the impelling force of these academic perspectives. They bore witness to the notion that spatial structures and territorial identifications are, indeed, relative and socially constructed.

Since spatial structures, such as political and geographical boundaries, are temporally and socially constructed phenomena, it is not far-fetched to make the same conclusion for cultural boundaries and cultural identities. These are, too, temporally and spatially specific and in that sense context-dependent. As pointed out by Jonas Frykman, cultural identity is not something that is, but instead, an issue of *when*, *where* and *how* (Frykman 1995: 6).

Indeed, researchers have become reluctant to see identities as objectivist lists of cultural traits and to view the study of identity as an exercise in the 'discovery' of such allegedly objective factors. Yet, the fact that identities are constructed in dialogues, interrelations or oppositions to each other does not simply mean that "If one is young, then one is not old; to talk about female qualities has meaning only because men exist" (Brück 1988: 79). Instead of being merely relational, identities are socially constructed categories and as such, constitutive of each other and negotiated in the discursive context of one another. For this reason, in addition to being an issue of *when*, *where* and *how*, the context dependence of the production and articulation of cultural identity is also – and emphatically so – an issue of *why*. In addition to the aspects of spatiality, temporality and modality, cultural identity, in order to exist, requires a motivation, a purpose, and an argumentative goal. When producing and reproducing categories of people on the basis of such identity factors as nationality, ethnicity, lifestyle, looks, language, dialect, party political or religious standing, territorial residence, etc., we do not merely make distinctions between 'us' and 'them', but we also make choices as to why such distinctions are made and maintained. In other words, the making of distinctions is argumentative by nature, as we have reasons for why difference makes a difference when it makes a difference, and why similarity does not always carry enough symbolic meaning to unite or integrate those that are similar.

The production and articulation of cultural identity takes place in rhetorical and argumentative processes of identification, which are in fundamental ways linked to questions concerning political and territorial loyalties and allegiances, social power, control of land, discursive ways of making historical continuity, and on geopolitics and geopolitical strategies. To put it simply, cultural identity is political identity.

As regards the role of loyalties and allegiances in the making of a cultural identity, some key factors here are the ways in which our various socially constituted loyalties suggest or determine when difference does or does not make a difference. Accordingly, the philosophical axiom of reality being socially constructed can be rephrased pragmatically to suggest that the interpretative frames of reality are to a significant extent constituted by and through various personal and intra-group, including national, loyalties. This makes both personal identity and group identity political in nature, as the question of who we are depends to a large extent on to whom we are loyal, and why.

Both on a personal and group level, including ethnic and national levels, such loyalties are morally founded. Loyalties are moral even when they represent the morality of an ideological minority whose morals are questioned by the majority as being, for example, xenophobic or racist. We express and construct moral loyalties, for example, when we argue that such differences as the ethnic origin should not make a difference, or that people who represent different genders, religious creeds, age groups, social classes or castes, sexual orientations, or economic and political values and interests, are all equal.

Then again, we also express and construct moral loyalties when we emphasize distinctions between 'us' and 'them' and celebrate 'our community' and 'our kind of people' against those who are foreigners or whom we regard in some other ways as outsiders. Consequently, we are moral whenever we express the universal social value and expectation of building a human community, regardless of what practical ideology of categorization it is based on. For this reason each and every human community can claim to be morally based, even though this must not lead to the cultural relativistic conclusion that all moral conceptions should be acceptable. While morality transcends politics, this transcendence is politically constituted. Collective symbols and traditions become valuable representations of cultural continuity because of their moral reference – even when they may contradict historical accuracy.

## Folklore, Identity, Politics

The concept of identity has become one of the most constitutive elements of both folkloristic and ethnological discourse. Jonas Frykman notes that the study of cultural identity came to dominate ethnology in the 1990s (Frykman 1995: 5). As for folkloristics, Elliott Oring claims that despite the recent origin of the term and its use, "identity has always been a central concern – in fact, *the* central concern – of the field" (Oring 1994: 223). Yet, in his quest to prove the presence of the 'project of identity' throughout the disciplinary history, as well as in his quest for thus constructing an identity for the discipline, Oring fails to distinguish between actual identity research and the politically motivated expectations that scholars and society at large have set for folkloric and folkloristic scholarship in order to have it provide evidence for collective identities. Rather typically in folklore studies, and echoing perspectives deriving from J. G. Herder, the identity that according to Oring is manifested in folklore materials is constituted by a collectively, mainly nationally, imagined set of characteristics, and by a shared mentality and ethos. There is no discussion in his article on how identities might be constituted by collective values and meanings deriving from and commenting on historically specific and politically motivated incidents of social action – whether by scholars themselves or the people they study.

Indeed, traditionally, studies on cultural identity have tended to ignore the politics of identity and the political dynamics in which, for example, local and group identities are constituted. Especially in the study of folklore, the study of cultural identity has generally meant the observation and analysis of those (decontextualized and depoliticized) texts, cultural traits, symbols, and performances of identity which appear to descend from previous generations and which are said – especially by the scholar of such traditions – to denote and strengthen the inner cohesion and thereby the identity of the social group or the cultural entity in question. Focusing on preconceived collectivities such as nations, ethnic groups, local communities and occupational groups, scholars have followed the discipline's modern sociological paradigm and placed much rhetorical emphasis on intra-group folklore as the foundation of positive and healthy collective identities – as well as employing this notion to legitimate their own scholarly practices in the representation of such groups. In addition to mostly ignoring the political implications of elevating particular identities and backgrounding others, folklorists have been bold enough to claim that studying collective identifications and providing material for them gives their field 'an identity bonus' in relation to other disciplines (see also Knuuttila 1994: 32–33).

However, folklore is not necessarily a collectively defined representation of a group identity, a manifestation of a coherent self-image of a preconceived group. Instead, folklore is a name for a type or act of communication produced in a situation or a process in which groups and collectivities are made through interaction between people belonging to different social categories and through the exercise of social power (Bauman 1972; Briggs & Bauman 1992). Instead of arguing how united a group may be because of its folklore, as this is often based on circular reasoning (see Abrahams 1981: 309), an alternative approach challenges the folklorist to discuss how folklore is employed in the *making* of groups, in the processes of categorizing people, in building boundaries in certain places and crossing them in others, and in defining relations between the categories thus created. Such category-making processes are both argumentative and political in character, and accordingly, the identities and identifications emerging from these categories are also argumentative and political. The same applies to the extent to which collective representations are collective. Folklorists may construct the discipline's identity on the premise that they provide material for 'positively evaluated' historical identifications, but they may also choose to come to grips with the political dynamics of identity processes and the conflict potentials of their representations.

To be sure, recent years have witnessed more and more reflection upon the political nature of the concepts of cultural identity and tradition as well as upon the politics of folklore research (see e.g. articles in Briggs & Shuman 1993; Bendix 1997; Naithani 1997; Bauman & Briggs 2003). This development represents a politically oriented continuation of the research trend generally labeled performance studies, which has accorded key roles to human agency and individual action for the understanding and analysis of folkloric communication. Sharing here some insights with Marxist and Gramscian perspectives (see e.g. Lombardi-Satriani 1974), performance approaches – or at least some practitioners – have been sensitive to the ways in which folklore is produced as an expression of social conflict and a form of social and political resistance (see e.g. Limón 1983a).

Political awareness in the discipline has also increased as scholars have reflected upon their own – or their colleagues' – metadiscursive textual practices (e.g. Briggs 1993). The questions of power and representation have been discussed especially in relation to gender (e.g. Mills 1990 and 1993). In addition to some folklorists participating in political activism and advocating for social change (see e.g. Kodish 1993), scholars in applied folklore have, as characterized by Abrahams, offered practical services in developing social welfare, alternative health care or legal assistance programs, and in public sector folklore displayed their fieldwork results in such public contexts as festivals, shows and exhibitions (Abrahams 1993b: 394; see also Baron & Spitzer 1992; Zeitlin 2000). Yet, to a large extent, the debates on politics and poetics in folklore scholarship have rather self-critically concerned the folklorists themselves and the political implications of their scholarly practices, instead of directing scholars to develop methodologies in the study of the production of identity in the context of situated political processes and political economy.

Undeniably, increased attention has been given to the politics of time and tradition, that is, the political and argumentative processes in which the meaning of the past and cultural descent is – instead of being 'handed down' by previous generations – constituted in the present. One of the starting points for this perspective in folklore studies was Dell Hymes's observation that in a process which he calls the active, dynamic and universal process of traditionalization (Hymes 1975: 353–354; see also Handler & Linnekin 1984), people make goal-directed historical links as well as breaks, foreground particular aspects of the past and background others in order to appropriate a given content of tradition for given argumentative purposes. Instead of being merely received, the past is thus actively – and often narratively – produced. Such a perspective on the active and interpretive production of tradition is emphatically different from the theoretical model formulated by Lauri Honko, according to whom tradition is "the stuff out of which cultures are made". By this Honko means that traditions exist in an inchoate state as material stored in museums, archives and the "library of the human mind", waiting to be selected, activated and thus transformed into culture (see e.g. Honko 1995: 132–136).

The perspective on the construction of the past in the present must also be distinguished from such categorizations as 'fakelore' or 'folklorism', as well as from the dichotomization of 'natural' and 'constructed identities' (see Honko 1988: 21–22), which all imply that authenticity awaits discovery somewhere outside and independently of the processes of traditionalization. Yet, it must also be emphasized that the purpose of research on the processes of traditionalization is not to 'reveal' that the phenomena that we call traditions are 'in reality' quite recent in origin and sometimes invented, that is, made up or fabricated (cf. Hobsbawm & Ranger 1983). Instead of classifying traditions into 'invented' or 'authentic' ones, we must be alerted to the selective and politically and morally argumentative nature of all traditions, both old and new ones, as well as to the fact that as social practices all traditions have a historical foundation and a point of origin. For these reasons, instead of regarding some traditions as inventions and others not, we should consider all traditions both inventions and human interventions in the sense that they are socially constructed categories with which people structure their experience and reproduce the social world.

The perspective on the politics of time and tradition exposes, among other things, the rhetoric embedded in the commonly employed biological metaphor of 'roots' and in the often expressed claim that our cultural identity is based and dependent on our 'roots' and on our 'awareness' of them. Although a source for some significant historical and political processes in the reorganization of global relations today, the general talk on 'cultural roots' has also created a great deal of unreflexive history, as it tends to naturalize – in the many senses of the word – a particular construction of history. On the one hand, the metaphor nullifies the possibility of alternative constructions and, on the other hand, it creates an illusion of particular modes of life and communities belonging, as it were, to the domain of natural history.

Then again, our focus on the processes of traditionalization should not lead us into thinking that all traditions are fake and inauthentic. We should avoid synonymizing or equating the social construction or the invention of culture and tradition with fiction and ontological fictionality. Instead, the perspective on the politics of time and tradition should help us observe the many ways in which people as social beings establish continuities and discontinuities, authenticate the past, and authorize its particular representations in images and actions. Yet, at the same time it must also be stated that this perspective does not grant the present autonomy in the definition of its past, because present definitions of the past are always influenced by past definitions of the past, and the present definitions of the past, by their very existence, are comments on these.

Today's folklorists, ethnologists, historians, anthropologists and others who study, for example, contemporary conflicts are well aware of the politics involved in the definition and appropriation of history and tradition in the service of present-day strategies and objectives. This does not merely concern those political movements that can be labeled 'traditionalist', 'neo-traditionalist', 'revivalist' or 'primitivist'. Perhaps more explicitly than ever before, battles are fought not only over territories and ideologies but also over cultural legacies and cultural identities, and here the very notion of 'tradition' has become a key issue. Indeed, tradition is today a highly contested identity space. In some places more explicitly than in others, much tension – even war – is created through the denials or claims over 'traditional' values, 'traditional' usufruct rights, 'traditional' customs, 'traditional' language, 'traditional' marching and parading routes, etc., which bear direct witness to the political and moral charge of the concept of tradition and its argumentative and rhetorical use in the making of particular policies. There is much controversy all over the world over the issue of what tradition is and how its contents are not only selected for political purposes but have direct political implications and consequences.

For example, in Northern Ireland today, a section of Protestant Unionists known as the Orange Order appeals publicly to the concept and idea of tradition in order to seek legitimation for its wish to continue – despite Catholic opposition – the 200-year-old practice of parading on July 12th through Catholic neighborhoods and celebrate the victory that their 'national' hero, King William III – also known as William of Orange – took over King James II and his Catholic troops in the Battle of the Boyne in 1690. As commented by Dominic Bryan, the parades give the appearance of timeless and unchanging commemorative events, while they have undergone many stylistic changes and their political status vis-à-vis the state has changed on a number of occasions (Bryan n.d.; Bryan 2000: 26, 155, 172; see also Tonkin and Bryan 1996). Bryan also points out that discourse on tradition is utilized by senior Orangemen, the community leaders, in situations in which they appear to be losing influence over the ritual events. The idea of historical lineage is thus employed to reassert not only cultural and political continuity for the group but personal control for its leaders (Bryan 2000: 177–178).

Northern Ireland is only one of the many places where current events show how, as put by Amy Shuman and Charles Briggs, "The process of traditionalizing culture (...) emerges as a locus of strategies for empowering particular groups, rhetorics, and interests" (Shuman and Briggs 1993: 116). Not only in conflict-ridden places but also in more peaceful environments traditions are selected and placed on display by groups of people in order to create and consolidate territorial identifications and use these representations as a means for political commentary. Whenever people make public presentations of their identity and show allegiance through cultural representations, they foreground some particular aspects and background others, which makes the presentation of self always argumentative in nature. Having a cultural identity does not, therefore, mean only an active production of context-dependent images of contemporary and inherited cultural styles. It means the production of images and representations through actions that have argumentative goals in the transformation of relations. As such argumentative production of relations, cultural identity is fundamentally political in nature, an issue of establishing, controlling and fighting over the meaning of symbols, exercising power, creating hierarchies and contesting them.

## The Nation and the State

Cultural identity is political not only because we employ various rhetorical means in the definition of the past and in the selection of cultural traits and symbols to denote a particular relationship between the past and the present. In other words, cultural identity is not a political issue only because of the argumentative nature of the process of traditionalization. Nor is it political only because the concepts of tradition and history are politically charged or because identities both manifest and constitute relations and hierarchies between individuals and groups. Cultural identities are political also because their constitution takes place within and in direct relationship with political events and actions, political processes, legislation, minority and majority policies, local, regional and national politics, the realm of civil society, and with state policies and politics.

Indeed, when we express our identity and indicate where we belong and with whom, we do not merely make distinctions and celebrate and perform difference on a 'cultural' level. Similarly, the places where we belong – or which belong to us – are not merely 'cultural units' solely defined by linguistic, religious or other 'cultural' factors. They are politically defined and marked areas and locales, and as such, always connected to issues of power, administration, social organization and control of territory. Individual identifications with these places – including personal narratives and life-stories about what has happened to whom and where, and how that which has happened has constituted or influenced social identities – are always part of larger and wider political fates and histories.

In disciplines such as folkloristics and ethnology, cultural identity has for a long time tended to be discussed in relation to such 'cultural issues' as nations, ethnicities and ethnic groups, and not in relation to such 'political issues' as the state and its hierarchical organization and administrative policies. This has rested on the traditional (but still modern) framework in which folklore is seen as coming in 'national packages', with the nation conceptualized as the organizing unit for folklore. Even when cultural identity has been discussed as an issue concerning nation-states, the emphasis has been on the nation as a cultural and symbolic unit instead of a political unit. Similarly, scholars have tended to classify territorial identifications into three levels, the local, the regional and the national levels, while ignoring the level of the state. Even though cultural entities and boundaries do not necessarily match with state entities and their borders, all people in the world live within the confines of some state, willingly or unwillingly, and in most people's lives the state plays an active role not only because of the law, the police, schooling, army, taxation, social benefits and bureaucracy, but also as an important unit of political and territorial identification. Therefore it is justified to say that the state as the context for both the constitution and understanding of traditions and traditional identities has not received the attention it deserves.

One of the main reasons for this lack of attention must be that folklore studies have conventionally conceptualized and constructed traditions as the cultural stuff that lies beyond the modern state or emerges from opposition to its presence, including industrialization, enlightenment and other effects and elements of modernization. The bias can also be witnessed in the centralization of those research approaches that conventionally belong to the 'humanities' and in the marginalization of 'state oriented' and 'state conscious' social scientific methods and approaches. A variant of this idea is present in the Western Marxist notion that the fundamental character of folklore is inherently opposed to state capitalism, its development and its social order (see Limón 1983b). The both implicit and explicit antimodernism of folklore study has been directed against the modern state but not against the modern nation. Folklore, as if by definition, concerns and celebrates the nation but not the state. The state is seen to be only interested in eradicating and changing, in accordance with the enlightenment ideology, those cultural expressions that ethnologists and folklorists have studied as traditions (see e.g. Ó Giolláin 1990). Such a perspective predicates power with negativity and places it outside the domain of folklore and the folkloric collectivity (see Linke 1995: 417, 437).

To be sure, folkloristic and ethnological research has been tangential to issues concerning the state. Cultural identity has been studied in the context of 'popular ethnic nationalism', which, as put by David Gaunt, "politically mobilizes an ethnic group in order to agitate for that group's own language and culture and eventual territorial sovereignty" (Gaunt 1992: 146). Accordingly, many of the nation-states that have the nationalistically oriented disciplines of folklore and ethnology in their academic curriculum, have emerged – or present themselves as having emerged – out of such popular ethnic nationalism. The societal relevance of these disciplines continues to be evaluated on the basis of how they consolidate the state with national symbolism and with research information concerning nationally contextualized culture and history. This means that the relationship between the state and the culture of its citizens is perceived through the state-legitimating ideology of nationalism and related questions of national identification and historical mythologization. Culture appears in the context of the nation, not the state.

As argued by, for example, Ulf Hannerz, the state is one of the most essential frameworks of the cultural process, "not as a bounded physical area but as organizational form" (Hannerz 1991: 112). The significance of the state as a factor in the constitution of cultural identities can be seen in, for example, the fact that the state as a social organization has customs, rituals, ceremonies and other collective traditions, symbols and values, which it may put on display for public and private celebration and reproduction. Such performances of identity and power are of great interest especially to historians, folklorists and ethnologists but also to political scientists and political historians (see e.g. Hobsbawm & Ranger 1983). Traditions and cultural identities, including ethnic identities, are both marked and constituted by political events and processes concerning states and their domestic and foreign policies, economy, legislation, the execution of laws and statutes, and other institutional elements of society making. It also worthy of note that many of the ways in which folklorists and ethnologists display the nationally significant traditions that they collect and study are established as symbolic traditions of the state and become part of its political mythology.

The significance of the state as a factor in the constitution of cultural identities can also be seen in the ways in which expressions of particular identities are supported by the state organization and its representatives. Indeed, in addition to creating common identification through 'state traditions', 'state folklore' or 'state mythology', state, local and regional governments encourage and fund cultural activities and the making of cultural identities – or rather, a particular type of discourse on cultural identity – when locally, regionally and nationally constituted cultural identities support and legitimate the political and administrative authority of the state organization.

The state thus employs cultural identity as a means to exercise state power, and this may be said to have its origin in the tendency by the post-medieval kingdoms and empires of Europe to collect 'antiquities' from among their subordinated peoples and employ these to legitimate the sovereign's control of the land. Indeed, as discussed by Roger Abrahams (1993a and 1996), one of the historical origins for the collecting of folklore was the use and advantage that medieval European states saw in folkloric products and objects as means for legitimating their territories with the emergent value of oral history. Similarly, Tine Damsholt places the political origins of Danish ethnology in the Enlightenment interest in the organization of the Danish state, albeit in the 19th century the political discourse was directed at the legitimation of the state with nationalism, and this came to be commonly regarded as the origin of ethnology (see Damsholt 1995).

On the other hand, the cultural – including linguistic and/or religious – identity of a local group or a minority may be constituted on the basis of their questioning the political and administrative authority of the state. In such situations, elements such as geographical features and location, traditional industries, local customs, historical background, language, and other cultural characteristics of a region can come to convey meanings that are politically charged because of this opposition. Indeed, the question of local and regional identity is more often than not linked to the politically charged question concerning the extent to which people are able to continue their 'traditional' or customary economic practices, hold usufruct rights over a given piece of land and other natural resources, speak a given language or dialect, adhere to their 'cultural and political heritage', or even maintain their basic human rights or rights of citizenship. Cultural identity, therefore, concerns discourse on political rights, and the refusal of a state to give certain groups or populations a right to 'express their culture', or live according to it, derives from the awareness of how political culture is.

## A Bias for the Local

In the present-day European context the perspective on the dialectic and dialogical relationship between the state on the one hand and the construction of tradition and identity on the other is utterly relevant and topical. Yet, this does not merely concern the processes of continuous state-formation within the European nation-states and the directly related issue of the nationalization of traditional culture in them. The present situation also challenges us to look into the ways in which the making of the European Union, along with its federalist overtones, relates to the continuous making of the national and the local.

Although European integration primarily appears to concern trade relations and the interconnectedness of state economies, some of its major challenges economically, politically, culturally and intellectually concern individual and collective territorial identifications, their interrelations and representations, and especially the status of the local and its representations. Indeed, the situation calls for research on the ways in which changes in the constitution of geographic and administrative regions, transnational networks in the production of goods and entertainment, and multi-state political organizations affect locally and translocally grounded collective identities and the constitution, selection and display of their cultural symbols.

A key word here is the local as a site of cultural production. In addition to the role of policies, politics and economic relations in the making of traditional cultures – or modern traditional cultures – an important aspect in the reorientation that the recent dramatic changes in Europe have demanded of us is the reconceptualization of the category of the local. Instead of viewing the local as an isomorphic, monolithic and traditional unit in the peripheries, or an endangered species on the verge of extinction because of homogenizing globalization and postlocalization, recent world-system theories and other globally sensitive ethnographic approaches have foregrounded a perspective which sees the local and its constitution in a direct relationship with issues larger than the local. On the one hand, the making of the local takes place in the dialectics of continuous globalization and localization, as well as continuous homogenization and heterogenization. On the other hand, the definition of the local, as well as the selection of its symbols, is a translocal process in which each locality creates its identity in the context of more or less similar identity processes elsewhere, both within nations and states and across them. In these processes, localities employ localized competitive strategies and a heightened sense of awareness of what makes a place special and gives it a competitive advantage (see e.g. Löfgren 1989, 1993a; Hannerz & Löfgren 1992; Friedman 1994b).

Recent perspectives in folklore scholarship have also questioned the traditional view of the local as a phenomenon of isomorphism and emphasized that such a view has been an obstacle to the study of the politics of culture of which the constitution of the local is part (see e.g. Shuman 1993). Accordingly, folklorists have looked for ways to incorporate into their methodology the fact that the local is always made up of constituents larger than the local. Here the insights provided by the study of 'public culture', the invention of cultural identity space in the context of global cultural flows and deterritorialized, hybrid, creolized, heterogenic and cosmopolitan cultural production and consumption (e.g. Appadurai 1990, 1996; Hannerz 1991; Hanson 1993; Kapchan 1993, 1996; Löfgren 2003), have increasingly attracted scholarly attention.

The deterritorialization of culture means that cultures are to a lesser degree than before territorially, nationally, regionally or locally specific, and instead, more and more interconnected. Yet, the important role of transnational linkages and networks in the production of culture – including cultural traditions and identities – does not mean that people will not also continue to ascribe to territorially based state-related, national, regional and local identifications. The significance of cultural interconnectedness lies in its challenge for us to look at the ways in which the local as a site of cultural production is constituted by and stands in relation to larger social and historical processes.

Indeed, cultural identities, whether local, regional, national or state-related, are constructed on the basis of various loyalties and allegiances, economic and political interests and historically specific circumstances and relations, which are always locally experienced, albeit at the same time in many ways translocally, even globally, constituted. This also includes the invention and display of traditions, which operate within communities – as communities operate within traditions – not only in the context of the larger society, the nation and the state, but as ways of producing meaning and identity within transnational economic and political structures, center–periphery negotiations and global political economy.[7]

For this reason, in order to understand the locality and the sense of place of the people we study – and conduct fieldwork with – we must contextualize the constitution and production of their respective identities with those world historical processes of which they are a part. To show the relevant relations and contexts of meaning, we must be sensitive to both local and multi-local dynamics and observe the ways in which people create their sense of place and geopolitical identity in the contexts of nationalism, localism, global tribalism, modernism and traditionalism, postmodernism and postcolonialism, local and state policies and politics, local organization of industries, transnational and trans-state conjunctions and disjunctures, world politics, economic world-systems and global cultural flows. It is in the context of a variety of competing ideologies, political processes, social and commercial networks, that vernacular cultural production, the constitution of local cultural and territorial identity as well as the construction of local history and historical imaginations take place.

# 7. Globalization and Nationalism

The term globalization has many meanings, and as one author commented, "The more we read about globalization from the mounting volume of literature on the topic, the less clear we seem to be about what it means and what it implies" (Amin 1997: 123). Generally, globalization can be said to contain the denotations of internationalization, universalization and transnationalization. Yet, it is much more than their total sum of meaning. Both 'international' and 'transnational' refer to things that reach beyond national boundaries or concern relations between different nations or states. While internationalization is generally understood as an increase in cultural, economic, and political contacts between different countries or their representatives, transnationalization suggests a comparative perspective on that which transcends national boundaries and emphasizes the constitutive roles that similar elements have upon each other within different national cultures (see e.g. Hannerz 1990).[8]

'Universal', on the other hand, refers to that which extends over the whole world or exists and occurs in all things. Universalization thus denotes the process by which things that are first individual, particular, or local become general and collective and diffuse across lands and countries. When globalization is understood as a universalizing process, it stands for the expansion and diffusion of things and ideas (and people) on a global scale. In this sense, globalization can be taken to mean, for example, the spread of modern Western institutions or marketed products to the rest of the world. But instead of merely denoting diffusion on a global scale, the concept also contains the idea that due to such diffusion, as well as due to the technological development of transport and media communications and the acceleration of global trade, the world is compressed, made small and village-like. As defined by Roland Robertson, globalization is "the crystallization of the entire world as a single place" (Robertson 1987: 38).

However, instead of considering the concept from only the apparently obvious Western perspective, many scholars have emphasized that globalization is an age-old phenomenon which includes, among other things, the spread of Asian and Islamic civilizations to other parts of the globe, and the constitution of large cultural areas such as the Chinese cultural block, the Islamic cultural block, and so on. In this meaning, universalization is not merely an issue of dissemination but may also be used to refer to the discursive practice in which certain cultural processes and values are 'deprovincialized'. This term suggests a process by which particular social forms and practices are metadiscursively rendered powerful, naturalized, "projected as the universal bases of knowledge, truth, culture, nation, rationality, science, politics, and modernity – as unmarked, historically transcendent, and natural foundations of social life" (Bauman & Briggs 2003: 313). A postcolonial act in this regard would be to 'reprovincialize' that which has been deprovincialized; accordingly, the dominant Eurocentrism in the universalization of modernity would require the reprovincialization of Europe (see Chakrabarty 2000).

## Global Context

Since people experience the world as more compressed, there is increasing awareness and consciousness about global connections: global has come to us as an arena to be aware of. Environmental changes, for example, have increased global awareness as well as global concerns and responsibilities. Then again, being aware of the global connections of local strategies in the use and appropriation of natural resources is closely related to the increase in awareness of global connections in social practices and their political and economic aspects, as well as global connections in cultural production and exchange. One of the consequences of such globalization has been the challenge to modern sociology's conventionally set national framework (e.g. Turner 1990).

The same applies to many other disciplines, as scholars have learned to put and see things in their 'global context' and view them from a 'global perspective'. In academic conferences on the study of culture, a great number of issues are now being discussed from the fashionable viewpoint that binds together local and global. For example, in the American Folklore Society 1998 meeting there were panels and forums with the following titles: 'Local and Global Processes', 'Local Culture/Global Issues: Cultural Representation Through a Thematic Lens', 'Local Cultures, A Global Discourse: Native Strategies for Telling Northwest Indian Stories in English', 'Responses to Globalization: Local Traditions in the Global Ecumene', 'Global Materials, Local Adaptations in Material Culture', 'Witchcraft in Local and Global Perspective', 'Local and Global Connections for Northwest Teachers', 'Jokes in the Global Media', 'Music Local and Global', 'Africa Local and Global', 'Geographies of Eating: Tastes of Dispersal Local and Global', and 'Local vs. Global Perspectives on 'Lesbian' Presentations of Self'.

One manifestation of global awareness is the interest in so-called global ethics. Some years ago, when I was new to the modern world of the Internet, the search word 'global ethics' brought me to the Institute for Global Ethics, which presents itself with a mission to discuss ethics in 'a global perspective'. This is to discover and articulate the globally common ground of ethical values, and to analyze ethical trends and shifts in values as they occur worldwide. The Institute offers a four-step Ethical Fitness Seminar, which "helps you become ethically aware, define values, analyze ethics, and resolve dilemmas" (Global Ethics n.d.). A somewhat different enterprise was the theologically and ecumenically oriented Center for Global Ethics, which "coordinates the work of thinkers, scholars and activists from around the world, who are working to define, implement and promote policies of responsible global citizenship" (loc. cit). One of the cornerstones for their activity is the Declaration of a Global Ethic, written by Dr. Hans Küng (1993).

The rhetoric of global ethics resonates with the rhetorical construction of the 'global community' and 'world community', which are rather commonly used terms in world politics today. The Harvard University Professor Samuel P. Huntington, discussing the role of the West in what he terms as the clash of civilizations and cultures, has pointed to the ways in which decisions made in the United Nations Security Council or in the International Monetary Fund reflect the interests of the Western powers but are presented to the world as reflecting the desires of 'the world community'. Says Huntington: "The very phrase 'the world community' has become the euphemistic collective noun (replacing 'the Free World') to give global legitimacy to actions reflecting the interests of the United States and other Western powers." (Huntington 1996a: 16.) According to Huntington, the West, acting in the name of 'the world community', uses "international institutions, military power and economic resources to run the world in ways that will maintain Western predominance, protect Western interests and promote Western political and economic values" (op. cit.: 17). Instead of representing globally shared views, such Western dominance, according to Huntington, is an emergent source of conflict between 'the West and the rest', which Huntington conceptualizes as a conflict between different units in cultures and civilizations.

## Global Economy and Politics

While many scholars have wished to relativize the present discussion on globalization and its alleged newness by seeking corresponding phenomena in ancient civilizations and cultural imperialisms (ancient Mesopotamia, hellenization, pax Romana, etc.; see e.g. Friedman 1994a), some others have regarded globalization as a new period and stage in modernity. For many postmodern theorists, 'postmodern' did not merely represent a critical approach to modernity and modernism but indicated a transition to a particular civilizational or cultural state, a postmodern condition in the modern world. In a similar manner, globalization has been understood by some scholars as a new stage or phase after postmodernity, a global modernity constituted by globally organized space, global economy and global frameworks of social relations and cultural flows (see e.g. Featherstone, Lash & Robertson 1995). Accordingly, one can view the present-day academic interest in globalization as a new trend coming after postmodernism in social sciences and the study of culture. The change that has taken place within the last few years is quite drastic. For example, no panel or forum in the afore-mentioned American Folklore Society 1998 meeting carried the term 'postmodern' in its title.

116

One of the basic ways in which globalization is understood today concerns current cultural, economic, and political changes and transformations, which are generated by the latest technological advances in mass communications, and by increased mobility and transfer of both people and goods across cultural and economic units and state borders. These changes are regarded as being unprecedented in both speed and volume, touching almost every country, province, city, neighborhood, and person on the globe. Yet, instead of merely indicating a global – that is 'worldwide' – impact of the latest developments, globalization is understood to signify the formulation of a world system of production and consumption, the emergence of global capitalism organized into networks and arenas that transcend the territories of the nation-states and national economies, connecting the local production of goods and culture into worldwide systems of relations.

Such a system of global economy is, however, hardly founded upon any global consensus. In addition, it mainly concerns global investments in currency speculations instead of investments in local production in other national units. A large portion of currency speculations has no relation to the sphere of actual production. This, according to such critics as David C. Korten (1997), means that global capitalism has replaced the market economy.

In essential ways, globalization stands for the increased speed and volume in investments on stocks and capital on a global scale and the creation of worldwide markets. One of the symbols of such globalization – and a highly controversial issue within the discourse of economic globalization – is the planned Multilateral Agreement on Investments (MAI), which would guarantee unrestricted flow of capital across national borders, so that there would not be any difference or discrimination between domestic and foreign investments. Consequently, this would also reinforce the separation of economy from the state.

This shows that we are witnessing a large-scale restructuring of economic and political power in which nation-state governments yield much of their control of economy and economic policy to multinational corporations – of which many are larger than many nation-states and their national economies – in order to gain some of the benefits that the multinational corporations may provide for national economies in the form of paid taxes and employment (see e.g. Hirst 1997). The multinational corporations may have a 'home base' in their national origin. In the national *Öffentlichkeit* (public sphere) of such a country, this can be appropriated as cultural capital and made into a source for national identification and symbol making. For example in Finland, the international success of the Nokia Corporation, the renowned manufacturer of cellular phones, receives many of its meanings through the discourse on Finnish national heroes. In this discourse, heroic figures are successful in international arenas. Such a discourse must obviously play down the fact the Nokia is 90% foreign-owned (e.g. *Helsingin Sanomat, International Edition*, June 10, 2002) and thus a 'global company'.

Although globalization diminishes the meaning of the state, government politicians choose to present such globalization as a process that is both inevitable and prosperous – a 'new global deal' that will bring wealth and prosperity to all. In Finland, Mr. Ole Norrback, Minister of European Affairs in the late 1990s, stated that a global economic system based on mutual interdependency would promote international peace and stability (Norrback 1998). A similar assertion was made by Mr. Alpo Rusi, the political advisor of President Martti Ahtisaari of Finland, who wrote that the stock market crash of the late 1920s gave an impulse to build obstacles to world trade, which then caused the emergence of Nazism in Germany, the Stalinization of Soviet Communism, and the strengthening of militarism in Japan (Rusi 1998). According to Rusi, this indicates the threat that national processes of identity production and economy pose to humankind. Therefore, it also demonstrates the benefits of free world trade and globalization. The logic of such a view (and the construction of historical narratives in accordance to it) is that by being global and trading globally, new totalitarian governments are prevented from emerging.

It must be acknowledged, however, that economic globalization, together with global investments based on stock market speculations and quick transfers of capital from one country to another, may also threaten the political balance of national economies, and shake political stability. For this reason, globalization can easily come to mean the loss of local and/or democratic means in economic policy making. As a global-scale political operation controlled by mostly Western industrial and post-industrial countries, it may represent a new form of colonialism. But on the other hand, a rearrangement in the global political and economic relations may enhance the decline of Western hegemony. The growing influence of non-Western countries in global economics and global politics through industrialization, tourism, and the control of natural resources may at least to some extent challenge the old center–periphery structures that the colonizing West established in its modernization and industrialization process.

It is obvious for these reasons that globalization cannot create a unified worldwide economy, but instead, promotes increased competition between large market areas, such as the European Union, the United States, and Japan. Accordingly, it has been predicted that the future competitors in the global economy will be entire continents. Such constellations are not without meaning for world politics or for collective or individual political and cultural identifications. According to Samuel P. Huntington, the world is divided by civilizations and cultural differences, and Western-based globalization is not going to undo these differences, but on the contrary, act upon them. Huntington's main argument is that alignments defined by ideology and superpower relations are giving way to alignments defined by culture and civilization, and that political boundaries are redrawn to coincide with cultural ones: ethnic, religious, and civilizational (see Huntington 1996c). Moreover, after the Cold War, "the principal conflicts of global politics will occur between nations and groups of different civilizations" (Huntington 1996a: 1).

By this Huntington means that despite the increase in global relations in economy, nation-states will continue to be important political entities and they will increase their political alignments on the basis of 'cultural' factors. Such factors are made of "history, language, culture, tradition, and most importantly, religion" (Huntington 1996a: 4). According to Huntington, increased interaction, greater communication and transportation, will not produce homogeneity, but instead, "interaction frequently reinforces existing identities and produces resistance, reaction and confrontation" (Huntington 1996b: 63).

The civilizational paradigm, according to Huntington, accounts for "many important developments in international affairs in recent years, including the breakup of the Soviet Union and Yugoslavia, the wars going on in their former territories, the rise of religious fundamentalism throughout the world, the struggles within Russia, Turkey and Mexico over their identity, the intensity of the trade conflicts between the United States and Japan, the resistance of Islamic states to Western pressure on Iraq and Libya, the efforts of Islamic and Confucian states to acquire nuclear weapons and the means to deliver them, China's continuing role as an 'outsider' great power, the consolidation of new democratic regimes in some countries and not in others, and the escalating arms race in East Asia." (Huntington 1996b: 58.)

Following Huntington, Marju Lauristin, formerly an Estonian political activist and now Professor of Political Communication at Tartu University, claims that the East-European revolution of 1989 and the collapse of the Soviet Union was to a significant degree an outcome of a 'civilizational conflict' between the Soviet Empire and the East European nations: the Russian-Soviet Empire represents a "New Byzantium of the 20th century", while the Baltic states and other East European nations represent "the Western traditions of individual autonomy and civil society" (Lauristin 1997: 28–31). Such a 'cultural' explanation makes the regaining of political power and independence for the linguistically and ethnically defined communities in the respective Baltic states a 'natural' phenomenon. In addition, it continues the pre-World War II thinking about the Baltic states (as well as Finland) as being the last resort of Europe against 'the evil forces of the East'. Therefore, for the Baltics, their regained independence appears as a return to 'Europe' and 'European civilization', while Russia is excluded from it by making it represent the Byzantine and therefore a 'non-European' heritage.

## The Global and the National

Because of the drastic and dramatic changes in world economics and politics, globalization has generated much discussion on identity and identification: individual, local, national, translocal, transnational, cosmopolitan, etc. The discussion on globalization and identity has especially concerned the relationship between identity and territory. There are two basic approaches in this discussion. The first is the notion that globalization leads to the end of cultural differences and to the beginning of global similarity. Globalization can thus stand for worldwide homogenization of culture (see Hannerz 1991), which may be conceptualized as 'the end of traditions' or 'the end of local cultures' or as 'McDonaldization'. Although the discussion on 'McDonaldization' in cultural studies may be sensitive to the worldwide changes in

119

economic structures (see e.g. Ritzer 1996), the discussion on the worldwide homogenization of culture tends to be based on the observation that given items of merchandise are now available even in the most 'peripheral' places. This is a diffusionistic approach to globalization based on the polarization of change and continuity. While novelties, seen as the elements of change, are observed to spread and diffuse more and more rapidly, and appear in places where they didn't use to be, the elements that are conventionally regarded as signs of continuity – such as local traditions and traditional cultural heritage – are felt to be more and more threatened. Globalization is here seen as an issue of consumption, but the term 'consumption' directs the observer's gaze only to the imported goods, not to the local construction of tradition and heritage in their political contexts. Indeed, we are accustomed to seeing the merchandise on shop shelves as commodities, while we tend to disregard the construction of collective traditions and symbolic heritage as a form of commodification.

For this reason, we may think that globalization and the preservation of traditional culture are in opposition to one another. But instead of constituting an opposition, they can also be seen as presenting two aspects of the same development. For example, establishing world heritage sites is a means to bring local culture into global processes of producing value and meaning. On the other hand, the continuation of a local identity within global integration does not automatically mean that the elements of local identity are or even should be 'traditional'. On the contrary, the category of the 'traditional' has itself become a global construction – especially on the global markets of tourism, trade and symbol production concerning traditional music and traditional arts and crafts. Indeed, there is another approach to globalization that emphasizes the deterritorialization of the production of identity and culture and of consumption. Accordingly, much emphasis has been placed on such processes as interstitial identities (Bhabha 1994), reflexive modernization (Giddens 1994), detraditionalization (Heelas, Lash & Morris 1996) and reflexive traditionalization (Welz 2001). Along the same lines, Néstor García Canclini suggests that globalization stands for a passage from modern territorial and monolinguistic idenies to postmodern transterritorial and multilinguistic identities (García Canclini 2001: 28–29). The former are imposed by nations and states, while the latter are structured by the logic of the markets.

One of the most heated topics generated by the processes of globalization concerns the future of the nation-state and nationalism, as well as the possibilities of global citizenship and global democracy. Globalization has meant a drastic decline in the importance of many institutions and strongholds in national economies and administrations, including institutions of democracy. Yet, the question that is in this context particularly interesting and challenging is the factual simultaneousness of both deterritorialized and highly territorial identities. Is one of them increasing at the expense of the other?

For many present-day researchers, the deterritorialization of culture and identity indicates a decrease in the significance of the national as a framework in the constitution of identity. For Arjun Appadurai, for example, it is an indication of postnationalism and the movement towards nonterritorial principles of solidarity (Appadurai 1996: 165). For Scott Lash and John Urry, the global present appears as marked by various kinds of flows: flows of information, flows of migrants and refugees, flows of capital, flows of commodities, and flows of culture. From this perspective, the recent developments denote a change from space to flow, from spaces to streams, from organized hierarchies to disorganization (see Lash & Urry 1996).

For Appadurai, electronic mediation and mass migration, in their present-day forms and meanings, represent a fundamental rupture between past and present, and one of their most essential aspects is that "Neither images nor viewers fit into circuits or audiences that are easily bound within local, national, or regional spaces" (Appadurai 1996: 4). To replace these, Appadurai presents five dimensions of global cultural flow that he has termed 'ethnoscape', 'technoscape', 'finanscape', 'mediascape' and 'ideoscape'. 'Ethnoscape' refers to the variety of people on the move across cultural boundaries; 'technoscape' to the positioning of multinational enterprises, factories, power plants, etc. and their work force across national and cultural borders and wage systems; 'finanscape' to the flow and disposition of capital across currency markets and stock exchanges; 'mediascape' to the distribution of electronic capabilities to produce and disseminate information through newspapers, television stations, film production studios, etc. as well as the narrative-like images of the world created by these media; and 'ideoscape' to the diaspora of political images composed of such narratively constructed Enlightenment-related ideas and terms as 'freedom', 'welfare', 'rights', 'sovereignty' and 'democracy' (Appadurai 1990; see also Appadurai 1996).

Discussing deterritorialization, Appadurai describes Turkish guestworkers in Germany watching Turkish films in their German flats, Koreans in Philadelphia watching the 1988 Olympic Games in Seoul through satellite feeds from Korea, or Pakistani cabdrivers in Chicago listening to cassettes of sermons recorded in mosques in Pakistan or Iran. It is in such situations that, according to Appadurai, "moving images meet deterritorialized viewers". In other words, immigrants who consume objects made at 'home' or objects that convey important symbolic references to the home country, are, according to Appadurai, deterritorialized, and as such, not easily bound within local, national, or regional spaces. This, according to Appadurai, speaks against the importance of the nation-state and its role in the production of social changes (Appadurai 1996: 4).

For Appadurai, territorial nationalism has no essential role in many of the present-day ethnic or national movements or conflicts. For example, "Serbian nationalism seems to operate on the fear and hatred of its ethnic Others far more than on the sense of a sacred territorial patrimony" (Appadurai 1996: 165). Similarly, according to Appadurai, "Palestinians are more worried about getting Israel off their backs than about the special geographical magic of the West Bank" (loc. cit.). Thus, territoriality for Appadurai appears to refer to a rather irrational religiosity, which can therefore be dismissed as a foundation and motivation for rational political action. Yet, we may wish to ask why the occupation of particular territories would not be important to these or other groups, since, in the case of population settlements, getting somebody off your back means, more often than not, to be left alone in spatial and geographical terms. As far as the motives for Serbian aggression are concerned, many others have pointed to territorial aggrandizement as their explicit goal (see e.g. Kirkpatrick 1996: 52).

A related issue concerns territorial control, as someone always controls territories – also those territories occupied or inhabited by diasporic populations. In fact, there can be powerful reterritorialization processes taking place in diasporic situations. While migration has received an almost metaphorical and metonymical status for deterritorialized global modernity, migrated populations may wish to put up monuments or symbols to commemorate their migration and settlement in order to become rooted in their new environments and receive support for their demands for political rights in their new neighborhoods.

As far as today's economic development is concerned, its global dimensions can certainly be described as economic pragmatism stripped of national loyalties. In many arenas, and perhaps we can say that in an increasing number of arenas, economic and commercial interests surpass instead of foreground national frames of reference. Yet, we may still wish to ask, how encompassing are these arenas, or do those speaking in favor of the loss of meaning for territorial identification represent only various sorts of elites? This is in fact suggested by Orvar Löfgren, according to whom there are new transnational and intellectual elites, "cosmopolitans who are at home in the world and have fewer loyalties to their old nation or home ground. They travel business class through life and across the world. Against this new elite we find an increasingly marginalized working class, trying to defend themselves against globalization by becoming more national, regional, or home-loving. They opt for the seeming safeness of place and ritual belonging, and in this nostalgia they become both more inward looking and more xenophobic." (Löfgren 2001: 3–4.)

There is reason to believe that despite internationalization, postnationalization and the pluralization of identities, identification with the national territory and the national community continues to be one of the major dimensions of social identification. In the previous chapter I wrote that even though – or probably just because – the media are becoming more and more delocalized and postnational, that is, independent of national loyalties – some of their most popular products, especially the international sport competitions, explicitly foreground and encourage national frames of reference and national identification and in that way discourage what is called the fragmentation of identities. Another reason for the continuation of the nation as the preferred imagined community is the strength of particular systems of thought inherited from the philologically influenced philosophy of nationalism developed in the late 18th and early 19th centuries. These concern the politically charged connections constructed between language and culture, on the one hand, and language and culture and the state, on the other. They may constitute a much stronger factor in the continuation of the national framework than expected, even if they seem modernist and therefore *passé* to the critics of nationalized modernity.

On one level, the continuation of such systems of cultural and political thought may mean the strengthening of the 'civilizational framework' in the construction of nationally constituted political and cultural entities. At least Samuel P. Huntington believes that "Faith and family, blood and belief, are what people identity with and what they will fight and die for" (Huntington 1996b: 67). Yet, as commented by Fouad Ajami (1996: 34), "States avert their gaze from blood ties when they need to; they see brotherhood and faith and kin when it is in their interest to do so." Still, it is one thing what the representatives of a state might argue and another, what mobilizes the masses. As noted by Unto Vesa, Huntington's arguments reproduce the images of threat built upon the mythology of the crusades (Vesa 2000: 490–493).

In this highly politicized context of making culture, the significance of cultural interconnectedness lies in its challenge for us, first, to look at the ways in which the local and the national as sites of cultural production are constituted by and in relation to larger historical and political processes and global political economy. Cultural identities, whether local, regional, national or state-related, are construed on the basis of various loyalties and allegiances, economic and political interests and historically specific relations, which are always locally experienced, albeit at the same time in many ways translocally, even globally, constituted. Another challenge lies in the ideological constitution of such loyalties, for which reason we must look, for example, at the roles that kinship, 'genetic belonging', and the metaphors of family continue to play in the construction of cultural and political units. Accordingly, the many arenas in which globalization is both encouraged as well as used for ideological purposes, alert us to acknowledge that despite the fact that there is only one globe, the global is a highly contested category.

# 8. Cultural Homogeneity and the National Unification of a Political Community

When discussing globalization, present-day Nordic policies vis-à-vis ethnic diversity, European integration, and the influx of refugees, asylum seekers and immigrants, we can hardly ignore the ideological foundations laid down by the 19th century national movements and state-making processes in the respective Nordic countries. Such discussions call for the examination of the role and continuing impact of the ideas of 'romantic' or ethnic nationalism – as especially expressed and promoted by the German philosophers Johann Gottfried Herder (1744–1803) and Georg Wilhelm Hegel (1770–1831). These ideas seem to have a lasting influence not only on the conceptualization of national identities and the discourses on national characters and history, but also on the legislation concerning citizenship and immigration, democratic principles, and popular attitudes regarding ethnic, religious or linguistic minorities and foreigners.

From both a Nordic and a global perspective, Finland provides an interesting example for discussing the historical foundations for the inter-relationship between what have been termed 'ethnic-genealogical' and 'civic-territorial' conceptions of the nation (Smith 1991). The former refers to the Herderian ideas of shared ethnicity and common genealogy, that is, common language, religion, history, customs and race, as the prerequisites for membership in a national community. The latter refers to the principle of legitimate participation in the political community of the territorial state (and the nation), with rights and duties determined regardless of ethnicity, race or ancestry. These distinctions have sometimes – but rather arbitrarily – been called 'eastern' and 'western' types of nationalism; East Europe being the location for ethnic nationalism and West Europe, for political nationalism or state nationalism. The recent developments both east and west have indicated that such a categorical distinction is not quite valid.

What is present-day Finland was part of the Kingdom of Sweden since the 12th or 13th century, until in 1809 the area was annexed to the Russian Empire and made an autonomous Grand Duchy, which gained political independence as the Republic of Finland in 1917. Developed from a disputed border area between Sweden and Russia (or first Novgorod) into a nation-state of its own, Finland exemplifies a country in which the idea of ethnic homogeneity and the sense of ethnic solidarity continue to play a significant role in the construction of the national and the selection of its representations and symbols. Instead of diminishing in its significance in the present age of globalization and globalism, the on-going European integration and the consequent decrease in the role of the state have given new impetus to cultural and ethnic nationalism.

In this situation, a variety of related topics have emerged for both academic research and general debate. Within research into immigration, refugees and ethnic diversity, a great deal of attention has been directed at intercultural encounters and especially at the adaptation of the immigrated or displaced people in the receiving country as a minority population. In addition to sociopolitical and legal issues, questions concerning cultural identity, especially its preservation and modification in the new social and cultural environment, have prevailed.

Much attention has also been paid to the attitudes that people in the receiving country express towards incomers. Here especially the apparent exclusivist and even racist sentiments against immigrants, asylum seekers and refugees have been a much-debated issue. In most surveys, research reports and scholarly essays, tolerance is called for and the multiculturalization of the nation-state is suggested as the political solution. These stand in open opposition to the demands of anti-immigration activists and their supporters to delimit immigration and the reception of asylum seekers and refugees and to deport those 'outsiders' who have already entered the national space.

According to statistics and polls, a large portion of the population in Finland has a somewhat negative attitude towards the recent growth of immigration and the reception of both refugees and asylum seekers. Often these attitudes bespeak a fear for increasing competition in the labor and marriage market, but there is also an explicit fear – even media-bred hysteria – for an unjust distribution of social benefits between the nationals and the newcomers. Foreigners in general tend to be regarded as posing a threat to the country by, allegedly, increasing criminality, trafficking drugs and spreading AIDS. In Magdalena Jaakkola's much publicized survey from 1998, approximately 20% of the 1,000 persons interviewed favored the principle that people from different cultures should not mix, and 42% believed that "people of particular races are unfit to live in modern society" (Jaakkola 1999: 183). In the comparative surveys of Finnish attitudes sponsored by the Centre for Finnish Business and Policy Studies (EVA), published in 2003, 43% in 1992 and 34% in 2000 were found to agree with the proposed statement that increasing immigration will lead to a disadvantageous mixture of races and weaken the vigor of the nation (Haikonen & Kiljunen 2003: 239, figure 6–9 C; see also p. 217).

How do we explain the popular negative attitudes and fears regarding the recent increase in the number of foreigners? In Finland, one of the most commonly suggested explanations is selfishness caused by the economic recession and high unemployment of the early 1990s. Other publicly aired suggestions include the idea of a national identity complex based on low self-esteem, a lack of multicultural policies in society, as well as a lack of satisfactory models of adulthood and ego for the youth. Ethnocentrism, intolerance of differences in cultural behavior and physical appearance, and prejudice against foreigners and foreign cultures in general have also been seen as manifestations of a particular 'Finnish mentality', which would make these attitudes and fears intrinsically Finnish.

I would suggest that in addition to being manifestations of historically specific international currents of exclusionist ideas (see Stolcke 1995), the attitudes and fears concerning immigrants and refugees, and foreigners in general, have to do with the way in which 'the national' is discursively constructed in a particular nation-state context. The explanations for the popular negative attitudes, therefore, call for research into the history of nation making and the policies and discourses regarding the ethnic, religious, cultural and political constitution of the national population.

As part of such an 'ethnopolitical' research agenda, the present chapter takes up for scrutiny the generally held conception that Finland is a nation-state of small cultural differences, and therefore, homogeneous – even "extremely homogeneous" (e.g. Kajanoja 1993: 21; Peltonen n.d.). In present-day academic discussions of Finnishness, which has gained momentum especially due to the collapse of the Soviet Union in 1991 and Finland's new membership in the European Union since 1995, the idea of Finland's homogeneity is both denied and confirmed (see e.g. articles in Laaksonen & Mettomäki 1996 and Alasuutari & Ruuska 1998; cf. Saukkonen 1999: 235–239). Yet, the conception of Finland's relative homogeneity may be supported by 'simple' population statistics:

Population statistics (source: Statistics Finland, www.stat.fi)

|  | 1998 | 2002 |
| --- | --- | --- |
| Total population | 5,16 million | 5,2 million |

Population by language:

|  | 1900 | 1998 | 2002 |
| --- | --- | --- | --- |
| Finnish | 86,75% | 92,61% | 92,14% |
| Swedish | 12,89% | 5,68% | 5,58% |
| Sámi | 0,06% | 0,03% (1,688 persons) | 0,03% |
| Russian | 0,29% | 0,45% (23,220 persons) | 0,64% |
| Other | 0,01% | 1,22% (62,865 persons) | 1,61% |

Population by religion:

|                          | **1900** | **1998** | **2002** |
|--------------------------|----------|----------|----------|
| Lutheran Protestants     | 98,1%    | 85,4%    | 84,6%    |
| Orthodox                 | 1,7%     | 1,1%     | 1,1%     |
| Other                    | 0,2%     | 1,1%     | 1,1%     |
| No religious affiliation | –        | 12,4%    | 13,1%    |

Foreign residents:

|          | **1990** | **1998** | **2002**  |
|----------|----------|----------|-----------|
|          | 26,255   | 85,060   | 103,682   |

The statistics clearly show, that in relation to the great majority of Lutheran Finnish speakers, the others represent only small minorities. In this sense it may be accurate to characterize Finland as a homogeneous country – 'homogeneity' being here a biological metaphor indicating lack of 'major' or 'significant' cultural variation or diversity. Yet, the statistics do not explain why Finland is a homogeneous country or why there is no 'major' cultural variation. Neither do they explain why the existing minorities are only minorities or why their minority positions have been deemed so 'insignificant' that they have yielded to a dominant image of homogeneity.[9]

If Finland is homogeneous, we may ask whether its homogeneity is a primordial state, dating from prehistoric times, or a historical consequence of particular homogenizing policies. In what way has Finland become homogenous or at least come to be viewed as such? If it is a narrative construction, what kind of rhetorical ways of narrativizing and mythologizing history have been employed in the production of homogeneity? Have the nationalized representations of traditional culture, produced by such academic disciplines as ethnology and folklore studies, helped promote ethnic and cultural homogenization? What role have the philological theories of the relationship between language, culture and territory and race played in this? What is the connection between such theories and the modern, mainly early 20th-century, 'race hygienic' measures taken, for example in eugenics, to secure 'purity' in the 'genetic heritage' of the national population? What kind of legislative actions have been taken to tone down ethnic and/or religious differences and make them less visible? How has the government's policy in granting citizenship affected the ethnic, linguistic and/or religious composition of the national population? Has the ideology and practice of modern democracy increased or decreased the cultural homogenization of the national population? Have 'geopolitical realities' and images of threat from across the national borders been used to legitimate ethnic and cultural homogenization? What sort of unifying campaigns have been launched in society by the state and its leaders – by those attempting to increase their own political power and influence – to create a sense of cultural homogeneity that transcends the differences in language, political objectives, and social class? How do these unifying campaigns employ the ideas of heritage and heredity, and extend their symbolism over the national population?

The idea of nations being homogeneous, or at least being regarded as such, is not a new one, as cultural homogeneity has been considered one of the central objectives in and prerequisites for the creation of political unity in nation-states. The production of a synonymy between national culture and the cultural homogeneity of a nation-state follows what has been called 'homogeneism', a term coined by Jan Blommaert and Jef Verschueren (1998) to refer to the ideological foundation of the discursive production of national homogeneity. According to Blommaert and Verschueren, homogeneism is "a view of society in which differences are seen as dangerous and centrifuged and in which the 'best' society is suggested to be one without intergroup differences. In other words, the ideal model of society is monolingual, mono-ethnic, monoreligious, monoideological." (Blommaert & Verschueren 1998: 194–195.) In homogeneism, that which is seen to manifest desired homoge-neity is established as 'the national tradition', which can then be used as a symbolic means to consolidate national political unity, while diversity and its manifestations are seen to threaten this unity.

The historical production of national cultures has been critically exam-ined in some of the most influential works in historical and cultural research in the late 20th century (e.g. Anderson 1983; Gellner 1983; Hobsbawm & Ranger 1983; Hobsbawm 1990). These critical works entail taking up a deconstructive perspective that also concerns the historical production of cultural homogeneity. The fact that this process has been constantly charged with heterogenizing forces, tendencies and preferences makes it a historical instead of a natural state of affairs. Since it takes place in contexts where there are at least theoretical, if not practical, alternative ways of making so-cial reality, it is also political.

The present-day academic interest in the problematization of nationness and its political and cultural constitution, together with the attention given to the politics of identity and multiculturalization, provide a framework in which I find it relevant to focus on a particular nation-state, Finland, and study how homogeneity – or belief and persuasion in its existence – has been produced historically and narratively. Since this mainly concerns the ethnic, linguistic and religious composition of the national population, it is closely linked to the ways in which the national culture has constructed and established cul-tural Others both within and beyond the territory of the state. Accordingly, one of the central issues in the study of ethnic diversity and heritage politics within a nation-state is this: How and why are some similarities within the heterogeneous or diverse ethnic, linguistic and religious reality employed to make nationally significant intercultural links, while others are employed to make breaks? In other words, what are the politics of difference in the cultural variation of the nation-state?

I have to point out, however, that my purpose here is not to take a com-parative approach to describe how the Finns constitute a group that is either similar to or different from other national groups. In other words, my aim is not to examine 'what the Finns are like' and come up with a new definition or characterization of Finnishness or 'Finnish mentality', on the basis of which I could then argue why the Finns are distinct from other people. This is, according to my interpretation, the research agenda outlined by some leading Finnish folklorists in the book *Gender and Folklore: Perspectives on Finnish and Karelian Culture*. The editors of this book write as follows:

> Finland's entrance into the European Union in 1995 has once again set in motion the process of national self-definition; this may explain the sharp increase in the number of university students enrolling in folkloristics. Folk poetry and folklore researchers are called upon to answer the same sorts of questions that they were a century ago, when the discipline emerged around the work of Julius and Kaarle Krohn. In these questions, the focus is once again ethno-cultural identity: who are the Finns in relation to the Other, what sorts of differences or similarities does our culture share with other cultures in Europe and the world? (Apo, Nenola & Stark-Arola 1998: 24–25.)

Even though I participate in the same disciplinary framework as these writers, I disassociate myself from this approach for two reasons. First, the role of folklore studies in modern society lies, in my mind, in its potentiality in offering insights into the *research* of identity production rather than consolidating and propagating for particular identifications and identity constructions. Second, the comparative methodology that the statement implies is descriptive instead of analytical. It would mean taking the categories of 'the Finns' and 'the Other' as given, as predetermined and innately separate 'ethno-cultural' entities, while my purpose here is to discuss their historical and ideological construction – including the very question of why culture and ethnicity are linked in a way that appears to produce a separate 'ethno-cultural identity'. Instead of studying the 'Finnish mentality', I am interested in scrutinizing historically developed mentalities that are employed in the ideological construction of Finnishness. My concern is to study the argumentative processes of producing nation-ness, rather than promoting such processes. This includes taking distance from the rather common discursive practice, typical also in the academic discussion on Finnishness, of constructing national identity space with the use of the first person plural. The rhetorical 'we' tends to cover up the politics of its composition.

Obviously, the present work cannot answer all of the questions listed above. Yet, I seek to contribute to their examination by paying attention to some elements in the discursive production of Finnishness since the creation of the Finnish state in 1809. The chapter will discuss how particular definitions of Finnishness – with its inclusions and exclusions – are adopted and employed as political means to manipulate or modify society, its population, territory and identity space, whether by the state through legislation or by civil activity, including academic discourse. Here, one of my major focuses is the ideological use of conceptions of race, language, religion and folk tradition in the production of national homogeneity and the related interest in making symbolic links and breaks between both peoples and territories. The present analysis of these issues is an attempt to put into practice what I have above, in Chapter 6, outlined about the political study of cultural identities and their argumentative and hierarchical nature.[10]

## Common Genetic Heritage

Even though my explicit purpose here is not to discuss the cause and effect relationship between Finland's alleged homogeneity and present-day attitudes towards immigration and multiculturalization, it is necessary to point out how the recent drastic changes in the number of immigrants and other foreign-born inhabitants (although they are far less drastic in Finland than in most other European countries) may function as a point of reflection against which earlier elements of ethnic diversity disappear from sight. Finland (like the other Nordic countries) has been traditionally perceived as a country of emigration, not immigration. Yet, a number of factors speak for continuous migration into the country.

It is an oft-repeated story how the area of present-day Finland was gradually settled during the last 9, 000 years since the Ice Age. It is a much less often told story how the heterogeneous sources of the settled populations have over the millenniums and centuries produced a culturally, ethnically and even genetically coherent community – or given grounds for a dominant image of such coherence. For example, during the second millennium A. D. , after the Viking period and strong Scandinavian influence, the area of present-day Finland has been settled and populated by Roman Catholics, Protestants, Muslims, Jews, Greek Orthodox, the Rom (Romanies or Gypsies), the Sámi, Russian speakers, Finnish speakers, Swedish speakers, and others. During the Hanseatic period in the Middle Ages, immigrants included Germans, Swedes, Danes, Dutch and Scots. The present wave of migration from abroad started in the 1980s, increasing rapidly in the early 1990s. The sudden diversification of the population, in terms of cultural background and languages spoken, appears to have created an image of a rapid heterogenization after an allegedly original state of homogeneity.

The most recent wave of diversification has helped bring some of the country's earlier heterogeneity to the surface and provided new forms of publicity for discussing the country's old linguistic and religious minorities. At present, the 'national minorities' are Swedish speakers (or 'Finland's Swedes'), the Sámi, the Rom, the Jews, the Old Russians and the Tatars. The Rom came to Sweden in the early 16th century, and in the 17th century they were ordered to settle in the eastern part of the kingdom, present-day Finland. The so-called Old Russians are descendants of the Russian civil servants, military officers and merchants who settled in Finland during the country's autonomous period (1809–1917), as well as of the emigrants of the Russian Revolution in 1917. Those who have come after the collapse of the Soviet Union in the early 1990s are commonly called New Russians.

Jews were first allowed to settle in Sweden in 1782, but only in the three cities of Stockholm, Gothenburg and Norrköping, and a little later to Karls-krona. These were all located in the western part of the state, which meant that that eastern part of the kingdom, today's Finland, remained off limits to Jews (Harviainen 1999: 333). The Jews of Finland came first to so-called Old Finland, which was part of the Russian Empire at the end of the 18th century. During Finland's autonomous period, more Jews came as tradesmen and craftsmen or retired officers of the Imperial Army. They were granted full citizenship only after Finland became a sovereign state. Until 1930 the Jews in Finland registered Swedish as their first language. The first Tatars arrived during the early years of Finland's autonomous period, when they were used as labor force in the construction of fortresses both on the Åland islands and in Helsinki. Groups of merchant Tatars migrated from Russia between 1870s and 1920s.

There is thus plenty of historical evidence to argue that Finland has always been ethnically diverse instead of homogeneous, albeit that the diversity has been rather small in numbers. Yet, the idea of Finland being a homogeneous country instead of a heterogeneous one is not merely a defensive rhetorical image created to oppose present-day immigration. Its roots can be placed in the ideological and political foundations of Finnish nationalism and nation-making, but also further back in history, in the Protestant Reformation of the 16th and 17th centuries and the consequent consolidation of the Swedish state. In addition to these factors, particular theories produced within comparative linguistics in the 18th and 19th centuries and in genetics in the 19th and 20th centuries have supported ideas according to which the population of Fin-land – of which 'the Finns' is at the same time both a matter-of-fact and an ethnopolitically charged denomination – is a uniform linguistic-ethnic-racial group distinct from their neighboring 'Indo-Europeans'. This distinction making functions even today as one of the prominent ways – although not always the politically dominant way – of conceptualizing, historicizing and territorializing Finnishness and Finnish identity. In a recent study on popular attitudes in Finland by Pentti Kiljunen of Yhdyskuntatutkimus Oy, sponsored by the Centre for Finnish Business and Policy Studies (EVA), it was found that 75% of the 2,133 people who responded to the mailed questionnaire in 2002 agree (and 14% disagree) with the proposition that Finns should ef-fectively protect their distinctive culture against globalization. In the same survey, 74% regarded it as a privilege to be a Finn, while only 44% felt that being a Finn also means being a European (see Kiljunen 2003, Chapter 5.1.; figures 40a, 40b, 40c).

One of the main reasons for emphasizing ethnic and racial homogeneity in Finland has been the political call for national unity. This was expressed most clearly by one of the pioneers and most influential experts in modern sociology and social policy in Finland, Heikki Waris, who in his 1940s and 1950s textbook wrote that "when one compares Finnish society to, for ex-ample, countries in Central and Southern Europe, which have many kinds of racial mixtures and consequently, social problems that are difficult to solve, one must acknowledge the great strength provided by the racial uniformity of our people. The racial uniformity of this people is an indispensable support to the unity and solidity of the nation-state." (Waris 1952: 24, quoted in Pentikäinen & Hiltunen 1997: 19, my translation)

After the racialized conflicts between Swedish and Finnish speakers over linguistic hegemony in the 1920s and 1930s, the debate on race has gradually changed into an interest in genetics and the national significance of genetic heritage. It is not at all uncommon to find in printed presentations of Finland articles or essays on the population's genetic composition. *Facts about Finland*, a semi-official guidebook to Finland distributed by the Finnish Ministry for Foreign Affairs, is a good example of this (see Saukkonen 1999: 158–160). The Internet pages of the Foreign Ministry, called *Virtual Finland*, also contain a long article on the genetic composition of the Finns (http://virtual.finland.fi). The most recent edition of Eino Jutikkala and Kauko Pirinen's book on the history of Finland in English is supplemented with findings from 'objective' genetic research (Jutikkala with Pirinen 2003: 20–22), while the earlier editions' discussions on the Finns belonging to the East Baltic race and partially to the 'Nordic' race (Jutikkala with Pirinen 1962: 7; Jutikkala with Pirinen 1984: 13) have been dropped.

Geneticists have played an important role in the definition of Finnish national identity by, for example, emphasizing the distinct nature of the Finns vis-à-vis the 'Indo-Europeans'. Yet, genetics have also yielded the conception that there is no major difference between 'the Finnish genotype' and the general traits of other European peoples (e.g. Kajanoja 1993). The latter emphasis has emerged to counter the claim that Finns are not members of the 'Europeid' or 'White' race (see Kemiläinen 1998). Here the ideas of race and civilization are linked, as the 'Western genetic heritage' of the Finnish population is used as an argument for Finland's belonging in West-European Civilization. According to one theory, instead of being genetically 'Uralic', the Finns are Indo-Europeans who have adopted the Finno-Ugric language of a previously settled population (Sajantila 1997: 354; Horn n.d.).

The emphasis on the Westernness of the Finns is a recent phenomenon. As observed by Pasi Saukkonen (1999: 159), the 1991 edition of *Facts about Finland* linked language and genealogy to create a sense of the Finns' 'originality' and 'non-Europeanness'. In the first chapter of the 1996 edition, the section entitled 'The Origin of the Finns' (note the singular form of the word 'origin') begins with a statement that 65–75 % of Finnish genes are European and 25–35 % are Asian. Saukkonen concludes that the new formulation 'moves' the Finns westward in regard to their physical traits. Elsewhere Saukkonen has suggested that such a research finding makes Finland's membership in the European Union appear as a 'return to Europe' (Saukkonen 1996: 17).

While Finland's political move to 'Europe', joining in the European Union, is justified with an 'appropriate' genetic heritage, the homogeneity of 'the Finnish genes' is emphasized to the extent that the presence of more than 30 congenital diseases is said to make up a 'pathological heritage' (Savontaus n.d.). According to Marja-Liisa Savontaus, who has written about Finnish genetics in *Virtual Finland*, the reason for this problem is the small number of the original settlers and the isolation caused by such a low population density. In addition, "our geographical location, just as our culture, language and faith, have limited the number of immigrants" (Savontaus n.d.).

Although it is now often stressed that language relations and biological relations are separate issues and linguistic ties are not necessarily an indication of genetic kinship (e.g. Savontaus n.d.), the language of genetics operates with the linguistically constructed categories of the Finno-Ugric and the Indo-European. They are also conceptualized as genetic categories. The relationship between genes and language is, however, denied when discussing the Sámi, whose difference from the Finns is emphasized even though they also speak a Finno-Ugric language. 'The Sámi genotype' is found to differ from all other European peoples as well as other Finno-Ugric peoples. This difference is said to be based on the genetic 'Sámi motif' (Savontaus n.d.).

This can be taken as an example of the ideological primitivization of the Sámi, which is one of the discursive means of producing Finnishness and its Others. Another example of such cultural othering is the interpretation that the primitive 'Fenni' described by Tacitus in his book *Germania* from the year 98, refers to the Sámi, not the Finns. Regardless of whether this is a fact or not, it is noteworthy how the Finns are emphasized to have been at that time on a much higher level of cultural evolution. (See e.g. Uino n.d.; cf. Ruuska 1998; Tuulentie 2001: 84; cf. Mathisen 2000, 2004.) Cultural evolution is used as an argument for making ethnic distinctions.

## *Linguistic and Cultural Affinity*

The 19th-century nation building in Finland has sometimes been compared with simultaneous developments in Estonia and Latvia, which were also part of the Russian Empire and in which the dominant social class spoke a different language from that of the majority of the population. Despite the many factual similarities, however, Risto Alapuro (1997a, 1999) emphasizes the differences. These were, first, the existence of Finland as a separate political unit within the Empire; second, the growth of its economic wealth especially towards the end of the 19th century; and third, the class structure dominated by extensive peasant land ownership, which was a legacy of the Swedish social system.

One of the most characteristic viewpoints on 19th-century Finnish nation making has been the attribution of great significance to J. G. Herder's ideas of nationalism (see e.g. Wilson 1976). Among folklorists, this is commonly understood to mean a close 'romantic' link between folklore collecting and the use of collected materials for national symbolism and collective identification. This follows the Herderian notion according to which national cultures are manifested in the oral traditions of the lower classes, the folk, and such traditions convey the history of the nation and speak for its innate unity. As a political conclusion in scholarship, great value is placed on small cultures and ethnic minorities and their struggle for cultural or political independence (see e.g. Siikala 1998, 2000).

The nation in Herderian nationalism is seen as a 'natural', 'family-like', and an 'organic' unit of people, and homogeneous in ethnic and genetic terms. States are artificial unless they are founded upon an ethnically homogeneous nation, for which reason the ideal state is one in which all citizens are genetically related (Nisbet 1999: 79–82). As a consequence of this premise, much emphasis is put on shared ethnicity, common genealogy, common language, religion, history, customs and even race as the prerequisites for membership in a national community. In this respect, Herderian nationalism downplays both the value and visibility of cultural diversity.

In Finland, these perspectives are manifested, among other things, in the exclusive character of the category of the Finn and in the popular tendency to think of only Finnish-speakers as 'real' Finns. This discursive practice defines Finnishness 'culturally' and biologically, on the basis of genetic and social kinship, and makes the Finnish speakers the 'core nation' within the nation-state. Such a perception is discursively reproduced in continuous examinations, debates and public lectures on the Finnish language, cultural roots, 'Finnish genes' and the close interrelation seen between these. There is a clear difference when comparing Finland in this regard to many other countries. Pasi Saukkonen has contrasted Finnish discourses on nation-state identity with those in the Netherlands and concludes as follows:

> To be a 'real' Finn, one should speak Finnish, have 'Finnish' ancestors or genes and live according to 'Finnish' social rules. (...) In the Dutch case (...) [l]anguage and religion do not work as explicit criteria. (...) Ancestry and genes, very important issues in the Finnish discussion, are almost totally lacking in the Dutch debate. (Saukkonen, n.d.; see also Saukkonen 1999: 142, 158–160, 252.)

Yet, as emphasized by Risto Alapuro, employing concepts made famous in the research on nationalism by Anthony D. Smith (1991), Finland can be characterized as a mixture of ethnic-genealogical and civic-territorial conceptions of nationality. This can be seen, for example, in the way in which, in the making of the Finnish nation-state in the 19th century, the former functioned as a means to construct symbolically and ideologically the 'people', who in the latter came to be regarded as the democratic holders of power in the modernizing state and the emerging civil society. According to Alapuro, the Finnish nationalists perceived citizenship as an issue of "legal equality of rights and duties, especially rights to social and political participation" (Alapuro 1999: 116), but still, ethnic solidarity conditioned the principle of political participation. For this reason, "the idea of citizenship (*kansalaisuus*) became intimately related to that of nationality (*kansallisuus*)" (Alapuro 1999: 114). This intimate relationship can also be seen in the close lexical similarity of the two terms.

Because of 'ethnic solidarity', the conceptualization of Finnish nationality continues to contain discursive elements that enhance the preservation and perseverance of the category of the Finns as compact and homogeneous; in other words, as unaffected by diversifying elements and factors from that which is categorized as 'the outside'. It is my contention that this is one of the reasons why and how nation making has made and continues to make diversities almost invisible. The Finns (meaning the Finnish-speaking Finns) are regarded as being similar to each other while all others are considered essentially different (see also Saukkonen 1999: 239–241). At the same time, those people who have come from elsewhere tend to remain non-Finns even if they become Finnish citizens – some groups of people even after generations of original settlement. Because of the sharp distinctions often drawn between citizenship and ethnically and 'culturally' conceptualized nationality, the fact that the state grants citizenship – which for the 'real' Finns is a hereditary right based on *jus sanguinis*[11] – does not necessarily encompass the incomer in the 'cultural' category of the Finns. For this reason, despite the expectations that immigrants 'integrate', integration is in practical terms prevented or hindered by the very fact that the new member of the state is excluded from the symbolically central ways of conceptualizing nationality, Finnishness as a cultural category.

The construction of Finns as an ethnic-genetic-linguistic category, a national organism analogous to the family, in the Herderian sense, has thus had serious repercussions in terms of how ethnic diversity has been conceptualized in Finland. Rendering the ethnic-genetic-linguistic Finns synonymous with the national Finns has not only excluded incomers but made all other 'ethnic-genetic' and linguistic groups living in Finland, for example the Sámi and the Swedish speakers, appear as foreigners or non-nationals. At the same time, there is a politically motivated emphasis on close cultural connections with linguistically related populations in Karelia and elsewhere in Russia and a consequent argument for 'family ties'. This is the idea of the 'Finnish tribe' that is considered to be constituted by all people speaking Finnish and related languages.

The linking of the question of citizenship with ethnic-genealogically conceptualized nationality is clearly visible today, for example, in the case of Ingrians, a Finnish-speaking population on the southern and eastern shores of the Gulf of Finland in Northwest Russia. They are descendants of the people who moved there in the 17th century from what is presently Finland or what was part of Finland before the end of the Second World War. In April 1990, in the middle of the political turbulence in the Soviet Union and the rest of Eastern Europe, President Mauno Koivisto (in office 1982–1994) told reporters in a television interview that Ingrians who wished to move to Finland should be regarded as returnees or ethnic remigrants (see also Laari 1997; Forsander 1999: 59–61; Lepola 2000: 96–99). This meant in practice that that their moving should be financially assisted by the Finnish state and the necessary bureaucratic procedures should be eased. The Finnish immigration law was eventually modified to accommodate the President's personal wish. Accordingly, the immigrating Ingrians were legally categorized as returning migrants and as such, expatriate Finns. In other words, they came to be regarded as Finnish nationals who had been residing outside Finland and were now returning to their home country.

There were a number of reasons for general acceptance of the President's suggestion to view any Finnish-speaking Ingrian as a potential returning migrant (see also Lepola 2000: 98–99). One of these reasons was the anticipated need for a cheap labor force competent in the Finnish language. Another one had to do with the idea that the Finnish state had to somehow compensate for the deportation of those Ingrians who had resided in the country during World War II. Finland had a 'debt of honor' to repay. This was the motive given in 1999 by President Koivisto himself in an interview published by *Helsingin Sanomat*, the country's largest newspaper (*HS Kuukausiliite* February 6, 1999). The sense of kinship between Finns and Ingrians was also involved in this, especially since the legal status of returning migrants was not only granted to those families whose members had been deported, but was extended collectively to all the descendants of those people who had moved to Ingria in the 17$^{th}$ century, including those who had been forcefully transported from there to Siberia in the 1930s. The Finnish immigration law concerned thus the 'whole Ingrian people', who now were adopted by Finnish law as members of the Finnish nation, and were on these grounds eligible for immigration and applying for citizenship.

The Finnishness of the returning migrants was, however, soon questioned. They were acknowledged as 'kinfolk' and 'relatives' but regarded as having been 'contaminated' by Russianness. They were thus Finns and non-Finns at the same time. In addition to the lack of need for cheap labor, due especially to the economic recession that started in the early 1990s, criticism against Ingrian immigration increased in the mid- and late 1990s due to repeated reports in the public media that many incoming 'returnees' from Ingria and elsewhere in Russia, who may have qualified in terms of biological kinship ties, did not speak a word of Finnish (see also Hakamies 2004: 43; Pöysä 2004: 57–59). As noted in an early July 1999 editorial of *Helsingin Sanomat*, their identity has been found to be 'completely Russian'. The Finnish consul Rauno Pietiläinen in St. Petersburg made a comment to the same effect on Finnish television in September 1999 (see Heikkinen 2003: 160–161). Such comments revealed that the Finnish-speaking Ingrians – Russian or Soviet citizens – were not only assumed to be similar to the Finns of Finland but were expected to identify with the Finnish nation and national culture. Their ability to speak Finnish was taken as an indication and guarantee of this. Their inability was taken as an indication that they were not 'real' Ingrians or relatives of the Finns. As put by the English-language Internet pages of *Helsingin Sanomat* on February 12, 2002, they lacked "true ties to Finland" (Interior Minister 2002). As a result of public demands for putting limits to this migration, the Ministry of the Interior decided in summer 1999 that the immigration law would be altered to make competence in the Finnish language a requirement (see also Lepola 2000: 108).[12]

The presence of Russianness within the category of the Ingrian represents one of the basic dilemmas in the political linking of Finnish-speaking Finns in Finland with Finnish speakers across the national borders. According to a common conception, if the 'relatives' of the Finns are partially Russian, they are partially non-Finns. Such a categorical approach has many roots. It partially derives from the centuries-old rivalries between Sweden and Russia over the control and taxation of the people in Finnish-speaking territories and the strong anti-Russian sentiment in Sweden in the 18$^{th}$ century. In the early

19th century Finns were generally loyal towards Russia (see Klinge 1997), but there was also a strong interest in constructing a Finnishness clearly distinct from Russianness (as well as from Swedishness). At that point, one of the central political goals was to ward off any attempt at standardizing Finland's social and political institutions with the rest of the Russian Empire. Yet, according to most recent research, it was only towards the end of the 19th century and the beginning of the 20th century that the Finnish Russophobia became 'ethnicized', concerning all Russian persons and everything deemed Russian (see Tarkiainen 1986; Immonen 1987; Karemaa 1998). For most of the 20th century, the political opposition to Communism has conditioned the ethnic, cultural and linguistic otherness of Russianness.

The aboriginal Sámi (or Lapps) in Northern Finland provide a somewhat different case from the Ingrians. The Sámi have been recognized as being linguistically related to Finnish speakers, but both genetic and cultural relationship to the Finns has been denied. In the making of Finnish national culture, the symbolic role that has been designated to them has been that of the primitive Other (see e.g. Isaksson 1997; Lehtola 1997; Ruuska 1998; Tuulentie 2001: 93–99). There is a presumption that the words 'saame', 'suomi' (Finland) and 'häme' (Tavastland) are related (see Koivulehto 1993) and a conception that the Sámi and the Finns have at some point in history constituted common peoplehood, but neither one of these have brought the Sámi close to the 'ethnic-genetic' Finns in the history of Finnish nation making. Vis-à-vis the Sámi, the consolidation of the category of Finnishness has also required a clear geographical distinction. The denial of a constructive role for the Sámi in the building of the nation has continued the 16th and 17th century policy of the Swedish state to push the 'primitives' towards the margins, to more inhospitable types of land, in which they have only recently started to gain political rights (cf. Tuulentie 2001: 81–93).[13]

Pekka Isaksson locates the exclusion of the Sámi from the nation-state project towards the late 19th century (Isaksson 1997). According to him, the marginalization of the Sámi can be mainly attributed to the historian and journalist Zachris Topelius, who in his highly influential writings excluded the Sámi both from the concept of the people of Finland (in Swedish *Finlands folk*) and that of the Finnish people (*det finska folket*). The latter included only the Finnish speakers, while the former has comprised of both the Finnish and the Swedish speakers as well as the Russians, Germans, French, etc. who have settled in Finland. However, the Jews and the Gypsies as well as 'other strangers' living in the country, which, among others, meant the Sámi, were excluded from both categories (Isaksson 1997: 54; see also Saukkonen 1998b: 33–34; Saukkonen 1999: 202–206). Topelius's categorizations can be regarded as being indicative of the growth of democracy in the late 1800s and the consequent desire to specify the membership criteria in the *demos*, the people conceptualized as the democratic subjects of the state.

The basic reason for the Sámi's exclusion, according to Isaksson, has been their nomadism (Isaksson 1997: 60–62). For 19th-century Finnish ethnographers and historians, who followed common contemporary Western ideas about non-Western and 'primitive' peoples and cultures, only agriculturalists had history and political organization, both of which were regarded as signs of national subjectivity. As a nomadic people the Sámi were regarded as having failed to make any progress since the Stone Age, which also meant that they lacked history. In addition, they were viewed as belonging to a different race than the Finns (Isaksson 1997: 63). This distinction making continues, for example in Finnish genetics, despite the common agreement of the lack of any scientific basis for such racializing discourses.

The nomadism of the Sámi has undoubtedly contributed to their denial of a constructive role in the Finnish nation-state project, but the history of their exclusion extends further back than Finnish nation making. In Elias Lönnrot's original vision of the historical basis of the *Kalevala* epic, the Finns and the Sámi (the Lapps) are seen as warring enemies. This both represents and reproduces the centuries-old hierarchies in which the Sámi, some of whom used to inhabit southern and central parts of present-day Finland up to the 16th or 17th centuries, were from early on distinguished from the 'Finnish tribes', that is, the regional groups that came to constitute the Finnish people (*det finska folket*). According to Jouko Vahtola, nomadic hunting was not a factor in the categorization that has existed at least since the Bronze Age. Those that have been called the Lapps were different ethnically, that is, linguistically and racially (Vahtola 1999: 111–113; see also Sammallahti 1999). Still, Seija Tuulentie emphasizes that the othering of the Sámi does not mean that they would be regarded as enemies of the Finns. The Sámi identity, according to Tuulentie (2001: 99, 273), complements Finnish identity. As such, its most characteristic feature is its constitution in the framework of Finnish national identity and its position as 'our' minority.


## Karelians as Finns and Non-Finns

In the Finnish politics of culture and construction of national mythology, the treatment of the Sámi has been radically different from the central symbolic position granted to the Karelians – and to some extent, the Ingrians – across Finland's eastern border. The Karelians are seen as having given the Finns the folk poetry that forms the foundation of the Finnish national epic, the *Kalevala*. Yet, the national romantic conceptualization of the Karelians as the 'cradle' of what has been defined as 'Finnish culture' demonstrates that the Karelians have also been othered and primitivized into a people without history.

Unlike the Finns, who are considered modern, both the Sámi and the Karelians have been regarded as living in tradition and in nature. While the Sámi are a primitive Other on the margins of Finnish settlement in the north, the Karelians (especially Viena or Archangel Karelians in Russia) have been primitivized and exoticized by othering them to their assigned role of reflecting ancient Finnishness and serving as a present-day representation of it. Their traditional culture thus stands for the history of the Finns, thus depriving them of a history independent of Finnish nation making. In this role, the Karelians have simultaneously been regarded as Finnish and yet fundamentally distinct from the Finns by being characterized as Homeric figures, innocent and noble savages, and a perpetually indigent people in need of Finnish-based – but not Russian-based – enlightenment and modernity. According to Seppo Knuuttila, they are noble as the truly civilized, but still belong to the category of nature rather than that of civilization (Knuuttila 1994: 106–107; see also Tarkka 1989; Varpio 2002).

The distinction made between Finland and Karelia can be described in oppositional pairs. Finland is rich, but Karelia is poor. Finns live in culture and history, while Karelians live in nature and tradition. Finns are modern, while Karelians are traditional. While the Finns have a nation that has developed into a state, the Karelians, as put by Topelius, are "children who lag behind the Finns in national development" (quoted in Sihvo 1994: 28). Both the Sámi and the Karelians have been othered on the grounds of lacking the key elements in defining Finnishness: history, national development, modernity, and nation-state identity.

According to Kaija Heikkinen, the long line of portrayals of Karelia continues to reproduce an arrangement in which Karelians are seen as part of the category of Finns, in accordance with the ideological construction of Finnishness (Heikkinen 2003: 158; see also Heikkinen 1989: 37). Indeed, located on both sides of the present-day Finnish eastern border, Karelia is emphatically seen to constitute a segment of the Finnish national space – even though most of its territory or population has never belonged to the Finnish state, and a large area of Finnish-speaking Karelia that was once part of the Finnish state was ceded to the Soviet Union in the Second World War. Simultaneously, Karelia has been seen to contain elements that are deemed alien to it.

The perception of Karelia as Finnish has a number of interrelated historical roots. Ever since the time of Mikael Agricola, the main reformer in Sweden's Finnish-speaking areas in the 16th century, the literati have paid attention to Karelian folk poetry and regarded it as representative of the oldest layers of Finnish-language folk poetry. This interest eventually led to the compilation of the *Kalevala* epic by Elias Lönnrot in the 1830s. As a Finnish national symbol, the epic established Karelia – especially Viena or Archangel Karelia, the main geographical source of the epic materials – as the 'origin' or 'cradle' of Finnish culture. To be sure, this corresponds well with the established historical links between Finnish settlement and Viena Karelian culture, especially in folk poetry (Siikala 2002a: 38–42; see also Pöllä 1995). The historical facts are not, however, geopolitically neutral. As phrased by Hannes Sihvo, Lönnrot's work joined the *Kalevala* and Karelia together "seamlessly" (Sihvo 1969: 29), which meant that Karelia was in increasing ways seen as part of Finland. The cultural linking of Karelia to Finland gained momentum thanks to National Romanticism and Karelianism of the late 19th century, when nationalistically oriented artists, scholars and intellectuals, members of the Finnish upper class and educated elite, traveled there from Helsinki to look for the "origins of Finnishness", "original Kalevala life", and "former Finnish 'Golden Age'" (Sihvo 1969; Sihvo 1999: 183–185). They sought to use what they saw as material in the creation and consolidation of Finnish national arts in a period that came to be called its 'Golden Era'. In this process, "neo-romanticist paintings (Akseli Gallen-Kallela), realist photography (I. K. Inha), bombastic musical compositions (Jean Sibelius) and political writings about Greater Finland (Ilmari Kianto) together created a picture of Finland originating from the Karelian backwoods" (Lehtinen 1994: 149).

Another foundation for Karelia's belonging to Finland lies in 18th-century comparative linguistics, which established the idea of the Finno-Ugric family of languages. This aroused ethnographic interest in documenting and studying the language, folk poetry, customs, religion, rituals and mythology of the populations speaking these languages. This scholarship can be – and certainly is – lauded for indispensable collections of historical information and premodern mythology. Still, the collected materials have not merely been objects of historical study. In addition, scholars have been seeking in these materials "the fundamental character of Finnish culture" (Siikala 1994: 9). They have been keen on establishing cultural links of identity-political significance between the ethnographic past and the scholarly present. Especially with regard to the idea of the Finno-Ugric family of languages and nations, ethnography – including folklore scholarship – has not only described similarities or differences between populations, their cultures, religious ideas and beliefs, worldviews and histories, but established lineages that have become some of the key elements of identity in the construction of Finnishness and the identity space of Finnish nationalism and national culture.

The linguistic connection and its politicized meanings have had serious repercussions even in the foreign policy of the Finnish state, since the interest in the ethnography of the 'kin peoples' was from early on linked to the idea of defining Finland's geographical extensions. Because the Finnish-speaking Karelians were given a central symbolic position in the making of Finnish-language national culture, they were emphatically viewed as Finns – despite the fact that the people in Russian Karelia identified themselves as Russians and regarded the visiting Finnish literati, as well as the other people living in Finland, as Swedes, in accordance with the centuries-old political borders between Sweden and Russia (see e.g. Sihvo 1969: 24–25; Pöllä 1991: 169; Björn 1993: 166). The fact that the Finnish literati identified the Finnish-speaking Karelians as Finns – and their culture as that of the 'ancient Finns' – made Karelia an irredenta, a territory that had been 'unnaturally' separated from its Finnish-language context and which, therefore, should be 'reunited' with Finland (Sihvo 1969: 38; cf. Sedergren 1996; Jukarainen 2004: 30–36).

For a number of scholars and activists in the mid-19th century, Lönnrot's work in collecting folk poetry became an argument for questioning the existing political border between the Grand Duchy of Finland and the rest of the Russian Empire. The political meaning given to linguistic and cultural affinity came to be expressed in aspirations for joining all of Karelia to Finland and, eventually, for creating a joint political unit that would join the Finnish-speaking and Finnish-related people and areas into one nation – under the same government, that of the Finnish state. The idea of a Greater

Finland became highly influential in the nationalistic politics of the late 1910s through the early 1940s (see e.g. Alapuro 1973: 91–101; Manninen 1980; Ahti 1999: 127f.; Sihvo 1999: 195–196; Bazegski & Laine 2000: 42–45; Pimiä 2003: 74).[14] The idea was first presented in 1844 by two student activists who, together with the young journalist Zachris Topelius, were influenced by the thoughts of J. G. Herder and argued that the Finnish people can only be united when Finland is 'complete', containing also Eastern Karelia in Russia. The geographical extensions of Finnishness were laid out in greater detail by, among others, August Ahlqvist, Professor of Finnish language, who, under the pen name A. Oksanen, published in 1860 a poem entitled *Suomen valta* (The Realm of Finland). According to this text, which was highly influential in the Finnish nationalist movement up to the Second World War, the territory that belongs to the Finns of Finland on the grounds of linguistic and cultural affinity extends from the Gulf of Finland to Lake Onega in Aunus (Olonets) Karelia, and from the Gulf of Bothnia to the White Sea beyond Viena Karelia.

Such extensions for Finland and Finnishness have remained an unfulfilled dream, except for a short period during the Finnish-Soviet conflict in World War II, when Finland occupied parts of Eastern Karelia across the Soviet border with the intention of annexing them to Finland (see Manninen 1980). At that time, scholars were sent out to collect information about local Finnish-related folk culture, in order to preserve it in museums and archives as well as to create national consciousness among the un-exiled local population (see Laine 1993). Yet, the collecting of traditional verbal art, or folklore, was not the only means in the pursuit to legitimate the inclusion of this territory in the Finnish state. More weight was placed on geography and botany to provide 'natural' grounds for the argument for 'natural' borders (Laine 1993). This was in direct line with the argument presented by Topelius, according to whom Finland must have 'natural' borders, founded upon elements of geography, geology and flora and fauna (see Tiitta 1994). A. V. Ervasti, among others, spoke for the same notion in his travelogues from Karelia (Ervasti 1884: 212; see also Nygård 1978: 21–22; Varpio 1997: 95; Valenius 1998: 34; Ahti 1999: 128).

In the final turmoils of the Second World War, Finland lost a great part of Karelia to the Soviet Union, which led to one of the largest evacuation campaigns in European history, as well as to an immeasurable amount of national nostalgia on the Finnish side of the new border. Many Finnish geopolitical discourses of the post-war years, as argued by Anssi Paasi, "are drawn together by one theme, the question of the location of the Finnish-Russian border (Paasi 2000: 91; see also Alasuutari & Ruuska 1999: 120–123). After the collapse of the Soviet Union, the question of the Finns' rights to reclaim the lost Karelian territories became a heated topic. Yet, as noted by Pertti Joenniemi, "the state actors have been reluctant to engage themselves in talks on restitution of those parts of Karelia ceded to the Soviet Union in the Paris Treaty of 1947", while the issue "remains mainly of interest to Finnish civil society" (Joenniemi 1998: 183). The closely related question of Karelia's Finnishness is a prime example of the complexities in the politics of identity

– in the competition between neighboring states over territories and over the territorial identifications and political loyalties of their populations. Karelia's Finnishness is in Finland founded upon the discursive practice of asserting national authority over areas that are regarded as having traditionally been within the Finnish-speaking cultural sphere. Such assertions have strongly denied the validity of all other definitions of these areas' cultural and political history, as well as competing definitions of heritage.

While there has been a strong interest in asserting national authority over Karelia, the role and position given to it in the making of Finnish national culture has at the same time been that of a symbolic center and a cultural Other. Since Karelia is seen to represent the oldest layers of Finnish culture and folk poetry, the national value attached to it is highly past-oriented – which has by no means decreased in the post-World War II longing for the lost territories. As phrased by Lotte Tarkka (1989), Karelia's landscape is that of Finnish national nostalgia. The past-oriented image of Karelia is an image appropriated in early 19th-century Finland for the writing of Finnish national (non-Swedish, non-Russian) history, and it is continued and further consolidated in present-day ethnographically oriented tourism that provides for opportunities for Finns and tourists in Finland to visit those places in Russian Karelia that have been symbolically central in the history of Finnish nation-making (Lehtinen 1994: 155; Anttonen & Kuusi 1999: 297–305; Virtanen 1999; Stark 2002). The main motif in this tourism is visiting the 'folklore-villages' or 'Rune Villages' in which Elias Lönnrot collected folk poetry in the 1800s (see e.g. Nieminen 1995). Following Lönnrot's footsteps is the basic metaphor for the touristic experience, which combines historical comparisons with cheap shopping, hiking and ethnographic recording. Another related motif is the presence of Finnish and German military forces in the same area in the early 1940s. There is a growing interest in visiting such war sites, inaccessible to foreigners until the early 1990s, as well as the memorials that have been erected there recently (cf. Raivo 2000: 144–147).

Such heritage tourism may boost the economy in the impoverished regions of Viena or Archangel Karelia, but as described and discussed by Laura Stark, it may also have negative repercussions when it privileges and favors only one ethnic group in the trans-ethnic infrastructures of the local communities (see Stark 2002). The inclusion of Karelians in the category of the Finns and the objectification of their culture as 'our past' represents a local variation in the global discourse on 'cultural roots', in which the focus is placed on "recording and gathering the heritage of related peoples in the process of extinction" (Salminen 2003: 276). Historically, ever since the mid-1800s, this discourse has been framed in a geopolitically charged competition between Finnish civilization and Russian/Slavic civilization over the definition of the area as well as its economic utilization. The competition has been about Karelia's history and prehistory (see Sihvo 1999: 190–194), the question of who gets to civilize and modernize its 'natural state' (Tarkka 1989: 246) and the changing meanings of the Finnish-Russian border (see Paasi 1994, 2000; Alanen & Eskelinen 2000; Bazegski & Laine 2000; Brednikova 2000). From this perspective, one may hope that the strong identity-political and even stronger economic interests expressed within the Finnish civil society do not conflict with the local production of identity, based on a rather different approach to Karelian history, modernity and the question of cultural diversity in the area's cultural, linguistic, religious and ethnic heritage.[15] Instead of a disputed boundary and a hinterland, Pertti Joenniemi sees the European integration bringing an opportunity for Karelia: a transformation into a transborder frontier that is "part of a continuous economic, social and cultural landscape" (Joenniemi 1998: 198).

## Innate Unity in Prehistory

Yet another kind of cultural othering has been projected onto the Swedish speakers, who have conventionally been seen as – and criticized for – belonging to a higher social class than 'the ordinary Finns', to use an expression that has become common in recent years for denoting Finnish speakers. The marked distinction has continued to be drawn regardless of the various attempts to consolidate the cultural and political link between the Swedish-speaking and the Finnish-speaking populations. In many everyday contexts, Swedish speakers are distinguished from Finnish speakers by calling the former Finland's Swedes and the latter simply Finns. 'Finn' and 'Finnish' tend to denote only Finnish speakers, thus making all others non-Finns.

The position of the Swedish language and its speakers continues to be one of the core issues in the making of the Finnish nation and in conceptualizing Finnishness and Finnish culture. Swedish was the official language of the autonomous state in the 19th century, but gradually Finnish gained ground and surpassed it in national significance.[16] Since Swedish was the language of state in the Finnish-speaking areas for centuries, many Finnish speakers adopted Swedish as their first language. This may be suggested as one of the reasons why Swedish speakers in Finland cannot in any 'objective' terms be regarded as constituting an ethnic group of their own. Yet, the relationship of the Swedish speakers to the Finnish speakers has been dealt with in ways that have ethnicized the differences. When Finnish speakers are regarded as an ethnicity, the Swedish speakers become their ethnic Other – that which needs to be distinguished from the category of the 'Finn' and which therefore becomes a constitutive element in the construction of this category. On the other hand, the collective identification of the Swedish speakers – as well as their collective efforts in gaining and/or preserving their political and linguistic rights – has adopted elements from the discourse of ethnicity and its representational practices. The Swedish speakers have become an ethnic group in their ethnopolitical and language political self-definition.

Yet, the ethnicization of the Swedish speakers has also been intentionally prevented with language policy. As pointed out by Alapuro (1997a: 24), the maintaining of Swedish as a national language after Finland became independent prevented the Swedish-speaking agriculturists, fishermen and working class from discrimination. They were thus spared from having to organize ethnic movements, unlike many other linguistic minorities elsewhere in the world. Similarly, according to John Westerholm, the making of Swedish into a national language was a means to prevent irredentism and oppose the call for making the Swedish-speaking areas in Finland autonomous cantons in the Swiss manner. By granting equal linguistic rights, the dominant population 'bought' the loyalty of its minority (Westerholm 1999: 282).

One of the basic questions regarding the relationship between Finnish and Swedish speakers has been, and continues to be, how a national community can have two national languages. The intimate link established between the national units, its territory and its language, is one of the key points in Herderian nationalism, and its main political function is not only to indicate cultural homogeneity in the national community but also to convey its political unity. Accordingly, the national movement in Finland has since the 19th century strongly rallied for the ideology of 'one nation, one language', as well as for 'one nation, one mind'. This has created a conception, held even today among many Finnish speakers, that Finland's official bilingualism is somehow 'unnatural', since only a small minority, less than 6 % of the population, speaks the other of the two languages as their first language. It is by no means uncommon to hear Finnish speakers complain how the large majority is obliged to study in school the language of a small minority. Official bilingualism is even seen as signaling the continuation of 'Swedish colonization'.

The position of the Swedish speakers in Finland, and their role in the production of the category of the national, must be seen in the historical framework established in the process of the state and nation building of the early and mid-1800s. In the new political situation, the making of the Finnish nation meant, first and foremost, the construction of an idea of Finnishness that would be recognized as fundamentally different from both Russianness and Swedishness. This political goal was epitomized in the famous slogan "Swedes we are not, Russians we do not wish to become, let us therefore be Finns", which has been commonly, either correctly or incorrectly, attributed to the political emigrant Adolf Ivar Arwidsson (1791–1858). For some 19th-century nationalists (Fennomans) and their descendants, this eventually came to also include the Swedishness (or alleged Swedishness) of the country's Swedish-speaking population. The slogan also laid down the foundation for the discursive practice of defining Finnishness through negation: on the basis of what it is not and what it is separated from, giving Finland a border identity between Sweden and Russia. The political logic of this boundary making was to institutionalize a language of symbolism that would unite the population under a single national identity. In practice it also meant the marginalization of some of the culturally and linguistically heterogeneous elements of this population.

Ideologically, the construction of Finnishness meant the establishment of a national culture that would be recognized as being founded only on 'Finnish' elements. At the same time, as put by the political scientist Teija Tiilikainen, "the focal political principles of the Swedish era were handed down in the structures of the administration and legislation that Finland was entitled to maintain" (Tiilikainen 1998: 120). Yet, the symbolic significance of these political institutions was downplayed, while the symbolic significance of 'Finnish' history and Finnish-language folklore was emphasized (Engman 1999: 169). In addition to being indicative of the selective and politically motivated nature of national symbolism, this contributed to the development of the notion that nationally significant Finnish culture is only constituted by the history and culture of the Finnish speakers. For such a conception the nationalist activists also sought acknowledgment from abroad, for example, with help of the *Kalevala* epic, which was raised to the status of a national symbol immediately upon its publication (in 1835) and adopted as "a *magna carta* to nationhood" (Engman 1999: 168).

Although the Finnish state was established before the emergence of the national movement called Fennomania, patriotic and 'Fennophilic' ideas had been presented before this. These were aired, for example, in written accounts on economic-historical issues in towns and parishes, and in 18th-century works by such historians as Daniel Juslenius (1676–1752) and Henrik Gabriel Porthan (1739–1804). To some extent they carried on the order given to the clergy by the Council on Antiquities, founded in 1666 upon the decree issued by the Swedish king Gustav II Adolf, to obtain information about 'ancient relics', which meant, among other things, historical narratives, old beliefs, folk poetry, songs, and archeological treasures (see Chapter 5). The explicit goal of the antiquarian campaign – modeled after similar actions taken elsewhere in Europe – was to use local history to glorify the Swedish state, but it was at the same time a direct response to a similar call made earlier by King Kristian IV of Denmark. As such, it was part of the conflict of power between the two Nordic kingdoms. The 'colonization' of history was simultaneous with the European colonization of lands across seas.

The early interest in Finnish issues became of great significance in the 19th century, as one of the key elements of Fennoman nationalism was the projection of its own history far back in the prehistory of the state. The Herderian link between language, history and the nation was not the only politico-philosophical foundation in this. The German philosopher G. W. Hegel's ideas of the national spirit, the spirit of the people (*Volksgeist*) that has developed in the course of history (see Karkama 1999: 148), and the conception of an exemplary heroic age in the ancient past were also instrumental. Accordingly, various historical and quasi-historical ideas of the (Finnish-speaking) Finns' Golden Age as a once powerful and wealthy people – a lost kingdom – were produced. The imaginary national history depicted in the *Kalevala* epic served the same purpose of providing a myth of origin that would present Finland as a primordial and an innate national unit, founded upon a common language – Finnish. The rhetorical device of projecting the foundation of the Finnish nation into prehistory made it appear as if the nation had existed first, before the emergence of the state, and had existed since time immemorial. The state came to be seen as having formed as a result of a natural – albeit an arduous – national development. Especially for J. V. Snellman, the leading figure in the Fennoman movement in the 1840s and 1850s, this was a struggle for regaining political power to an innate entity that was a chosen people, a nation by the grace of God (see Kemiläinen 1980: 4), but whose nationness had been suppressed for centuries by forced Christianization and Western civilization (see Snellman 1928: 12; see also Skyttä & Skyttä 1981: 128).

The projection of nationalism into prehistory (especially into the prehistory of the state) was based on the idea and belief that the Finnish nation is not so much constituted by a political organization, common jurisdiction and centrally governed economic structure as it is by a common language, culture and history – in other words, by common genealogy. The perceived unity of language and culture purportedly contained the historical project of the nation-state, in which, in Hegelian terms, the agent-subject was the historically developed national spirit within the individuals (see Karkama 1999). In the decades to come, both in the late 19th century and early 20th century, the 'cultural' argument would be used much more vigorously than the idea of a political contract between different social classes and interest groups to produce a sense of national unity. Such a 'cultural' projection has also played an important role in the conceptualization of Finland and Finnish culture (more precisely, the culture of the Finnish speakers) as homogeneous, as it has emphasized the intimate link between language, territory, bloodlines, national consciousness and worldview.

It was the search for national political unity that turned the nationalist intellectuals of the 19th century to prehistory, away from actual, documented history, which was regarded as not national and therefore not symbolically useful. This history was 'plagued' by foreign domination (Sweden) and a foreign religion (Catholicism). The denial of both the 'foreign' history and the hegemony of contemporary Swedish-language culture politically motivated the nationalists to make a symbolic turn to the uneducated Finnish-speaking population, who came to be viewed as the 'people' as both *ethnos* and *demos*. As argued by the Fennoman leader Yrjö Koskinen (later Yrjö Sakari Yrjö-Koskinen, originally Georg Zacharias Forsman, 1830–1903), the Finnish 'people' had a history that could be adopted as national history; accordingly, his textbook on Finnish history from 1869, *Oppikirja Suomen kansan historiassa*, presents the ethnically defined Finnish people as a historical subject (Majander 2000: 501). Koskinen's radical program stressed the idea that a nationally significant Finnish culture is constituted by the culture and history of the Finnish speakers only. All others are Others.

The symbolic turn was exemplified in the historians' quest for 'Finnish' themes and motifs in Finland's 'foreign' history. Koskinen called for writing a new national history that would seek evidence of 'Finnish national aspirations' and 'Finnish heroism'. As noted by Mikko Majander, with reference to the tropic analysis of historical narratives by Hayden White (e.g. 1987), such themes and motifs would serve the function of synecdoche; they would witness of the innate capacity of the Finns to provide competent men for important tasks in society (Majander 2000: 508–509). One of the early examples of the new trend was the interest in the peasant uprising called the Club War (1596–1597). Koskinen's doctoral dissertation from 1858 (republished in 1877) – the second dissertation written in the Finnish language – offered an interpretation in which the Finnishness of the rebelling peasants and their struggle to maintain their freedom and Protestant religion were some of the central points. The spirit of national independence that Koskinen saw in the actions of the rebelling peasants is indicative of his Hegelian frame of reference (see e.g. Koskinen 1877: 590–591).

I will discuss in a forthcoming book (see also Anttonen 2004b) how a similar process of historicization and heroization was applied to the narrative of the 'birth' of Finland, depicting the killing of Bishop Henrik, the allegedly first Christian bishop, in connection with the allegedly first crusade to Finland from Sweden in 1156. Over the centuries, both in Catholic times and during the Enlightenment, this incident (or rather, the clerical legends and popular narratives concerning it) had been viewed as an example of the stubbornness and hardheadedness of the Finns to accepting Christianity – and by extension, other tokens of Westernness and modernity. In the course of the new nationalistic history writing, the bishop's murder gradually came to symbolize the desire of the 'free Finnish peasant' to liberate Finland from the 'foreign' religion of Catholicism.

Indeed, it is no coincidence that the Swedish historian Erik Gustaf Geijer (1783–1847) presented similar ideas concerning the meaning of the Catholic era in Sweden. Geijer had argued that the medieval Catholic Church had destroyed the previous social organization that had rested on democracy and equality. Reformation, therefore, meant the restoration of the democratic institutions of the peasant society (Stråth 1994: 57). The Protestant denial of Catholicism's political and cultural heritage was, thus, part of the common transnational grammar of nation making in the Nordic countries. In this respect, the making of Finnishness in Finland did not differ from the making of Swedishness in Sweden.

## Symbolic Lack of Class Hierarchies, and the Elite as Others

For the Fennoman nationalists, the making of the Finnish nation meant the political integration of Swedish speakers and Finnish speakers, as well as that of the different social classes within the territorial unit. This entailed, among other things, the adoption of Finnish as a state language and the symbolic use of the 'people's culture' or 'folk tradition' in the construction of the national heritage. This would not, however, mean that civilization in Finland should be based on the cultural achievements of the Finnish-speaking folk. The national significance ascribed to selected representations of folk culture did not mean that the elite would reject their education-based culture for the culture of the uneducated. Echoing the views of J.V. Snellman, Gabriel Rein emphasized in his Presidential Address to the Finnish Literature Society in March 1842 that he identified himself first as a member of the intelligentsia and second as a Finn. The educated elite remained distinct from the 'people' but identified with it in the project for a national language and culture, in the name of consolidating the national entity.

This positioning eventually produced a double-sided discourse of both creating and dismantling class differences, which to a great extent characterizes Finnish society even today. The double-sided discourse can be regarded as a mixture of elitism and populism – or it can be seen as an indication of the elite's ambivalence, as Alapuro has suggested (1998). Snellman and Rein's position eventually came to be regarded as elitism, because, as put by Alapuro, in accordance with the populism of Fennoman nationalism, "the educated class had to be culturally one with the people" (Alapuro 1999: 114). Accordingly, the Fennomans started to include themselves in the same category of 'Finnishness' that they had constructed for the 'people', and by doing so, they placed both the 'people' and themselves in opposition to the 'foreign' upper class that spoke a 'foreign' language (Alapuro 1998: 181). Language and class thus became major factors for distinguishing between not only 'Finnishness' from 'Swedishness' in Finland but also between the people (as both *ethnos* and *demos*) and those excluded from it.

Satu Apo considers it quite a miracle how the performers of folk poetry, "quadrupled Others" across the dividing lines of language, culture, social class and race, could have provided illusions of a united Finnish people and culture (Apo 1998: 94; cf. Valenius 2004: 189). One can try to explain this 'miracle' by pointing to some of the key ideological elements in the production of folkloric national culture and symbolism in Finland. These elements include the use of folk tradition in the construction of national ancestry and the discursive practice of drawing politically desirable links to the ancient speakers of Finnish and Finnish-related languages. What is most characteristic in these elements, as far as social dynamics is concerned, is that they bypass the question of social stratification. The trend of drawing ancestral links from the Finnish speaking agrarian 'folk' of the earlier centuries to the present-day 'ordinary Finns' is a discursive act in the art of creating solidarity that is supposed to transgress markers of social class within a given language group. The same applies to the similarly common tendency to speak of only the Finnish speakers of earlier centuries and millennia – or the ancient speakers of Finno-Ugric languages – as the forefathers of present-day Finns.

As put by Gaela Keryell, there was a rhetorical turn in which the Others of the 19th century became the Ancestors of the 20th (Keryell 1999: 264; see also Maure 1996: 68–69). Because of the wish to be "culturally one with the people", as noted by Alapuro, the Fennoman elite started to perceive the peasants as 'us'. In the discourse on the national in the imagined national community, 'their' oral culture and folklore became 'our' traditions and heritage. The elite, in other words, created a symbolic image of themselves as if originating from the (Finnish-speaking) people and claimed both participation and ownership in the people's culture that they had raised to a central position in national symbolism (see also Sulkunen 2004: 26–27).[17]

One can also examine these processes with regard to language myths. According to the taxonomy suggested by Vivien Law, language myths can be grouped into language-intrinsic myths and language-extrinsic myths. The former include beliefs about a language's purity, elegance, euphoniousness, expressiveness, and its lexical resources, such as the size of its vocabulary (Law 1998: 175, 188). The latter include beliefs about a language's origins, antiquity, genetic affiliations, destiny, and its match to its speakers or to Nature (Law 1998: 175). The language-extrinsic myths are intertwined with ethnic myths, myths of origin, of descent, of homeland, etc., and thus equate the category of the ethnos with that of a particular language. According to Law, language-intrinsic myths connect with inclusive nationalism, while language-extrinsic myths are both favored and deployed in exclusive nationalism (Law 1998: 195–196).

Fennoman nationalism did not merely contribute to the changing of the state language of Finland from Swedish to Finnish. Because of close links to particular ethnopolitically charged theories of linguistic relations, the gradual change of state language was accompanied by a change in the ideological position of language in the nation-state. In the mid-1800s, the Finnish language was, despite the claims for language-intrinsic myths, still regarded by most educated people as unfit for education, civilization and modern artistic expression. The use of selected representations of folk tradition, such as the *Kalevala* epic, to argue for the suitability of Finnish for these purposes both modernized and antiquated the Finnish language – or more precisely, modernized it by antiquating it. While it was lexically developed to meet the requirements of a state language as well as communication in modern industry, trade and education, it was at the same time embedded with language-extrinsic myths about its origins and antiquity, as well as the origins and antiquity of its speakers. 'Ancient Finns' – the authors of the antiquated genres of oral poetry (cf. Stewart 1991: 7) – became the predominant image of ancestry, history and authenticity, signaling the history of the kind of Finnishness that was to constitute a crucial part of the symbolic capital in the construction of the country's modernity.

The both modernized and antiquated Finnish language became one of the most central ideological 'glues' within the nation-state, and the myths about it became some of the central elements in the ideological construction of Finnishness and the making of the Finnish speakers the 'core nation' in the nation-state. In addition to its new position as a state language, the Finnish language received its modern legitimization from its alleged antiqueness and its ethnic-genetic affiliations.

In other words, in addition to the Herderian idea of the 'folk' being romantically regarded as a site of cultural authenticity, the social and political significance given to the representations of the 'folk' was based on their assumed role in the making of 'Finnish' national heritage, the constitution of which had now, instead of the Swedish speakers, become the privilege of the Finnish speakers. On the one hand, as described by Apo (1998), the "four-times-othered performers of folk poetry" of the 19th century, especially in Karelia, represented to the elite the margins of society, the Other in terms of class and culture. Yet, they came to be valorized as the keepers of the heritage of the ancient Finns, the Ancestors (Keryell 1999: 264). Their local traditions were now seen as the survivals of an age-old national patrimony. The connection across the centuries and millennia was the antiquated Finnish language, which in addition to antiquity pointed to modernity, as the antiquated representations of Finnish-language culture could be used to argue for the Finnish-speakers' modern capabilities.

One of the political consequences and manifestations of these heritage discourses is the present-day tendency among Finnish-speakers to negate any privileged statuses within the language group. Instead of social stratification, there is a common emphasis on political consensus, cultural homogeneity, lack of class differences, and lack of cultural hierarchies in taste (e.g. Mäkelä 1985; Karkama & Koivisto 1997). In addition to the belief in 'democratic' access to upward social mobility, high value is placed on social equality and the wish to avoid – or fear to express – elitism, as this is regarded as causing social tension. Especially since the 1960s, when many of the presently influential homogenizing processes were launched by the Social Democratic welfare state, the idea of social equality has become one of the most loaded political concepts.[18] For the same reason no (Finnish-speaking) intellectual in Finland dares to count him or herself in the class of intelligentsia, because that would be regarded as indicating snobbism, social distinction, and lack of solidarity within the language group (see e.g. Alasuutari 1998: 154). According to Pertti Karkama and Hanne Koivisto (1997: 10), there is a reserved or a negative attitude to intellectuals in the society. Indeed, researchers may turn intellectuals and intellectualism into objects of study, but few Finnish-speaking intellectuals feel at ease with the notion of designating themselves as intellectuals. Intellectual discourse on Finnishness is criticized – by intellectuals themselves – for exemplifying an elitist interest in drawing a distinction between themselves and the 'ordinary people'. Indeed, according to Pertti Alasuutari (1998: 165), attributions given to the 'ordinary people' – unlike in other countries such as Britain, Germany and France – constitute in Finland the core contents of the stereotypical category of the national.

These are some of the reasons why the Finnish-speaking elite are not regarded as a 'real' elite, and the members of such an elite tend to negate their own privileged position. Since the Swedish-speaking elite are regarded as a 'real' elite, such categorizations speak for the continuation of a language-based dichotomy – and myth – according to which members of the elite in Finland are foreign and foreign-based and speak foreign languages. Ethnic solidarity among Finnish speakers is expected to both describe and prescribe the assumed lack of class differences within the language group, but at the same time it describes and prescribes lack of class solidarity across the language boundary. Class differences are strongly emphasized when language is a factor, but de-emphasized within a language group.

This dichotomy has its historical basis in the 19th-century nation-building process. Yrjö Blomstedt characterizes the historical situation of the 1850s as being drawn by two opposite and dialectic social forces: Finnishness as a 'democratic force' and Swedishness as an 'aristocratic force' (Blomstedt 1980: 300). Since this opposition encapsulates a wider framework, one can infer that the Swedish-speaking elite came to appear 'more elite' than any Finnish-speaking one because the Swedish speakers' elite positions, due to the linkage with the 'aristocratic force', came to be regarded as being hereditary, while the elite positions of the Finnish-speakers could be regarded as resulting from upward social mobility, permitted by increasing democracy. Even in an elite position, a Finnish speaker would embody the democratic idea of the people, the amalgamation of *ethnos* and *demos*.

This bias is reflected in the emerging national politics of heritage and the selection of folkloric representations as heritage symbols. Heritage, as discussed by Regina Bendix, is associated with the preservation and celebration of ethnicity, locality, and history (Bendix 2000: 38) and with the idea of the absence of power – as is the Fennoman idea of Finnishness and its representations. Heredity, however, is embedded with power – as are the Swedish speakers that are distinguished from the idea of Finnishness. As put by Bendix, heritage appears more democratic than heredity, doing away with "the particulars of history and heredity, who governed and who was governed" (Bendix 2000: 42). When Finnish speakers, as distinct from the Swedish speakers, are associated with heritage and not heredity, they appear without hierarchies. The assumed lack of social hierarchies within the language group is then supposed to speak for national unity and homogeneity – as well as to consolidate the ethnopolitical idea that the 'democratic' and 'non-hierarchical' Finnish speakers constitute the core nation within the bilingual nation-state.

However, the idea of heredity is also adopted for the Finnish speakers, but again in a 'democratic' sense in contrast to the Swedish speakers and foreign nobility. This is the process that Regina Bendix refers to by calling attention to the ways in which the idea of heredity has been transferred from genetic to cultural 'bodies' in national projects. The heredity of blood lines and the conceptualization of the Finnish speakers as a genetic category foreground the sense of sameness and the consequently assumed ethnic solidarity, which is also expected to encourage political consensus within the civic-territorially conceptualized nation-state. While meeting these ends, it simultaneously creates hierarchies and a sense of power vis-à-vis those that are actively denied a part in it.

## A Nation Divided?

It has been my purpose in this chapter to discuss thematically how homogeneity has been historically produced through discourse, with both language and action, in Finland. Some of these homogenizing processes have been so successful that their end results have been taken for granted as national characteristics. Yet, some others are likely to reveal that the political unity that has been aimed at has not been achieved. The Fennoman nationalist call for 'one nation, one mind' may have been symbolically significant for creating political unity – based on both assumed and imposed cultural sameness – but it appears to have created only a rhetorical image of such unity.

There have been a number of national projects of homogenization that have at the same time been national projects of unification. The project established by the Fennoman intelligentsia in the mid-1800s aimed at unifying the bulk of the population through the identification of the Swedish-speaking elite in the same nation with the Finnish-speaking majority. This project included the comprehensive education of this majority and the creation of a national culture in its language. The project of unifying the people after the Civil War of 1918 aimed at bridging the marked class divisions that the war and the political developments prior to it had created and brought to the front stage. This eventually meant the integration of the political far Left to the confines and constraints of parliamentary democracy, mainly because it was considered the best strategy with regard to national security. As put by Alapuro, "A large part of the Communist party – a legacy of the failed revolution in 1918 – was integrated into the Finnish political system, thereby reinforcing the internal cohesion of Finnish society in the face of Soviet pressure" (Alapuro 1999: 119). Class divisions have been further bridged with various sociopolitical measures, such as eradicating the mobile agricultural labor force in the early 20$^{th}$ century and the comprehensive school reform in the 1970s. National unity has been further built rhetorically through repeated narratives of historical events in which collective participation is said to indicate the innate quality of the Finns in their ability to unite when facing an outside threat.

However, the many national projects of unification have hardly reached a point where they are no longer found to be necessary. Although class is not a big divider today, language still is. Language and culture have been presented, in the Herderian fashion, as uniting factors, but the problematic relationship between the ethnic-genealogical and the civic-territorial conceptions of the nation continues to be a source of suppressed conflict. The idea of Finnishness continues to be – and perhaps is in increasing ways – divided over the question of whether the 'real' Finnish religion in the national sense is Lutheran Protestantism or pre-Christian paganism. The highly valued political consensus in the country can be taken to signal fear of the re-emergence of class divisions among Finnish speakers – that is, among those who are expected to embrace 'intrinsic' ethnic solidarity. Instead of the nation being unified, it is characterized by a perpetual fear of being divided – perhaps because of the traumatic memory of the 1918 Civil War (see e.g. Peltonen 1996, 2003). The potential for such a division was one of the major concerns in the 1994 referendum on the country's membership in the European Union.

The observable fact that there are many national projects meant to unite the Finnish people can be interpreted as a sign that speaks for the lack of such unity, rather than indicating its successful presence. The rhetoric of uniformity and homogeneity tends to cover up the fact that membership in 'the national We' has been determined in rather complex and even contradictory ways. It has mainly emphasized the unity and homogeneity of the Finnish speakers and at the same time constructed a number of Others not only outside but also inside the political boundaries of the nation-state. The idea of homogeneity thus conceals, in the name of national and cultural unity, the many dividing lines that continue to exist in the collectivity of the nation.

It would be tempting to conclude from this that the people in Finland make up a population that is preoccupied with its own unity. This would, however, be yet another attempt at capturing multitude in a single characterization. Yet, the history of the nation can be described – and of course, constructed – as a series of unifying and homogenizing projects that share the observable characteristic of symbols of unity being eagerly consumed. The divided nature of the nation has not only increased attempts at national unification and homogenization but has also increased the production and consumption of collective symbolism.

This consumption also characterizes the representation of folk tradition and the use of such representations in constructing modernity. In fact, folk traditions provide for some of the central commodities in the modern consumption of symbols of unity and homogeneity in the collectivity of the nation. At the same time, folklore and the oral traditions of the 'people', whether conceptualized as an *ethnos* or *demos*, a social class or a democratic constituent, have played an important role in the construction of sameness in a nation-state's cultural and political heritage.

A number of scholars (see e.g. Bakhtin 1981:147) have discussed the modern tendency to first imagine a most preferred future and project it into a mythical past, which then becomes the tradition that the people in the present feel they have lost. Such a process of historical inversion, mythologization and construction of tradition and heritage characterizes the reception of the *Kalevala* epic in Finland, as one of the major aspects in the use of its historical or mythical interpretation has been its adoption as a political symbol of national unity.

The *Kalevala* epic, intentionally edited into a novel-like genealogy of the Finnish nation by its compiler, Elias Lönnrot, is a narrative of national unity on a number of levels. First, it is a narrative about the unity of a heroic people, the people of Kaleva, against a single enemy, the people of Pohjola. Second, its textualization process symbolizes national integrity, as it is compiled of elements deriving from different geographical areas in what is claimed to be the national territory. Third, it is compiled in a way that is meant to give the impression that instead of coming from the compiler's desk, it has come from the 'people'. The 'people' in the historic-political context of 19th-century Finnish nationalism did not merely refer to the illiterate 'folk' as distinct from the educated classes, but also the Finnish-speaking population which was to be integrated both politically and culturally into the autonomous nation-state and the category of the Finns – and which as such was expected, within the emerging modern democratic political culture, to give political legitimacy to those in charge of the administration of the state.

As a product that appeared to have come from the 'people', the *Kalevala* epic was meant to speak for the people's innate cultural capacity and encourage the 'people's' role in the building of the Finnish nation-state and in the writing of its national history. Accordingly, the epic came to be used by the nationalists and their various organizations in enlightenment and folk education as a symbol with which they would argue for national unity and at the same time present themselves as the guarantors of this unity. Throughout the 20th century, the epic continued to provide a mythical image of prehistoric origins, which was, on the one hand, presented as a lost tradition but was supposed to offer a model for an aspired political reality and future, on the other. The unity that the *Kalevala* was taken to illustrate was used as a rhetorical image with which political and cultural activists could argue for common interests and values between such conflicting interest groups as the elite and the lower classes, the Swedish-speaking and the Finnish-speaking sections of the population, and across the class difference between the opposite parties of the 1918 Civil War.

However, instead of indicating national unity, the use of the *Kalevala* as a political symbol of national unity has rather paradoxically suggested a lack of such unity. The historical interpretation of the *Kalevala* both derives from and further supports the idea that Finland as a political unit is united on the basis of intrinsic links between language, history, genes and national tradition. Because of this, the nation is also expected to be one in political terms, but the political reality – including the presence of two national languages and various ethnic Others – does not support this expectation. Together with other national symbols, the *Kalevala* is expected to signal that the nation that 'belongs together' in linguistic, cultural and even biological terms must also be united in a political sense. If the political unity is lacking, the symbols of linguistic, cultural and genetic unity are expected to create such political unity. If they cannot do this, they are expected to at least inspire people with hope for such unity. It is the element of hope or wishful thinking for the unity of those that 'should be united' that makes such symbols appealing for repeated consumption, for example as folkloric and heritage-political representations, publications and performances. Indeed, symbols of unity are eagerly consumed in community-making projects. In Finland, the political divisions within the nation have not only increased attempts at national unification and homogenization but also increased the production, consumption and commodification of collective symbolism. In this, that which is made to symbolically encourage unity is already seen as its fulfillment.

# 9. Folk Tradition, History and 'The Story of Finland'

Internationally, the most important work on the role of research on folk tradition in Finnish nation making and Fennoman nationalism is William A. Wilson's *Folklore and Nationalism in Modern Finland* (Wilson 1976). The book provides an outstanding and unsurpassed record of the extent to which 19th and 20th-century folklorists in Finland participated in political and militaristic propaganda concerning the Finnish nation, its history and folk traditions, national characteristics and geographic extensions. It well deserves the place it was given in the international discussion on folklore and politics in the 1970s and 1980s.

However, some of the book's theoretical weaknesses have only come to light in the course of the new perspectives on nationalism and the narrative construction of the national developed in the social sciences in the 1990s. Instead of critically analyzing 19th-century Romantic Nationalism, founded upon the ideas of Herder, or even considering other influential politico-philosophical doctrines, such as those by Hegel, Wilson recounts the history of nationalistically oriented literary activism in 19th-century Finland from a conspicuously Herderian perspective. He sees the role of folklore in Finnish nationalism as following the course of events that Herder described for Germany (e.g. Wilson 1976: 30). Accordingly, his "principal concern" in the book is to examine "the Finns' attempt, through folklore, to discover their past" (Wilson 1976: 6).

Because of this narrative agenda, the introductory section on 19th-century developments (entitled 'The Road to Independence') – which were originally meant to be Wilson's main focus in the book (see Wilson 1987: 408) – is more of a celebration of the national significance of folklore and folklore scholarship in Finland than an actual analysis of their political role in Finnish society. It functions as a means for Wilson to show his love for folklore scholarship and his respect for Finland (see Wilson 1987). Without in any way questioning the overall value of Wilson's seminal work, I wish to point here to a particular account of Finnish history that appears in the preface of the book. Describing the historical process by which Finland was annexed to the Russian Empire, Wilson writes as follows:

> Fragmented as they [the Finns] were into several dialect groups and lacking the binding ties of a common literature and a written record of their national past, they were ill-prepared to face the century of Russian rule and attempted Russification of their culture which lay ahead. Yet in a little over a century they had coalesced and won their freedom. (Wilson 1976: ix.)

This account conveys a number of arguments that are worth examining. First, it presents the Finns as one historical subject speaking one language, but fragmented into dialect groups. Elsewhere in the book, somewhat differently, Wilson (e.g. 1976: 27) says that the Finns were "divided into separate linguistic camps". Secondly, the Finns have a national past but no written record of it. Third, they have their own culture (note the singular), but this faces Russification. Fourth, they came together and became free.

Wilson's account corresponds well to a commonly held notion – a political myth, or an 'ethnomyth' (see Rihtman-Auguštin 2000) – that the nation-building process in 19th-century Finland followed Herder's ideas for what has since then been called cultural, romantic, ethnic or autonomist nationalism. According to this notion, the emergence of nationalism in Finland was a call for independence by an oppressed people with an indigenous culture, a folk tradition that speaks for the innate unity of the Finnish folk. The Finns are seen as making up a primordial but dormant nation whose history prior to its political independence constitutes a narrative about being on the road to that independence. This image thus conveys a heroic narrative about the Finns' historical project for modern nationhood.

From an ethnopolitical perspective, what is especially noteworthy in Wilson's arguments is that they at the same time both include and exclude the Swedish speakers from the category of the Finns. The notion of the people speaking one language but being fragmented into dialect groups refers to the Finnish speakers only. The same applies to the notion that the Finns had no written record of their past. However, those who are said to have coalesced are the Finnish speakers and the Swedish speakers. In addition, Wilson includes the Swedish speakers in the category of the Finns by describing the mostly literary-oriented nationalist activities of the educated Swedish speakers. These were "aspiring young nationalists" who brought "the wealth of [folk] poetry" to "the attention of their countrymen" (Wilson 1976: 31; see also Wilson 1996: 47).

Wilson is far from being alone in conceptualizing the Finns in a way that both includes and excludes the Swedish speakers. In fact, this is a paradox that characterizes much of the 19th-century (and in many ways still continuing) Fennoman perspective on Finnish national culture. It manifests the wish to acknowledge the contribution of the educated Swedish speakers in the making of Finnish-language folk tradition part of Finnish national culture, but it also manifests the simultaneous desire to define this national culture in ways that only acknowledge Finnish-language cultural products as its representations. Much of the national value of these 'Finnish' cultural products derives from placing them in opposition to the role of both Swedish-language culture and other 'foreign', such as Russian, elements and influences.

This opposition has contributed to making Finland a country in which the idea of ethnic homogeneity and the sense of ethnic solidarity (mainly between Finnish speakers) continue to play a significant role in the construction of the national and the selection of its representations and symbols of unity. Although Finland is officially bilingual, with the influence of the Swedish speakers far exceeding their present number in percentage, popular discourses on Finnish identity are characterized by the Herderian notion of an intimate link between the nation and the Finnish language (see also Saukkonen 1999). In the connection made between language, nation, history, folk tradition and cultural identity, it is mainly the Finnish language as well as the (constructed and reconstructed) pasts of the Finnish speakers that are to be shared in order for the Finns to make a nation and have a cultural identity of their own. Such a perspective tends to position the Swedish speakers, among others, as the 'heteroglossic Other' (Law 1998: 270, n. 4) and exclude their pasts from that which is to be shared.

## A Model for Nation Building

The opposition constructed between Finnishness and its constitutive Others yields a heroic ethno-nationalistic narrative of a struggle for independence that draws in decisive ways on folklore. This is a narrative that portrays the emergence of nationalism and nation building in Finland as a call for cultural and linguistic rights (and eventually political independence) by an oppressed and subordinated people. The 'people' here means the Finnish speakers, whose nationhood is, in Herderian fashion, regarded as being inscribed in their orally transmitted cultural traditions and the literary representations made of these. The narrative paints a picture of the Finns as a people that has constituted a Finnish-speaking nation since prehistory but which has been subjected to foreign domination and colonization throughout the thousand-year long historical period. In light of this narrative, the political independence gained in 1917 appears as a return to and a restoration of an allegedly original state of affairs, which in many scholarly imaginations, as discussed by Wilson (1976), is presented as an independent pre-Christian state or a kingdom existing before the historical period. Thus, instead of cultural capacity, the Finns only appeared to lack their original political power and sovereignty.

One of the numerous expressions of such a narrative was published in 1996 in the 80th anniversary issue of the weekly *Suomen Kuvalehti*, the most influential political periodical in today's Finland. The editor Tapani Ruokanen writes: "Our nation was born long before Finland gained political independence. It emerged from history: from the collective experiences of the people, common language, culture, values." (Ruokanen 1996: 3, my translation.) Ruokanen's idea of the immemorial Finnish nation is monolingual and culturally homogeneous. As such, it can be juxtaposed with the similar image portrayed by Zachris Topelius, albeit that for Topelius – rallying for 'one nation, two languages' instead of 'one nation, one language' – Finland was a multilingual instead of a monolingual country. According to Topelius, the Finnish nation had existed since the dawn of history, because God united the people living in Finland into one nation, and God has kept them together even though they speak different languages (Topelius 1985 [1875]: 17–18).

Ruokanen's perspective distinguishes between the historical foundation of the nation and the political independence of the state, but still it implies that the historical foundation of the nation *led* to political independence. Especially after Finland became an independent state (1917) and nationalistic history writing gained special force, the history and prehistory of Finland and the Finns came to be conceived of as a teleological narrative of a nation that had for centuries determinably moved towards political independence (Tommila 1983: vii; Engman 1999: 169; cf. Kalela 1993: 38).

The teleological narrative about the Finnish-speaking Finns' road to independence has also yielded an interpretation that Finland, because of its successful ethno-nationalist struggle, provides an apt model to be followed by other nations and ethnic minorities that lack a written history but aspire towards cultural and/or political independence. These populations mainly include the Finno-Ugric 'kindred peoples' in Russia, but the model is also said to apply to the making of states and national cultures in Asia and Africa. The idea was developed by Lauri Honko (see e.g. Honko 1980c: 42, 61) and adopted soon afterwards by a number of other scholars (see e.g. Hurskainen 1992). It also comes forward strongly in one of Honko's last articles:

> New nations wanted to have a history of their own, but its ingredients were not to be found in the documents kept by the conqueror. Other resources were needed, including folk poetry. In a sense, the story of Finland began to be carried out in many African and Asian countries, but while the Finns had a century's time to build up a cultural foundation for independence, a state in Africa or Asia only had up to two decades at its disposal. (Honko 2002: 7, my translation.)

Since it is not specified which countries in Africa and Asia have carried out 'the story of Finland', this is not a call for a comparative analysis in political development. Instead, the purpose appears to be to present Finland as a model of principle. The idea to be modeled is that the Finns – meaning the Finnish-speakers – lacked written history and therefore have "discovered their past through folklore", as William Wilson phrased it. Such a notion has found general acceptance, since a great number of present-day Finnish folklore scholars explicitly share and reiterate it.[19] Its popularity is by no means surprising as it basically repeats one of the fundamental tenets of the study of oral tradition, as articulated by Jan Vansina: "Where there is no writing, or almost none, oral traditions must bear the brunt of historical reconstruction." (Vansina 1985: 199.) Yet, when applied to Finland and its history of nation making, the application of this idea argues that ethnography on folk traditions has provided the Finns the necessary foundation for a national cultural identity, which has then supported the building up of a political identity. Folklore thus compensates for the lack of written (national) history, and folkloric collections in archives and museums provide national symbols of unity and character as well as sources of historical knowledge and political legitimization.

The logic behind the suggested global application of the 'Finnish model' comes from the wider Western notion that the political independence and decolonization of Third World countries in the mid-20th century has followed – and is expected to follow – the Herderian models allegedly employed in many of the European nation-states in the 19th century (e.g. Wilson 1998: 443). Such a notion does not merely point to the European origins of nationalism and nation-state making, but appears to locate Europe as the source of modernity and democracy as well as the model for legitimate state membership and civilized political cohesion. It also provides Finnish folklorists with an export product on a global scale: inherent know-how on the collecting and organizing of folklore in tradition archives and on the textual practices of making folklore collections into tokens and monuments of national patrimony.

The geopolitical charge of such a role may be compared with that of 19th-century Greek folklorists. As discussed by Michael Herzfeld, the nationalists in Greece in the 19th century, among them those who created the discipline of folklore, searched for traces of ancient heritage in order to obtain historical justification and intellectual reinforcement for nation building. This had a clear geopolitical aspect to it, as the search aimed at providing the independent Greek nation-state proof of direct descent in the Hellenic tradition and a corresponding role in European civilization (Herzfeld 1982). The geopolitical nature of this identification has also been elaborated by Jonathan Friedman, who has discussed how Greece was identified in the expanding polity and economy of Western Europe as the legitimate ancestor, and as such, the embodiment of the essence of European modernity (Friedman 1994b: 122).

When we compare the neo-Hellenic nationalization of Greece with nation building in the Nordic countries, we can observe that Greece was a periphery seen with symbolic significance in the construction of the center. The Nordic countries have also been incorporated into the expanding West as peripheries, but with much less symbolic value in the making of Europe – except as modernity's exotic edges and more recently, in an attempt to redefine the periphery, in the role of promoting the social democratic welfare state, 'modern' gender roles, moderate class distinctions and transparency in public policies and decision-making. The modernization of these countries, especially Finland and Norway – which, unlike Sweden and Denmark, have never been European super-powers on any scale – has manifested a geopolitical perspective emerging from their peripheral and symbolically less significant position. Accordingly, their nationalism carries elements that are indicative of a tendency to define selfhood as more or less distinct from European-ness and Western modernity. The relatively strong academic status of traditional folkloristics – unlike in Sweden, the most modern of the modern Nordic states (see Löfgren 1993b) – also bears witness to the ways in which modernity is produced in these countries within particular geopolitical configurations.

As far as the role of folklore studies in these configurations is concerned, the Finnish, Nordic or European practices may be compared for example to

Latin America. According to Néstor García Canclini, "many folkloric studies in Latin America were born through the same impulses that gave rise to them in Europe; on the one hand, the need to root the formation of new nations in their identity of their past; on the other hand, the Romantic inclination to rescue popular sentiments in the face of the Enlightenment and liberal cosmopolitanism" (García Canclini 1995: 150). García Canclini acknowledges that Latin America adopted a 'Finnish model' in folklore scholarship and in the apprehension of the popular as tradition. As a consequence, a vast body of empirical knowledge has been produced about "ethnic groups and their cultural expressions: religiosity, rituals, medicine, fiestas, and handicrafts. In many works a profound interpenetration with the Indian and mestizo world can be seen, an effort to give it a place within national culture." (García Canclini 1995: 149.) But García Canclini sees a major problem concerning the scientific quality of this European trajectory:

> The influence of the Finnish school on folklorists – under the slogan 'Leave theory behind; what is important is to collect' – promoted a flat empiricism in the cataloging of materials, the analytical treatment of information, and a poor contextual interpretation of the facts, even among the most conscientious authors. Therefore, most of the books on traditional handicrafts, fiestas, poetry, and music enumerate and exalt popular products without locating them in the logic present in social relations. (García Canclini 1995: 151.)

This quotation suggests that there is much more to the global politics of folklore than the narrative of Finland and its study of folklore as a universal model for postcolonial nation making. At the same time, it may be necessary to emphasize that it is not necessarily my purpose to object to the political logics of folkloristic discourse within nationalism. Yet, the constructed character of such logics calls for a more precise analysis of the ways in which national histories are created, how the nation is projected into its own prehistory and how particular configurations of center–periphery relations are created, transmitted and maintained – for example, in the context of the geopolitical and security political interests of the state. Instead of conceptualizing history as a narrative with a plot, regardless of how patriotic or morally appealing that might be, I seek to examine the social and political dynamics in which selections are made as to what counts as history or 'roots', whose history that is, and what arguments are employed to make the link between the present and the imagined past. Instead of merely stating that nationalist intellectuals were 'in search of their roots' or for 'a better understanding of the self', we can examine how certain landscapes and social practices (especially when they lie across the national borders) are appropriated into histories of the intellectual elites, projected ideologically onto those that come to constitute the 'people' for such elites, and are conceptualized as sites of their ancestry and heritage. Research into heritage politics and the study of political mentalities have a common task in investigating what sort of cultural models are being employed for such processes of thought and argumentation.

## Folk Tradition as 'People's' Culture

In making links between language, nation, history and cultural identity, the 19th-century – originally Swedish-speaking – national movement employed a variety of representations of Finnish-language folk tradition and peasant culture. Many of them continue to be used in national symbolism and rhetoric today to denote the national heritage of the (Finnish-speaking) Finns. Yet, despite the fact that the Herderian perspective presupposes a decisive role for folk tradition in the constitution of the nation, the extent to which such representations of the national have actually contributed to Finnish nation building and especially to the country's political independence is a matter of debate. The significance and political force of folkloric national symbolism tends to be overemphasized by those who participate in the production of such symbols and who assign themselves, also in the name of scholarship, to publicly persuade of their meaning.[20]

It is undeniable that the attempts to consolidate Finnishness characterized the development of Finnish society in the 19th century. Yet, the extent to which Finland's relation to the Russian Empire was that of a victim is open for discussion. Matti Klinge has stressed that the national culture of the Grand Duchy of Finland was built in the spirit of loyalty to the Russian Emperor, not of protest (see e.g. Klinge 1988a, 1997). Anti-revolutionary conservatism was exemplified by the stronghold of folklore collecting, the Finnish Literature Society (see Klinge 1988b; cf. Sulkunen 2004: 22). Emperor Alexander II in fact supported the Fennoman movement, partially as a reward for loyalty shown in Finland for Russia during the Crimean War in the 1850s and partially as a means to ward off political and ideological influence from Sweden. The ideology of Scandinavism and the Swedish anti-Russian sentiments were regarded as a much bigger threat in Russia than Finnish interest in promoting the Finnish language (e.g. Liikanen 1995: 103). The latter was actually seen as providing a barrier to the consolidation of the former, as far as Finland was concerned (Skyttä & Skyttä 1981: 212). Throughout the 19th century, the Fennoman nationalists consented to the power of the Emperor, while the mainly Swedish-speaking liberals, who opposed the Fennoman nationalists especially for their anti-Swedish language program, spoke for strict constitutionalism and were in favor of economic and religious liberties (Tiilikainen 1998: 127–131, 142–145).[21]

The construction of Finnishness and Finnish nation-state identity in the 19th century, especially towards the end of that century, reflected a general opposition to the censorship policies imposed on Finnish political life by the Russian Empire. As a consequence, many popular images of threat against Finnish sovereignty continue to be located across the country's eastern border. Yet, as far as the future and social position of the Finnish language and its speakers is concerned, an even more decisive factor has been its relation to the position of the Swedish language and its speakers in the Finnish territory. Discussion on this relationship has continued to flourish to this day.

It was characteristic of the autonomous Finnish state in the 19th century that, instead of political institutions being in the hands of those who represented the Russian Empire and the highest political power in it, the Finnish state was administered by a Swedish-speaking elite. The laws that had kept Swedish as the official language after the establishment of the Grand Duchy granted this status. The Swedish speakers made up the most active section of population in the nationalist movement (later known as the Fennoman movement) of the 1840s and 1850s. On the other side of the great social division within the autonomous state were the 'people', who for the nationalist Fennomans appeared as a distinct group of mostly uneducated Finnish speakers. They constituted the majority of the population.

The mutual relationship between these two population groups and social classes was determined by a number of factors. Risto Alapuro (1997a: 18–19, 1999: 113–114) emphasizes that since the hegemonic position of the elite was not based on land ownership, the elite depended upon the support of the 'people' in order to secure not only its own cultural and political hegemony but also the state and its political institutions against the assimilation policies of the Russian Empire. This also meant that the elite, instead of executing the politics of oppression, had to be attentive to the demands of the landowning peasants.

Especially for J. V. Snellman, the making of the Finnish nation meant the political integration of Swedish speakers and Finnish speakers, as well as that of the different social classes within the territorial unit. As state administrators, the Swedish-speaking elite identified with the state and saw it as their political task to unite with the 'people'. This identification had at least two political goals. The first was to make the Finnish-speaking sections of the population loyal to the state and yield from them political legitimacy to those in charge of state administration (Alapuro & Stenius 1987; Alapuro 1999). The second was to better secure the unit's political institutions from potential integration with the rest of the Russian Empire (Alavuotunki 1990: 9–10). The latter aspect was also stressed by Yrjö Koskinen (Rommi 1980: 313).

As pointed out by Alapuro and Stenius (1987), the adoption of the majority's language (Finnish) as the state language was regarded as the most productive means to achieve these ends. This entailed turning against the hegemony of Swedish-language culture and the power position of the Swedish speakers in society. The 'people', on the other hand, had to be endowed with political power, their level of education and civilization had to be raised, and their language had to be developed to meet the requirements of a future state language, a language of civilization.

The mostly Swedish-speaking Fennoman nationalists constructed nationhood with an enlightenment project that took, in the spirit of both Herder and Hegel, a symbolic turn to the 'people'. The people's culture – especially orally transmitted folk poetry – was appropriated to speak at the same time for both the long and ancient history of the national and the potentiality of Finnish as a modern language of literature and civilization. This argumentative role was a crucial basis for the eventual establishing of the sphere of folk tradition as well as its research, collecting and public display as some of the central symbolic elements in the Finnish civic religion and the consolidation of national loyalties. Folk tradition served both history and the future. Still, the elite would not replace their cultural achievements with the 'people's culture' that they were elevating to national significance. No effort was made to preserve or continue folk traditions where these existed. Instead, a nationalizing discourse was created that constructed and reconstructed antiquity for a markedly modern purpose. The educated nationalists documented folklore and put its representations – texts, material objects, architecture – in the service of the interrelated projects of nation making and the production of modernity: to speak for the nation and the national as well as to speak for the 'people' in the national and political sense of the word. 'Tradition' thus received its meaning in the context of producing modernity, in the making of modern political culture, as part of the modern discourses on society, state, class and national integration and the nature of modernity.

Here, folkloristic images came to serve both the national and the international marketing of the country. The most important product in this regard was the *Kalevala* epic that Lönnrot compiled from Finnish-Karelian folk poetry. In addition to becoming the Finnish national epic and gradually one of the country's most distinctive domestic symbols, its publication in 1835 was also acknowledged in literary circles abroad and contributed to making the concept of Finland internationally known. The epic was soon translated – in part or in full – into some of the major European languages (for a complete list, see Anttonen & Kuusi 1999: 151–165). In the latter part of the 19th century, many Finnish products in fine arts, crafts, modern industry and commerce were strongly embedded with folkloristic symbolism in name and/or style (see Anttonen & Kuusi 1999: 290–297). Finland's participation in World Exhibitions also became instrumental in this (see Smeds 1996; MacKeith & Smeds 1993). The political argument in the displays, especially abroad, was that Finland was a nation of its own, regardless of the fact that it was part of the Russian Empire. This was in line with the constitutionalist conception – which was much disputed especially in Russia – that 'in the law of nations' Finland was a state that was in a union with Russia (Tiilikainen 1998: 129).

In addition to drawing categorical boundaries towards Russia, nationalistic symbolism was employed to construct Finnishness as distinct from two other major directions. These were Swedishness (of Sweden) as a spatial Other, and medieval Catholicism as a temporal Other, both of which had been present in the country's medieval history that now came to represent a non-national element. Under the leadership of Yrjö Koskinen, Fennoman nationalists, formally organized as the Finnish Party since 1872, chose to foreground the symbolic significance of 'Finnish' elements in the country's documented but 'foreign' history. This trend contributed to the growing notion that nationally significant Finnish culture is mainly constituted by the history and culture of the Finnish speakers. Although the famous slogan 'Let us be Finns' by the Swedish-speaking nationalist activists in the early 1800s was meant to unite the heterogeneous elements of the population under a single national identity, it came to symbolize the aspirations for a culture that would be recognized as being founded on 'Finnish' elements only. For Koskinen, it would also require the elimination of bilingualism (Rommi 1980: 307).

However, despite the Fennoman project of making only 'Finnish' elements stand for the national, Finnish society in the 19th century continued to develop and strengthen its autonomous status as a nation-state in ways that were not all 'Finnish' in the Fennoman sense of the term. Finland had inherited a number of social and political institutions from the Swedish rule. Teija Tiilikainen, among others, has emphasized that when the Finnish provinces were annexed to the Russian Empire and made into a Grand Duchy, "the focal political principles of the Swedish era were handed down in the structures of the administration and legislation that Finland was entitled to maintain" (Tiilikainen 1998: 120). These structures included the constitutional status of the Lutheran Church and faith, granted in the Porvoo Diet in 1809. The class structure dominated by extensive peasant land ownership was another legacy of the Swedish political and social system (Alapuro 1997a, 1999). Similarly, Max Engman has argued that

> [t]he emphasis on Finnish language, folklore, history and symbols should not (...) overshadow the fact that Yrjö-Koskinen and his followers wanted to preserve the central institutions of the Swedish period: autonomy, laws, judicial system, social structure, Lutheran faith and educational traditions; concerning such matters, there was no Finnish alternative. (Engman 1999: 169.)

This demonstrates that the 'Finnish alternatives' in history, literature and folk tradition – meaning mainly the cultural practices (non- or semi-Christian religious beliefs, verbal arts, agricultural means and tools, vernacular architecture, etc.) of the rural Finnish-speaking population – did not, in precise terms, lay the foundation for national culture or the eventual political independence. Rather, folkloric symbolism served in the production of politically preferred distinctions and that way contributed to the consolidation of the already existing notion that Finland (as declared by Emperor Alexander I in 1809) constituted a nation of its own. Since the constitutional status of the autonomous Grand Duchy was a matter of dispute with the representatives of the Imperial administration (see Jussila 1987, 1999), Finnish nation building was comprised of actions that were to strengthen the country's separate identity within the Empire and make its rather abstract nationness more concrete. This concretization included a set of representations that could be jointly labeled national culture and/or national literature. The role that Finnish-language folk tradition had in this was to provide such representations.

In this discourse, the political institutions that represented documented and factual historical continuity did not carry the necessary ideological significance in the making of 'Finnish' national symbols. Such historical continuity was to be found elsewhere, in the culture of the Finnish-speaking 'folk', not in the culture of those in search of the 'folk'. The allegedly ancient culture of the folk came to stand for ancestry and heritage in a national sense, while the historical continuities of the country's political institutions were denied this function in national rhetorics. A distinction was drawn between the traditions of the state and the traditions of the nation, as 'national tradition' came to refer to folkloric symbolism concerning the non-Christian or semi-Christian and syncretistic religious beliefs, verbal lore and vernacular architecture of the rural Finnish-speaking population.

Still, the value of the folkloric representations was not only in their reference to history, ancestry and heritage. Even more important was the emerging notion and belief that such constructions of history and heritage could prove that Finnish speakers, too, can contribute to 'national life' and modern civilization. Because of this agenda, the central goal in the discourse on folk tradition was not its preservation as indigenous culture. Neither was it the promotion of cultural diversity. Instead, folklore was nationalized and made into a metonymy of a culturally homogenizing and politically unifying national community. Oral tradition was transformed through folkloristic collecting and its entextualization practices into 'pre-literate' literature, into written epics and other types of published collections – and eventually, into consumables of national tradition, history and heritage.

It is worth emphasizing that for Snellman, the value of folk tradition was not in its alleged capacity to manifest a 'natural' and therefore an unhistorical nation, as was argued by Herder. Instead, the value of folk tradition was in its potential to indicate the presence of a national spirit, which he considered to lead individuals to make "moral and rational social contracts" (Karkama 1999: 148) and thus promote national development and civilization (see also Karkama 2001: 188, 200–201). In addition to pointing to nationalized antiquity, the value of folk tradition lay thus in its capacity to promote and enhance modernity and a modern civil society. We could therefore argue, in present-day terms, that Hegel's idea of *Volksgeist* contained for Snellman more historical and political agency than Herder's cultural concept of the *Volk*. The former was seen as a force for historical change, while the latter, as discussed by Wilson (1976: 28–29), conveyed the idea that national characters – best expressed in language and folk poetry that are allegedly unspoiled by foreign influence – indicate cultural and political units that are to be defended against outside influences.

For the later generations of Fennomans, the use of folk tradition, such as the *Kalevala* epic, continued to stand for the antiquarian foundation of national civilization. The latter half of the 19th century was the period in which the study of folklore was established as an independent branch of scholarship, but the leadership in the Fennoman movement only saw symbolic and political value in the enterprise; representations of folklore served to legitimate both the national movement and the national polity (Sulkunen 2004: 204–205, 216–218). At the same time, the use of folkloric symbolism increased in a variety of organizational activities and commercial contexts (see Anttonen & Kuusi 1999: 290–297).

This was not, however, the only way in which folklore was political. Since folk tradition and the *Kalevala* were seen as coming from the 'people', the purpose of the use of folkloric elements as national symbols was linked to the argument that the Fennomans as a political party spoke on behalf of the people, and that they – better than anyone else – represented the people's will (see Liikanen 1995: 170–171, 280–282 *et passim*; Liikanen 1997; Sulkunen 2004: 169–171). Folklore functioned as a means to construct symbolically and ideologically the 'people', who to a gradually increasing extent came to be regarded as the democratic holders of representational power in the modernizing state and the emerging civil society. Because of this civic-territorial principle in constructing nationhood, folkloric symbols became an issue in the competition over political representation, in speaking for and on behalf of people and social classes.

## Language and Culture Point to the East

One of the basic reasons why the *Kalevala* epic was soon after its publication raised to the status of a national symbol was that the history read from it, supported by a historical interpretation of the rest of the folk poetry, served as an instrument, in the words of Robert Foster (1991: 241), "for uncovering and recovering an authentic and ancient definition of the national community as a distinct people". Yet, in addition to speaking for the (Finnish-speaking) Finns' distinctiveness as a people, it provided support for the emerging myth of origin that would present Finland as an innate national unit. In order to promote this myth, Lönnrot made the epic into a narrative about mythical incidents that he saw as being of historical importance. For him – and eventually for many others – they spoke of Finnish and Karelian national antiquity. In this antiquity, prior to the advent of Christianity and the establishment of Swedish rule, the Finns had constituted one tribe comparable to a nation – pure and authentic in the Fennoman sense of Finnishness. In accordance with the dominant philological methods of his time, Lönnrot created a textual representation of that allegedly original state by removing what he regarded as later influences.

Yet, even though Finland was regarded as a nation of old, Fennoman nationalists considered it unfulfilled in terms of its 'real' and original nature. Geographic extensions were one aspect of this. The Greater Finland ideology, influential since the 1860s and especially during the 1920s and 1930s, aimed to include all Finnish-speaking areas within Finland's political boundaries (see e.g. Sihvo 1973: 352; Wilson 1976: 137–161). Today, the popular resentment against the Swedish language among many Finnish speakers indicates a tendency to regard the development of the national position of the Finnish language as unfinished and incomplete. Despite its official status as a domestic language, and the international reputation of Finnish bilingualism as a model for other countries with linguistic minorities (especially for the minority groups, see Saari 1999: 273), Swedish continues to be viewed as a sign of foreignness in the Finnish-speaking nation. Examples of this can be encountered on a daily basis. According to Mirja Saari, a number of opinion polls show that one in every third Finnish speaker has reservations about Finland-Swedes or the status of the Swedish language in Finland (Saari 1999: 272).

Thus, rather ironically, although it was the Fennoman-minded Swedish speakers who were the original agents of Finnish nation making, with a purpose of integrating the two linguistic groups of Swedish and Finnish speakers into one national culture and create equality between the two languages, the Fennoman nationalist idea about Finland came to concern mainly the Finnish language and its speakers – and in many ways exclude the Swedish language and its speakers. In her recent history of the Finnish Literature Society, the stronghold of the Fennoman movement, Irma Sulkunen locates the beginning of this process in the early 1870s, when Snellman withdrew from his position as the president of the Society and Yrjö Koskinen's more strictly Finnish-oriented language policy gained hegemony (Sulkunen 2004: 169ff.).

Another important factor in this development was the scientific discovery of Finno-Ugric language kinship, which became an established linguistic category by the early 19th century (see Korhonen 1986: 28–33). This discovery gradually outdated the scholarly attempts at locating the origin of Finnish in the 'holy languages' of Hebrew, Greek and Latin (see Korhonen 1986: 25–27). Instead of the Europe of ancient civilizations, the history of the Finnish language now pointed east, to Russia, Siberia and Asia. This was not only a scientific reorientation, but marked the emergence of new language myths of primordiality.

In addition to becoming a dividing element in the relationship between the Swedish and Finnish languages in Finland, and by extension also elsewhere in northern Europe, the discovery of the kinship of Finno-Ugric languages resulted in the development of the academic fields of linguistics and ethnography, in which the relationship of Finnish language and culture with the rest of the Finno-Ugric family of languages was studied comparatively and was further consolidated. According to Kaisa Häkkinen, the linguistic kinship is the cornerstone of research on Finnish prehistory (Häkkinen 1997: 333–334). One of the leading pioneers in this development was Matthias Alexander Castrén, whose goal was to prove that there were historical-genetic relations between the Finno-Ugric peoples – even though it would mean, as he wrote to Snellman in 1846, "we are the offspring of those despised Mongols" (Korhonen 1986: 60). Indeed, as Castrén had feared, his findings, which established for a long time the idea that the Finnish nation had its cultural cradle in the east, contributed to the eventual rise of racial theories about the 'Mongolian' character of the Finns towards the end of the 19th century and the beginning of the 20th (see Kemiläinen 1998: 65–66 et passim).

The linguistic discovery and the subsequent cultural interest in the populations speaking Finno-Ugric languages did not merely concern historical developments. In addition, it came to be linked to emerging language-extrinsic myths (see Law 1998) that established preferred relations between particular ethnicities and nationalities. Among other things, these linguistic and cultural relations also sparked an interest in the idea of a pan-Finnic tribe, constituted by all people speaking Finnish and related languages. For Castrén, this served to indicate that the Finns are not alone in this world but "we are in kinship relations to at least one-sixth of the human population" (Snellman 1931: 119, my translation). In 1924 the right-wing nationalist Academic Karelia Society counted that there were 19 million of 'us', that is, members of 'the Finno-Ugric tribe'. This bears witness to the inclination to conceptualize the linguistic category as a political entity.

Today, the militaristic aspirations for the expansion of Finnish political territory, kindled by the Greater Finland ideology, seem like past phenomena. There is a growing trend to "avoid any inference that the present-day speakers of Finno-Ugrian languages have more in common with each other in terms of an unbroken, vertical inheritance of culture than they do with their neighbors of several centuries who may not speak Finno-Ugrian languages but with whom they have had close and regular contacts" (Branch 1993: 36). Still, a tendency continues – also among scholars – to place the origins of Finnish ancestry, national heritage, mentality and even genes in the assumed ancient origins of the Finnish language and the prehistory of the speakers of Finno-Ugric languages. In this discourse, the terms 'ancestor' and 'forefather' tend to be reserved for the Finno-Ugric elements in the history of the Finnish language and Finnish religious beliefs.[22] Cultural similarities with the other populations speaking Finno-Ugric languages denote family relations, while cultural similarities across linguistic categories denote borrowings – foreign influences instead of inherited tradition. A difference is drawn between a heritage of civilization and a heritage of culture. The spread of (Western) civilization appears as historical change, while (Finno-Ugric) heritage denotes an unmediated descent and inheritance of belief and knowledge.

Such rhetoric of ancestry undermines the role and significance of other historical sources in the constitution of the Finnish language and the population of Finland. Apparently, the political value of this rhetoric is to function as a means of producing national unity that homogenizes the diverse origins of the population into an image of a single origin, all having the same forefathers and ancestors in a cultural sense, if not in biology. At the same time, there is a different strategy for creating a sense of national unity across the linguistic division. For example, Elias Lönnrot, both in his work and his personality, is widely celebrated for his exceptional ability to mediate between the Finnish speakers and the Swedish speakers, as well as between the uneducated 'folk' and the educated elite (e.g. Karkama 2001: 88). The Finno-Ugric links, however, appear to exist without a need for such mediation by individual agency, even though, as put by Lauri Honko, "The distance between Finnish and Khanty approximates that between Swedish and Sanskrit" (Honko 1995: 139). The "fragile bond" or distant affinity perceived between Finnish and related languages, as well as the people who speak these languages, by no means negate the politically charged and morally grounded desires to speak on behalf of the Finno-Ugric minorities in Russia and support their "battle for ethnic survival" (Honko 1995: 140ff.). On the contrary, such desires – some of them based on a rather rigid distinction made between Finno-Ugric and Russian identities among these populations – serve to indicate the presence of active mediation between the cultural practices of the Finno-Ugric peoples and the Finnish discourses on the heritage of culture. Links are discursively asserted especially when the cultural traditions of a Finno-Ugric population and the research on these serve as sources for experiencing symbolic union and common belonging (see e.g. Siikala 1997: 58–60; Siikala 2000: 57, 76–77).

Regarding the political charge of Finnish research on the populations speaking Finno-Ugric languages in Russia, Timo Salminen has argued in his recent dissertation that in the late 19th century, Russia and Siberia were viewed as "Finland's scientific lands of conquest". According to Salminen, this constituted a parallel to "West European colonialist policies, even though the Finns felt they were involved in recording and gathering the heritage of related peoples in the process of extinction" (Salminen 2003: 276; cf. Pimiä 2003: 82). It remains to be debated, however, whether this is an either-or or both-and issue, and whether this approach in any way characterizes present-day Finnish ethnographic research activities across the Russian border (see e.g. Survo 2001).

Another consequence of the establishing of the Finno-Ugric language relationship since the late 18th century was a stronger link between a Finn and a Finnish speaker. For educated Finns in the 18th century, a Finn was a person who was born and raised in Finland, regardless of whether he spoke Finnish, Swedish or Latin (see e.g. Manninen 2000: 81–82, 88–89; Manninen 2002: 12). The same applied to the upper ranks of civil servants in the Grand Duchy of Finland in the first half of the 19th century, among whom, according to Kristiina Kalleinen, nationality was not linked with any particular language (Kalleinen 2002). For Elias Lönnrot, however, the term 'Finn' designated all those who speak the Finnish language, regardless of whether they lived in Finland, Russia, Sweden or Norway (Sihvo 1969: 39). Accordingly, when the political unit of the autonomous Grand Duchy established its cultural identity, and the educated elite of the Fennoman nationalists made their symbolic turn to the 'people', the nomination of the Finns came to have two meanings. On the one hand, it inclusively denoted both the Finnish and the Swedish speakers as common nationals, and on the other, the Finnish speakers exclusively. The national history and antiquity sought after in folk tradition was mainly provided by the culture of the Finnish speakers, those that were 'ethnically', 'genetically' or 'ancestrally' Finns. The Swedish speakers would establish their own folk tradition, which would not speak for the nation but only for the distinct culture (and more recently, for the ethnic identity) of the Swedish speakers.

## History and Periphery as Prerequisites for a Nation

When examining the role of folk tradition in the symbolic production of the Finnish nation, we need to address the methodological question concerning the relationship between historical reconstruction and history as a present-day construction of the past. In addition to being sensitive to the political nature of the concept of history, we must alert ourselves to the intertextual links that the discourses on history share with discourses on the modern, such as the politics of modernity. What constitutes history? How is history made an issue of ownership? How are given reconstructions of the past linked to preferred cultural and political relationships and ideological constructions of modernity?

Some historians in Finland have recently suggested that instead of the Finnish state being established as an end result of a successful nationalist (or ethno-nationalist) struggle, as the Romantic Nationalist narrative would have it, the state was formed first, practically as a 'gift' from Emperor Alexander I (see e.g. Klinge 1997; Engman 1999). This perspective follows the constitutionalist tradition of political thought that has argued, especially since the 1860s, that Finland was annexed to Russia in the form of a province but became a state through a mutually binding contract made in 1809 between the Finnish Estates and the Emperor of Russia (Tiilikainen 1998: 128–129). Forming the nation and establishing for it a distinctive cultural and political identity – which could then be used to consolidate the unit's nature as a state – were some of the new state and nation's initial political agendas.

In a similar vein, Risto Alapuro has pointed out that the national movement in Finland, unlike many other such movements in Europe, did not need to argue for a state-unit because it already existed (Alapuro 1997a: 18). What it did need to argue for, though, was history. History was considered the mark of civilization for a modern nation, and in Hegelian thinking national history, especially the heroic age in its antiquity, served to indicate the presence of the national spirit, which would guide peoples in their state formation.

In addition to the progression to nationhood from a heroic age in antiquity, history meant the presence and function of political institutions. In an evolutionary framework, peoples without history in the 'higher' national sense of the term were regarded as standing on a lower step of development. As stated by M. A. Castrén in his inaugural speech on being appointed to the chair of Finnish language in 1851, ethnography was the new science for the study of their history (Castrén 1857: 8; see also Vuorela 1977: 20; Isaksson 1997: 61; Pentikäinen 1997: 233; Isaksson 2001: 205). Instead of progression to nationhood, history in their context meant (evidence of) the continuation of immemorial oral traditions and traditional practices.

Finland as a 'Finnish' conception was in the first half of the 19$^{th}$ century considered by many intellectuals to lack a history of its own. One of these intellectuals was Zachris Topelius the younger, who in a public lecture in 1843 stated that a national history would require the self-consciousness of nationality and the existence of judicial and political institutions. According to Topelius (1845: 214–217), the Finnish people did not have these before 1809. Almost two decades earlier, the historian and philosopher J. J. Tengström had presented similar ideas but with reference to both Swedish and Finnish speakers (see Tengström 1931: 311–312). Even though Topelius changed his opinion and in many of his later literary works set out to depict 'Finnish' elements in pre-1809 history, the idea of the Finnish people – meaning the Finnish-speakers – lacking their own history remained influential. It is evident, for example, in the above-mentioned conceptualization of ethnography as a means to serve as the nation's history writing.

It is an unquestionable fact that the collecting of folk tradition has provided a significant share of cultural history where written history was lacking. Indeed, the value of folk poetry has since the 18$^{th}$ century been mainly placed on its ability to yield information on the history and culture of the common people. However, since history was in 19$^{th}$-century nationalism regarded as a major ingredient in making a people a nation, classifying the Finnish-speaking

Finns as a people without history in the 'higher' national (or Hegelian) sense of the term would go against the explicit political goal of making Finland a recognized national unit. Therefore, it was instrumental for the Hegelian-minded Fennomans to argue that the Finns (the Finnish speakers) have a national spirit and are able to create a 'national life'. In this project, ethnography on Finnish culture – in addition to providing the history of those who had no history – was expected to unearth the antique layers of the nation's 'childhood'. This antiquity, and the historical progression away from it, would then serve to legitimate the idea of Finland as a modern nation with history – a nation in which, in Hegelian terms, the agent-subject was the historically developed national spirit guiding individuals (see Karkama 1999).

Because of this political logic, Finnish ethnography and folklore collecting was not a mere quest for cultural survivals or the history of those without history. Neither was it a mere nostalgic project to collect emblems of tradition threatened to fall into oblivion, even though, as Seppo Knuuttila has pointed out, collectors and researchers of Finnish folklore have tended to engage in the rhetoric of decadence, locate themselves on the threshold of an ending era and witness the loss of immemorial traditions (Knuuttila 1994: 18–20). Despite the discourse on modernity as loss, Finnish ethnography has been committed to modernization, the spread of literacy and civilization, education and science, patriotic service of the modern nation-state – and to the use of these qualities as means of creating distinction.

Both this modernization and the related antiquation of Finnish language and tradition have been processes that set themselves against Matti Klinge's claim that Finnish national identity was built in the 19th century on landscape and poetry instead of history (e.g. Klinge 2003: 69). The romantic interest in landscapes and folk poetry appears to bypass and contradict history as the temporality of political institutions. Still, the image of the Finnish nation, in the Fennoman sense, was built upon a landscape of history that was regarded as opening up from Finnish-language folk poetry and its representations – even if this image was not in all details historically accurate. The in many ways modern (and antique) epic that Elias Lönnrot compiled from folk poetry was regarded as providing the nation with a history – as if from the perspective of the Finnish speakers. History in this context meant the nation's narrative or historical image about itself. At the same time this conveyed the idea that history comes in 'national packages', as national histories (see Wolf 1982). Since the *Kalevala* was looked upon as a narrative of a nation, as if depicting its genealogy in a manner familiar from Virgil's *Aeneid*, its existence was considered to prove Finland's nationness.

Among the many types of epics in the world, the *Kalevala* can be classified as a traditional one since the bulk of its contents correspond to the oral poetry on which its literary form is based. It serves to document some of the traditional folk poetry of the Finnish-speaking populations. Yet, at the same time it is a modern epic, since one of its major functions in the society in which it was published was to contribute to the production of national discourse on the basis of its traditionality. Since it was taken to suggest that Finland had an antiquity in its prehistory, it actually argued for contemporary

Finland's modernity. The link that it was said to create in time simultaneously stood for the distance between the Fennoman present and the past it imagined. The bygone-ness of the imagined antiquity was a central element in its social value, as it indicated historical movement. With antiquity in its past, the Finnish nation could be modern and develop further, unlike the peoples without history that were doomed to live in the past, in tradition, in absence of progress.

Such peoples were, among others, the Sámi, the Karelians and the Ingrians, who are both linguistic relatives and have lived on the margins of Finnishness. Unlike the Sámi, both the Karelians and Ingrians were integrated into Finnish nation making by giving them a role in representing Finnish antiquity (see also Tarkka 1989; Sihvo 1973: 356–357; Survo 2001). This antiquity did not provide them with history in the national – or the Hegelian – sense of the term. While Karelians, as characterized by Topelius, are "children who lag behind the Finns in national development" (quoted in Sihvo 1994: 28; see also Castrén 1857: 1–2), the Finns have a nation that has developed into a state. The 'kindred peoples' lack what is central to the definition of Finnishness: history, national development, modernity, and nation-state identity. Their culture points to the history of the (Finnish-speaking) Finns, but they are different from the Finns because they have stayed in that history.

It is noteworthy that when Topelius in 1843 gave a lecture on the question of whether the Finnish people have a history, he had regarded the (Finnish-speaking) Finns as political children. According to him, the Finnish people mentally constituted a nationality, but in their "thousand-year political childhood" they were unable to turn this unit into a state (Topelius 1845: 208, my translation[23]). The (Finnish-speaking) Finns were thus seen as being underdeveloped in the art of state formation. Later Topelius replaced the Finns with Karelians as such political children. This may be taken to speak for the very notion that the Fennomans vehemently opposed: that the historical development in the Finnish-speaking Finns' ability for state formation was due to the cultural influence of the Swedish speakers, thanks to the legacy of the Swedish rule (see e.g. Ahtiainen & Tervonen 1996: 34; Kemiläinen 1998: 160). In any case, Topelius emphasized that the historical progression of the Finns provides them with a leading position in 'their tribe' – that is, among all the peoples speaking languages related to Finnish (Tiitta 1994: 65; see also Isaksson 2001: 203).

Indeed, when political childhood is projected onto people in the periphery, the people in the center begin to look more advanced. The distancing and temporal othering of Karelia into a periphery of modernity made Finland the possessor of such a periphery. Such a strategy in constructing modernity is by no means unique to Finland. During the last two centuries, many instances of international and intra-national colonialism have shown that the possession of a non-modern periphery, and the power over its definition, makes the possessor modern and developed – and competitive in the modern category of nations (see e.g. Morris-Suzuki 1998: 17–34). In other words, tradition is put on display as an object of a modern gaze in order to make the subject of the gaze appear modern and as such, the possessor of the symbolic and political value of the objectified tradition. Finland is a good example of a discursive arena in which such displays are part of a competition over power, since the construction of the Finnish periphery has taken place in direct relationship with competing attempts at defining Finland as such a periphery. Timo Vihavainen gives an apt description of this:

> Nineteenth-century Russian scholars rather unanimously considered that the Kalevala reflected a very primitive state of society, where larger administrative and military units were absent. It did not, in their opinion, witness to an ability to create a state in the future either. For such Slavophiles as A. F. Hilferding and Nikolai Danilevsky, the conclusion was clear: the Finns were doomed to remain under Russian domination because they were not able to form a state. They also believed that the Finns were constitutionally unable to create a great culture of their own, but – this they benevolently granted – they could well be used as 'ethnographic material' for the Russian empire and thus contribute usefully to world history. (Vihavainen 1999: 120.)

This quotation shows how Russian intellectuals placed the (Finnish-speaking) Finns in an ethnographic framework that would have its theoretical and ideological premise in a clear distinction between the peripheral character of its objects, the members of an *ethnos*, and the modern and developed character of its subjects, the ethnographers, writers and other educated observers. It may appear ironical, but yet perfectly characteristic for ethnography that this was the same role that the Finnish ethnographers and other intellectuals were willing to impose on the Karelians, Ingrians and other 'kindred peoples' across the Russian border. The strong interest in heritage production within the kinfolk ideology has not been in opposition to the often paternalistic, patronizing or even colonizing approach in which Finnish ethnography has constructed its object. Instead, it has been another element or face in it. There are thus close similarities between Finnish and Russian intellectuals in the modern construction of periphery and the discourse on the role of folk tradition in conveying collective mental capacities in cultural production and political organization. The premises of argumentation are similar, but the political conclusions are quite different.

It may be necessary, however, to also consider the extent to which the Finnish discourse on Russian intellectuals' patronizing attitudes is a rhetorical construction of a foreign threat that presents Finland as an innocent victim – portrayed often as a maid in danger (see Valenius 2004: 132–163). In such constructions, Finnish folk tradition is given a role in national defense by allegedly providing proof of how mistaken those people are who have questioned the cultural skills of the Finnish-speaking Finns. Vihavainen's article serves as an example of the representation of the *Kalevala* epic as a product of a nation that speaks volumes for its cultural capacity:

> From the point of view of the 18th-century Enlightenment, the case of the Finns was rather discouraging. It was possible to maintain that this people had, during the course of history, produced nothing remarkable. (…) The Kalevala, appearing in the heyday of romantic thinking, changed everything at a single blow. (Vihavainen 1999: 119.)

## Finland is Modern by Having History

The idea of Finland having a history denoting both antiquity and progress is also present in the mid-20th century folklorist Martti Haavio's influential book *Viimeiset runonlaulajat* ('The Last Rune Singers'), which depicts in highly romantic fashion Karelian and Ingrian folk poetry and its individual performers. The book is filled with overwhelming nostalgia for a culture in decadence and its last representatives, but it can be argued that Haavio's main concern is not the nostalgic landscape of the dying culture *per se*, but the value that he sees in it for Finnish modernity and for Finland as a historical subject (see also Tarkka 1989: 244). The decadence that Haavio witnesses in Karelia and Ingria is not a loss for Finland as a nation-state. For Finland, it is a victory.

Haavio explicates this view by stating that the treasure Finland possesses in the folk poetry that Karelians and Ingrians have preserved for generations has helped Finland understand its antiquity and envisage its further historical development (Haavio 1985: 31, quoted also in Tarkka 1989: 244). This can be argued to show that even though Haavio includes the Karelian and Ingrian landscapes and people in the idea of Finnishness and the 'Finnish tribe', he also places them outside the modern national sphere of Finland. While Finland has antiquity in its past and progress ahead, the peoples that are seen to embody Finland's antiquity have only tradition – and now, in the decadence allegedly caused by diffusing traits of modernity and the Russification of their area of inhabitance, they face the inevitable loss of this tradition. They lack both modernity and progress and are soon to lose tradition. History for them is the continuation of indigenous traditions from generation to generation, as well as now their eventual loss, while for Finland history is a progressive movement from antiquity to the future.

As for M. A. Castrén and many other Finnish ethnographers after him, Finland for Haavio has a history that speaks for its status as a nation-state. Because of this status, Finnish patriotism draws a conceptual distinction vis-à-vis those that Finnish nationalism and the heritage political Finno-Ugric discourse symbolically unite. This puts the kinfolks' tradition, which the nation-state of Finland due to its development no longer has, in the role of an Other. One could say that it makes the kinfolk into 'sacred Others'; significant for the ancient history of the nation and its value in the sacralization of its mythology, but still set apart, distanced temporally and even placed on the same evolutionary level as nature and barbarism. (For discussions on such projections, see Tarkka 1989; Knuuttila 1994; Apo 1998[24]; for the concept of sacred, see V. Anttonen 1996 and 2000.) Speaking of the similar exoticization and mythologization of Ingrians, Arno Survo has characterized this aspect in Finnish ethnography as the nationalist production of a symbolic periphery (see Survo 2001: 26, 225–230).

In addition to making sacred peripheries, there have also been other methodological ways in which ethnography and folklore collecting have served to prove that Finnish culture is modern by having history – history as change, and as such, as a token of modernization. One of the main aspects in the emerging Finnish ethnography was both to study and further consolidate the relationship of Finnish language and culture with the rest of the Finno-Ugric family of languages. Comparing Finnish folk poetry with the ethnography on kindred peoples, M. A. Castrén concluded that Finnish poetry is abundant with "new materials and beliefs". According to the scientific methodology he established, the only way one can acquire a clear understanding of "the form of life of our ancestors" is to compare "the concepts to be found in Finnish folk poetry" with "the concepts of inter-related ethnic groups who had retained the purity of their original tribal characters" (Castrén 1857: 8; see also Vuorela 1977: 20; V. Anttonen 1987: 42). This tenet was eventually formulated into a "theory according to which kin relationship between different Finno-Ugric peoples was not based only on language, but other cultural factors as well. The theory implied that beliefs and practices that still prevail among technologically and socially 'less-developed' other Finno-Ugric peoples living in Russia and in Siberia can be used to shed light also on religious evolution among the Finns as well as among the Hungarians." (V. Anttonen 2005 forthcoming.)

The perceived loss of the 'original' forms in Finnish culture as well as of its 'tribal' characters has created a great deal of nostalgic rhetoric, but this loss has also served to indicate that contemporary Finnish culture – even among its own Finnish-speaking 'folk' – had undergone historical changes and has, therefore, been more modern than the culture of the Finnish speakers' linguistic relatives. In fact, the very act of doing ethnography and collecting folklore has proved the relative modernity of the Finns, especially when counting in the country's educated, Swedish-speaking elites. As I have written in Chapter 5, oral traditions do not become nationally symbolic merely by existing somewhere, but through their transformation into literature and literary collections, through their adaptation and entextualization into material objects of display to be preserved in nationally significant sites, such as archives, museums and universities.

Finland was relatively modern as early as the mid-19th century, since the institutions of education and cultural documentation were able to send out ethnographers to make comparative analyses among the traditional 'kinfolk'. They did not possess the necessary modern institutions, interests, funding or technology to engage in such activities. Until recently, they were not even expected to, as their role was to encounter the Western scholar from Finland in the framework of the close cultural affinity established between 'their tradition' and 'our prehistory'. The fieldwork conducted by the Fennoman-minded Uno Holmberg-Harva among the Udmurts in 1911 exemplifies well the denial of coevalness (see Fabian 1983) and the drawing of distinction. The fieldworker's (valid) historical interest in "unravelling the origin and development of early forms of religion among the peoples speaking Uralic languages" (V. Anttonen 2005 forthcoming) is justified by the conception that the Udmurts have lost their 'own tradition' due to the pressures of civilization (V. Anttonen 1987: 66). The same conception does not, however, apply to the fieldworker himself and the national entity that he represents. Even though he emphasizes a close cultural affinity and the existence of similar beliefs, these mark a temporal difference and denote progress for those for whom the affinity is prehistorical. Modernity is the privilege of the Westerner in search of links to nationalized prehistory in the landscape of non-modernity.

Anna-Leena Siikala has recently emphasized that the work of Elias Lönnrot and others who in the 19th century mapped Finnish language and cultural history must be viewed in the context of models deriving from the international tradition of ethnographic research expeditions (Siikala 2002b: 6–7; Siikala 2003). Siikala's point can well be seen as relating to one of the central factors that distinguish the Finns (both as Finnish speakers and as a national category that also includes the Swedish speakers) from the linguistic relatives they study as history and, in the discourses on cultural heritage, symbolically identify with.

The 'postmodern' conclusion to be drawn from this is that if there is a nationalistic or Fenno-centric 'story of Finland' to be promoted internationally, concerning the role of folk tradition in the making of the nation-state, it is a not a master narrative about an ethnonationalistic struggle and its victory, but a story that provides an account of the building up of modern democratic institutions, economic infrastructure, systems of comprehensive education, modernization of vernacular languages and the cultivation of civilization that, among other things, enhances and supports the practice of international ethnography and the related interest in the collecting of and studying representations of folk tradition. In the history of Finnish nation making, folklore has contributed to the construction of modern national identity as modern but antiqued cultural texts. The representation of these, as culture to be lost in modernization but valorized as the democratic heritage of the nation's Finnish speakers, has served the processes of state-making, democratization and national unification, but also those of national homogenization and the construction of ethnic and linguistic Others both within and around the national sphere.

The more recent process of Finland's participation in European integration and the expansion of the European Union can be regarded as being consistent with the country's nationalization and modernization. The persistent discourse on the Finno-Ugric heritage, for example, has not translated into political acts or agitation against EU membership or globalization. On the contrary, the Finno-Ugric discourse on heritage and antiquity contributes to the ideological role ascribed to the category of folk tradition as proof of the Finns' capability to become modern and European. This is radically different from the present-day situation in Hungary, where the Finno-Ugric linguistic theory and its cultural implications have come to be contested, especially in right-wing politics, as allegedly imposing on the Hungarians – first by the Habsburg regime and later by the Soviets – a belief in their primitive and non-European origins (The Controversy n.d.; Marsovszky n.d.; Marsovszky, personal communication, 2 June 2004). Instead of denoting the primitiveness of the present-day Finns, or linking their modern culture with Siberian hunter-gatherer nomads, the Finno-Ugric discourse in Finland rests on the antiquation of that heritage, which locates its foundation in the prehistory of the modern Finns. Thus, instead of tying Finns to their allegedly peripheral prehistory, representations of Finno-Ugric heritage discourse and mythology serve the national project of producing modern progress and distinction vis-à-vis the linguistic kin across the Russian border, and accordingly, the allignment of the country with the European political center.

This points directly to my main argument in this book, which is that in folkloristic discourse, tradition has not meant indigenous practices to be continued, preserved or revitalized, but instead, the concept has stood for representations of national antiquity that are to be valorized and nostalgized but also to be left behind in order to have them speak for a national capacity for historical progress towards statehood and modernity. Tradition has stood for reports and representations to be used for symbolic discourses with a modern political agenda. These symbolic and political discourses have then become some of the great traditions of nationalized modernity, signifying the ways in which tradition as both non-modern and modern cultural production has become not only accessible but also thinkable through modernity.

# *Notes*

1. 'Now' is a rather relative and elusive concept. The sense of 'modern' requires at least some permanence for the sense of 'now', but as pointed out by Ahmed Zewail, the shortest measurable unit of time, a nanosecond – one billionth of a second – has come and gone before we finish uttering the word 'now' (Zewail 2002: 2).

2. The broad and even boundless territory of folklore has come to serve for many folklorists as evidence of the discipline's vitality and of its central position in both academe and the rest of society. Some others have, however, felt that this has obscured the object of research (e.g. Virtanen 1993: 264). Barbara Kirshenblatt-Gimblett has noted that such terms as the folk group "live rhetorically", but "are dead analytically". "Attenuated to the point that *folk group* can refer to anyone, the notion is devoid of agency and analytic consequence, which is, of course, very consequential. Its sole purpose is to identify the enterprise as a folkloristic one." (Kirshenblatt-Gimblett 1998: 308.)

3. The transnational symbols that all nations are expected to have include the national anthem, the national flag, the national spirit, the national song, the national instrument, the national flower, etc. As regards the transnationalism of nationalism, it is also worth noting, as pointed out by Robert Foster (1991: 248) that the nation-state is a cultural form originally produced in Europe and then diffused throughout the world by processes of industrialization (see Gellner 1983), print-capitalism (see Anderson 1983), and colonialism (see Chatterjee 1986, 1993).

4. According to the American folklorist Alan Jabbour, "The word *folklore* conjures up many things to Americans. And no wonder: it compounds two venerable English words." (Jabbour 1988: 7.) During the 20th century in many non-English speaking countries, the term folklore replaced its diverse vernacular variants as the name of the academic discipline – for the apparent benefit gained in international standardization. That this constituted a novelty can also be taken as a metacomment on the discipline itself, as the foreignness of the term connotes modernity and presents the discipline as a stately modern enterprise.

5. Although the etymology of the word 'ecumene' leads to the religious concept of ecumenicalism, signifying unity and cooperation between the Christian churches, as a cultural concept it denotes regions of persistent interaction and exchange. Yet, as emphasized by Hannerz (1991: 107), an ecumene is not necessarily egalitarian but is made of centers and peripheries. Note how the previous name of the European Union monetary unit, the Ecu, an abbreviation of European Currency Unit and French for 'coat-of-arms' as well as 'coin', created a connotation through these symbolic and linguistic references of the idea of a European ecumene.

6. For an extensive historical study on the concept and idea of Europe, see Mikkeli 1994 and 1998. For discussion on the European Union and European identity, see e.g. *American Ethnologist* 1991; Macdonald 1993; Haller & Richter 1994; Delanty 1995; Wintle 1996; Anderson 2000; Shore 2000; *Ethnologia Europaea* 1999; *Etnologia Europaea* 2002.

7. For a discussion on localism and the production of culture and tradition on the margins of Scotland, see Nadel-Klein 1991; for a discussion on the making of folk culture in Newfoundland in the context of state policies and the world capitalist system, see Sider 1986.

8. Air and water travel across national boundaries, but water is international only in the concept of 'international waters', that is, water areas that lie beyond national boundaries and national water lines. Since air molecules cannot be nationalized on the basis of their place of origin, their travel across national boundaries is not regarded as an international event. Air is, therefore, international only in a metaphorical sense, denoting the atmosphere that people with different origins are felt to create when coming together.

9. The neutrality of statistics for showing 'plain figures' is often illusory. The above

number of the Sámi indicates only those who are registered as Sámi by language. When language is not the criteria, their number is estimated to be approximately 6,400 (Pentikäinen & Hiltunen 1997: 99) or 6,900 (Tuulentie 2001: 18, 78–79). The number of eligible voters in the Sámi Parliament elections in early October 1999 was 5,120. In the 2003 elections it was 5,147.

10  Regarding the same research agenda, see also Saukkonen 1998a: 220–222; Saukkonen 1999: 68–73, 116.

11  *Jus sanguinis* (law of blood) means the legal principle according to which a person's nationality is determined at birth by the nationality of his or her parents. In contrast, *jus soli* (law of soil) means the legal principle according to which a person's nationality is determined at birth by the territory in which he or she is born. Germany is a classic example of the former, the USA of the latter (see e.g. Alasuutari 1998: 159; Alasuutari & Ruuska 1999: 47–49).

12  The law that requires main applicants (but not dependants) to prove competence in either Finnish or Swedish came into force in 2003.

13  The act on the Sámi language from 1992 guarantees that Sámi may be used in legal proceedings as well as in state and municipal administration in the areas of the Sámi Homeland, where the Sámi have cultural autonomy.

14  After Finland became an independent state, Northern Norway, because of its Finnish-speaking population, was also within the desired extensions of Finland and Finnishness (see Ryymin 1998, 2003).

15  In 2002, according to the Official Government Server of the Republic of Karelia, 73,6% of the total population of 716,400 were Russians, 10% were Karelians, 3,6% Ukrainians, 2,3% Finns, 7% Belarusians and Vepps 0,8%. (Karelia n.d.)

16  Since the language manifesto of 1863, Finnish could be used when dealing with the authorities. From 1883 onwards civil servants were obliged to use Finnish when issuing documents, and in 1892 Finnish became an official language equal to Swedish. In 1906 Finnish became the first official language, placing Swedish second. After Finland gained independence as a state, the position of the Swedish language in society was guaranteed in the 1919 constitution and in the 1922 speech act. The Swedish language is not a minority language in legal terms, but a second national language besides Finnish.

17  The image of mutual bonding was shattered in the 1918 Civil War and in the political processes leading to it (see e.g. Sarajas 1962; Alapuro 1998; Apo 1998; Saukkonen 1999: 223–226). Yet, it has been reconstructed in the subsequent processes of creating national unity and homogeneity.

18  Homogeneity has also been valued negatively as indicating lack of variation in communicative signs (Tarasti 1990), lack of reflexivity and language play (Alapuro 1997b), and testifying to a low-context culture (Stenius 1995; Ehrnrooth 1996; Anttila 1993, 1996).

19  See e.g. Honko 1980: 42, 61; Apo 1998: 93; Apo, Nenola & Stark-Arola 1998: 16; Jääskeläinen 1998: 42; Karkama 2001: 240; Pentikäinen 1997: 233; Pentikäinen 1999b: 317–318; Siikala 1998: 194.

20  According to William Wilson, for example, the role of folk tradition has been decisive in establishing Finland as a sovereign political unit (Wilson 1976; see also Wilson 1998: 443–444). Lauri Honko has written that "In a way, Herder's wishful thinking came true in Finland. An epic created a nation." (Honko 2003: 8.)

21  The Fennoman movement by no means represented the perspectives of the entire population. The Swedish-speaking liberals, who were the main opponents of the Fennomans since the 1860s, opposed the idea of a dominant Finnish-language culture, and wanted to continue the Swedish cultural and political heritage in order to secure the consolidation of political institutions in Finland. While the Fennomans took many of their symbols of national unity from the *Kalevala* and other representations of folk poetry, the liberals established the Maiden of Finland (or the Finnish Maid) as the personification of Finland. This was adopted for much wider use than the Fennoman and national romantic *Kalevala* figures (see Reitala 1983; Valenius 2004).

22 Ulla-Maija Kulonen, Professor of Finno-Ugric Linguistics at the University of Helsinki, stated in her inauguration lecture in May 1999 (entitled, in English, 'At the Roots of Finnishness') that the study of the etymology, structure and development of Uralic languages increases our knowledge of the roots of our language and *the origin of our intangible heritage* (Kulonen 1999, my italics).

23 In the original Swedish text, Topelius writes that "finska folket har gått i tusenårig politisk barndom, utan att förmå i *staten* förverkliga den enhet, som andligen omslöt detsama i nationaliteten "(Topelius 1845: 208).

24 Some of this criticism has focused on blaming Haavio for not describing the performers of folk poetry as representatives of their own times, as ordinary agriculturalists, tenant farmers, cattle tenders, masters and mistresses or male and female farm aids, mothers and fathers – that is, as people falling more or less in the same category of human beings with Haavio (e.g. Apo 1998: 96). Viewing them through the imagery of Greek Antiquity as mediators of ancient heritage is, according to Apo, to distance them into representatives of Otherness.

# Sources

## Internet sources

Dyer, Gwynne 2001. A (Temporary) Love Affair With Death. *The Japan Times*. December 1, 2001. Tokyo, Japan. http://www.japantimes.com/cgi-bin/getarticle.pl5?eo20011201a2. htm. Last viewed 30 March 2004.

Fukuyama, Francis 2001. The West Has Won. Radical Islam can't beat democracy and capitalism. We're still at the end of history. In: *The Guardian*. October 11, 2001. http://www.guardian.co.uk/waronterror/story/0,1361,567333,00.html. Last viewed 30 March 2004.

Global Ethics n.d. http://www.globalethics.org/seminars/default.html. Last viewed 30 March 2004.

Haikonen, Jyrki & Kiljunen, Pentti 2003. Mitä mieltä, suomalainen? EVAn asenne-tutkimuksien kertomaa vuosilta 1984–2003. http://www.eva.fi/index.php?m=3&su bm=2&action=1&id=16. Last viewed 30 March 2004.

Horn, Frank. n.d. National Minorities of Finland. In: *Virtual Finland*. Produced by Ministry for Foreign Affairs of Finland. Department for Press and Culture/ Publications Unit. http://virtual.finland.fi/finfo/english/minorit.html. Last viewed 30 March 2004.

Interior Minister 2002. Interior Minister would simplify residence permit application process. http://www.helsinki-hs.net/news.asp?id=20020212IE8. Last viewed 30 March 2004.

Kalleinen, Kristiina 2002. Isänmaallisuuden, kielen ja kansallisuuden merkitys 1800-luvun alkupuolen suomalaiselle virkaylimystölle. *Ennen & nyt* 2/2002. http://www. ennenjanyt.net/2-02/kalleine.htm. Last viewed 30 March 2004.

Karelia n.d. http://www.gov.karelia.ru.gov/Different/karelia_e.html. Last viewed 19 November 2004.

Kiljunen, Pentti 2003. Vaatelias vaalikansa. Raportti suomalaisten asenteista 2003. http:// www.sci.fi/~pena/eva2002/sisluet.htm. Last viewed 30 March 2004.

Kulonen, Ulla-Maija 1999. Suomalaisuuden juurilla – kielitieteen tehtäviä ja keinoja (tiivistelmä). Virkaanastujaisluento 26.5.1999. http://www.helsinki.fi/hum/sugl/ kulonen/tiivistelma.htm. Last viewed 30 March 2004.

Küng, Hans 1993. Declaration of the Religions for a Global Ethic. http://astro.temple. edu/~dialogue/Center/kung.htm. Last viewed 30 September 2003.

Luddism 2002. Luddism and the Neo-Luddite Reaction 2002. University of Colorado at Denver. School of Education. http://carbon.cudenver.edu/~mryder/itc_data/luddite. html. Last viewed 30 March 2004.

Marsovszky, Magdalena n.d. The Ethnic Conception of Culture in Hungary. http://www. c3.hu/~ligal/ManaMagdalena5.html. Printed in *Culture Europe* (published by the Culture Europe Association) Nr. 38, 12/2002. Special Issue: Populist Right, Far Right and Culture. Last viewed 2 June 2004.

Peltonen, Arvo. n.d. The Population in Finland. In: *Virtual Finland*. http://virtual.finland. fi. Produced by Ministry for Foreign Affairs of Finland. Department for Press and Culture/ Publications Unit. http://virtual.finland.fi/finfo/english/populat.html. Last viewed 30 March 2004.

Savontaus, Marja-Liisa. n.d. Finnish Genes. In: *Virtual Finland*. Produced by Ministry for Foreign Affairs of Finland. Department for Press and Culture/ Publications Unit. http://virtual.finland.fi/finfo/english/geeneng.html. Last viewed 30 March 2004.

Statistics Finland. http://www.stat.fi/tk/tp/tasku/taskue_vaesto.html. Last viewed 11 September 2003.

The Controversy on the Origins and Early History of the Hungarians. http://www.hunmagyar. org/hungary/history/controve.htm#II.%20THE%20FINNO-UGRIAN%20THEORY. Last viewed 2 June 2004.

Uino, Pirjo. n.d. The Prehistory of Finland in a Nutshell. In: *Virtual Finland*. Produced by Ministry for Foreign Affairs of Finland. Department for Press and Culture/ Publications Unit. http://virtual.finland.fi/finfo/english/prehistory.html. Last viewed 30 March 2004.

Varpio, Yrjö 2002. 11. Jalo villi. http://www.uta.fi/laitokset/taide/opetus/suki_kurssi-materiaali/02-03/suuret_kertomukset/sk_a11.html. Last viewed 30 March 2004.

Wallgren, Thomas 1997. Emu ja infantiilin modernin loppu. http://www.kaapeli.fi/~veu/Thomas2.htm. Last viewed 19 November 2004.

# Literature

Abrahams, Roger D. 1964. *Deep Down in the Jungle...: Negro Narrative Folklore from the Streets of Philadelphia*. Hatboro, Pennsylvania: Folklore Associates.

Abrahams, Roger D. 1981. Shouting Match at the Border: The Folklore of Display Events. In: Richard Bauman and Roger D. Abrahams (eds.), *"And Other Neighborly Names": Social Processes and Cultural Image in Texas Folklore*. Pp. 303–321. Austin: University of Texas Press.

Abrahams, Roger D. 1985. Pragmatism and a Folklore of Experience. *Western Folklore* 44: 324–332.

Abrahams, Roger D. 1988. Rough Sincerities: William Wells Newell and the Discovery of Folklore in Late-19th Century America. In: Jane S. Becker & Barbara Franco (eds.), *Folk Roots, New Roots: Folklore in American Life*. Pp. 61–75. Lexington, Mass.: Museum of Our National Heritage.

Abrahams, Roger D. 1992a. The Past in the Presence: An Overview of Folkloristics in the Late 20th Century. In: Reimund Kvideland et al. (eds.), *Folklore Processed in Honour of Lauri Honko on his 60th Birthday 6th March 1992*. Studia Fennica Folkloristica 1. Pp. 32–51. Helsinki: Finnish Literature Society.

Abrahams, Roger D. 1992b. *Singing the Master: The Emergence of African American Culture in the Plantation South*. New York: Pantheon Books.

Abrahams, Roger D. 1993a. Phantoms of Romantic Nationalism in Folkloristics. *Journal of American Folklore* 106: 3–37.

Abrahams, Roger D. 1993b. After New Perspectives: Folklore Study in the Late Twentieth Century. *Western Folklore* 52 (2, 3, 4): 379–400. Special Issue. Theorizing Folklore: Toward New Perspectives on the Politics of Culture. Guest Editors: Charles Briggs and Amy Shuman.

Abrahams, Roger D. 1996. Historicizing Folklore in the Late Twentieth Century: The Place of Custom and Tradition in a Transnational World. *Suomen Antropologi* 21 (2): 23–28.

Abrahams, Roger D. 2000. Narratives of Location and Dislocation. In: *Folklore, Heritage Politics, and Ethnic Diversity: A Festschrift for Barbro Klein*. Edited by Pertti J. Anttonen in collaboration with Anna-Leena Siikala, Stein R. Mathisen and Leif Magnusson. Pp. 15–20. Botkyrka, Sweden: Multicultural Centre.

Adorno, Theodor W. 1991. *The Culture Industry: Selected Essays on Mass Culture*. Edited with an Introduction by J. M. Bernstein. London: Routledge.

Ahti, Martti 1999. *Ryssänvihassa. Elmo Kaila 1888-1935. Aktivistin, asevoimien harmaan eminenssin ja Akateemisen Karjala-Seuran puheenjohtajan elämäkerta*. Porvoo, Helsinki, Juva: Werner Söderström Osakeyhtiö.

Ahtiainen, Pekka & Tervonen, Jukka 1996. *Menneisyyden tutkijat ja metodien vartijat. Matka suomalaiseen historiankirjoitukseen*. Helsinki: Suomen Historiallinen Seura.

Ajami, Fouad 1996. The Summoning. In: *The Clash of Civilizations? The Debate*. Pp. 26–35. New York: Foreign Affairs.

Alanen, Aku & Eskelinen, Heikki 2000. Economic Gap at the Finnish-Russian Border. In: Pirkkoliisa Ahponen & Pirjo Jukarainen (eds.), *Tearing Down the Curtain, Opening the Gates: Northern Boundaries in Change*. SoPhi 54. Pp. 55–68. Jyväskylä: SoPhi, University of Jyväskylä.

Alapuro, Risto 1973. *Akateeminen Karjala-Seura. Ylioppilasliike ja kansa 1920- ja 1930-luvulla.* Porvoo, Helsinki: Werner Söderström Osakeyhtiö.

Alapuro, Risto 1982. Finland: An Interface Periphery. In: Stein Rokkan & Derek W. Urwin (eds.), *The Politics of Territorial Identification: Studies in European Regionalism.* Pp. 113–164. London: Sage Publications.

Alapuro, Risto 1997a. Kansallisuusliike ja valtio 1800-luvulla. In: Risto Alapuro, *Suomen älymystö Venäjän varjossa.* Pp. 13–24. (Article originally published in 1982.) Helsinki: Tammi.

Alapuro, Risto 1997b. Ensimmäinen ja toinen aste. In: Risto Alapuro, *Suomen älymystö Venäjän varjossa.* Pp. 184–191. (Article originally published in 1996.) Helsinki: Tammi.

Alapuro, Risto 1998. Sivistyneistön ambivalentti suomalaisuus. In: Pertti Alasuutari & Petri Ruuska (eds.), *Elävänä Euroopassa. Muuttuva suomalainen identiteetti.* Pp. 175–189. Tampere: Vastapaino.

Alapuro, Risto 1999. Social Classes and Nationalism: The North-East Baltic. In: Michael Branch (ed.), *National History and Identity: Approaches to the Writing of National History in the North-East Baltic Region Nineteenth and Twentieth Centuries.* Studia Fennica Ethnologica 6. Pp. 111–121. Helsinki: Finnish Literature Society.

Alapuro, Risto & Stenius, Henrik 1987. Kansanliikkeet loivat kansakunnan. In: Risto Alapuro, Ilkka Liikanen, Kerstin Smeds, Henrik Stenius (eds.), *Kansa liikkeessä.* Pp. 8–52. Helsinki: Kirjayhtymä.

Alasuutari, Pertti 1998. Älymystö ja kansakunta. In: Pertti Alasuutari & Petri Ruuska (eds.), *Elävänä Euroopassa. Muuttuva suomalainen identiteetti.* Pp. 153–174. Tampere: Vastapaino.

Alasuutari, Pertti & Ruuska, Petri (eds.) 1998. *Elävänä Euroopassa. Muuttuva suomalainen identiteetti.* Tampere: Vastapaino.

Alasuutari, Pertti & Ruuska, Petri 1999. *Post-patria? Globalisaation kulttuuri Suomessa.* Tampere: Vastapaino.

Alavuotunki, Jouni 1990. Miten J. V. Snellman suhtautui Venäjään suuren ulkomaanmatkansa aikana 1839–1842. In: Heikki Viitala (ed.) *Snellman, valtakunta ja keisarikunta.* Snellman-instituutin julkaisuja 10. Kuopio: Snellman-instituutti.

Albertsen, N. 1988. Postmodernism, Post-Fordism, and Critical Social Theory. *Environment and Planning D: Society and Space* 6: 339–365.

Alsmark, Gunnar 1982. Folktraditionens roll vid utformandet av nationell och regional identitet. In: Aili Nenola-Kallio (ed.), *Folktradition och regional identitet i Norden.* NIF Publications 12. Pp. 25–39. Turku: Nordiska institutet för folkdiktning.

Alver, Brynjulf 1979. Nationalism and Identity: Folklore and National Development. *NIF Newsletter* 2/1979 (vol. 7): 3–5.

Alver, Brynjulf 1980. Nasjonalisme og identitet. Folklore og nasjonal utvikling. In: Lauri Honko (ed.), *Folklore och nationsbyggandet i Norden.* NIF Publications No. 9. Pp. 5–16. Åbo: Nordiska institutet för folkdiktning.

*American Ethnologist* 1991. Representations of Europe: Transforming State, Society, and Identity. *American Ethnologist* 18 (3).

Amin, Ash 1997. Placing Globalization. *Theory, Culture & Society* 14 (2): 123–137.

Anderson, Benedict 1983. *Imagined Communities: Reflections on the Origin and Spread of Nationalism.* London: Verso.

Anderson, Malcolm 2000. *States and Nationalism in Europe since 1945.* London & New York: Routledge.

Anttila, Jorma 1993. Käsitykset suomalaisuudesta – traditionaalisuus ja modernisuus. In: Teppo Korhonen (ed.), *Mitä on suomalaisuus?* Pp. 108–134. Helsinki: Suomen Antropologinen Seura.

Anttila, Jorma 1996. Onko suomalaisuudessa samastumiskohteena mitään erityistä? In: Pekka Laaksonen & Sirkka-Liisa Mettomäki (eds.), *Olkaamme siis suomalaisia.* Kalevalaseuran vuosikirja 75–76. Pp. 201–210. Helsinki: Suomalaisen Kirjallisuuden Seura.

Anttonen, Pertti 1982a. Massakulttuuria vai uusia traditioita? *Kanava* 10 (8): 489–491.

Anttonen, Pertti 1982b. Kansanmusiikkia – elävänä tai kuolleena. *Suomalainen vuosikirja* 83: 46–60.

Anttonen, Albert [Pertti] 1985. Masskultur, motkultur eller nya traditioner? *Nord Nytt* 24: 28–34.

Anttonen, Pertti J. 1992. The Rites of Passage Revisited: A New Look at van Gennep's Theory of the Ritual Process and its Application in the Study of Finnish-Karelian Wedding Rituals. *Temenos* 28 (1992): 15–52.

Anttonen, Pertti J. 1994a. Ethnopoetic Analysis and Finnish Oral Verse. In: Anna-Leena Siikala & Sinikka Vakimo (eds.), *Songs Beyond the Kalevala: Transformations of Oral Poetry*. Studia Fennica Folkloristica 2. Pp. 113–137. Helsinki: Finnish Literature Society.

Anttonen, Pertti J. 1994b. Metaforer för värde och makt inom nordisk folkloristik. *Nord Nytt* 55 (1994): 5–22.

Anttonen, Pertti 1998. Seksistinen vitsi ja humoristisen kommunikaation poliittinen luonne. In: Jyrki Pöysä & Anna-Leena Siikala (eds.), *Amor, Genus & Familia. Kirjoituksia kansanperinteestä*. Tietolipas 158. Pp. 367–396. Helsinki: Suomalaisen Kirjallisuuden Seura.

Anttonen, Pertti 2002. Kalevala-eepos ja kansanrunouden kansallistaminen. In: Pekka Laaksonen & Ulla Piela (eds.), *Lönnrotin hengessä 2002*. Kalevalaseuran vuosikirja 81. Pp. 39–57. Helsinki: Suomalaisen Kirjallisuuden Seura.

Anttonen, Pertti 2003. The Perspective from Folklore Studies. *Oral Tradition* 18 (1): 116–117.

Anttonen, Pertti 2004a. Kalevala etnopoeettisesta näkökulmasta. In: Anna-Leena Siikala, Lauri Harvilahti & Senni Timonen (eds.), *Kalevala ja laulettu runo*. Pp. 375–394. Helsinki: Suomalaisen Kirjallisuuden Seura.

Anttonen, Pertti J. 2004b. A Catholic Martyr and Protestant Heritage: A Contested Site of Religiosity and its Representation in Contemporary Finland. In: Anna-Leena Siikala, Barbro Klein & Stein R. Mathisen (eds.), *Creating Diversities: Folklore, Religion and the Politics of Heritage*. Studia Fennica Folkloristica 14. Pp. 190–221. Helsinki: Finnish Literature Society.

Anttonen, Pertti & Kuusi, Matti 1999. *Kalevala-lipas. Uusi laitos*. Suomalaisen Kirjallisuuden Seuran Toimituksia 740. Helsinki: Suomalaisen Kirjallisuuden Seura.

Anttonen, Veikko 1987. *Uno Harva ja suomalainen uskontotiede*. Helsinki: Suomalaisen Kirjallisuuden Seura.

Anttonen, Veikko 1996. *Ihmisen ja maan rajat. 'Pyhä' kulttuurisena kategoriana*. (The Making of Corporeal and Territorial Boundaries: 'Sacred' as a Cultural Category). Helsinki: Suomalaisen Kirjallisuuden Seura.

Anttonen, Veikko 2000. Sacred. In: Willi Braun & Russell T. McCutcheon (eds.), *Guide to the Study of Religion*. Pp. 271–282. London & New York: Cassell.

Anttonen, Veikko 2005 forthcoming. Harva, Uno. In: *The Encyclopedia of Religion*. 2nd Edition. Editor-in-Chief: Lindsay Jones. New York: Macmillan.

Apo, Satu 1998. Suomalaisuuden stigmatisoinnin traditio. In: Pertti Alasuutari & Petri Ruuska (eds.), *Elävänä Euroopassa. Muuttuva suomalainen identiteetti*. Pp. 83–129. Tampere: Vastapaino.

Apo, Satu & Nenola, Aili & Stark-Arola, Laura 1998. Introduction. In: Satu Apo, Aili Nenola & Laura Stark-Arola (eds.), *Gender and Folklore: Perspectives on Finnish and Karelian Culture*. Studia Fennica Folkloristica 4. Pp. 9–27. Helsinki: Finnish Literature Society.

Appadurai, Arjun 1990. Disjuncture and Difference in the Global Cultural Economy. In: Mike Featherstone (ed.), Global *Culture: Nationalism, Globalization and Modernity*. A *Theory, Culture & Society* special issue. Pp. 295–310. London: Sage.

Appadurai, Arjun 1996. *Modernity at Large: Cultural Dimensions of Globalization*. Minneapolis: University of Minnesota Press.

Aris, Reinhold 1965. *History of Political Thought in Germany from 1789–1815*. New York: Russell & Russell.

Asad, Talad (ed.) 1973. *Anthropology and the Colonial Encounter*. London: Ithaca Press.

Babcock, Barbara 1980. Reflexivity: Definitions and Discriminations. *Semiotica* 30: 1–14.

Bacchilega, Cristina 1988. Folk and Literary Narrative in a Postmodern Context: The Case of Märchen. *Fabula* 29 (3/4): 302–316.

Bakhtin, M. M. 1981. *The Dialogic Imagination. Four Essays.* Translated by Caryl Emerson and Michael Holquist. Edited by Michael Holquist. Austin: University of Texas Press.

Baron, Robert & Spitzer, Nicholas R. (eds.) 1992. *Public Folklore.* Washington, D.C.: Smithsonian Institution Press.

Baudelaire, Charles 1989. Modernin elämän maalari. In: Jaakko Lintinen (ed.), *Modernin ulottuvuuksia. Fragmentteja modernista ja postmodernista.* Pp. 24–65. Helsinki: Kustannusosakeyhtiö Taide.

Baudrillard, Jean 1975. *The Mirror of Production.* St. Louis: Telos Press.

Baudrillard, Jean 1983a. *Simulations.* New York: Semiotext(e).

Baudrillard, Jean 1983b. *In the Shadow of the Silent Majorities, or The End of the Social and Other Essays.* New York: Semiotext(e).

Bauman, Richard 1972. Differential Identity and the Social Base of Folklore. In: Américo Paredes and Richard Bauman (eds.), *Toward New Perspectives in Folklore.* Pp. 33–41. Austin: University of Texas Press.

Bauman, Richard 1983. Folklore and the Forces of Modernity. *Folklore Forum* 16 (2): 153–158.

Bauman, Richard 1989. American Folklore Studies and Social Transformation: A Performance-Centered Perspective. *Text and Performance Quarterly* 9 (3): 175–184.

Bauman, Richard 2001. Tradition, Anthropology of. In: Neil J. Smelser & Paul B. Baltes (eds.), *International Encyclopedia of the Social and Behavioral Sciences*, Volume 23: 15819–15824. Amsterdam: Elsevier.

Bauman, Richard & Briggs, Charles L. 1990. Poetics and Performance as Critical Perspectives on Language and Social Life. *Annual Review of Anthropology* 19: 59–88.

Bauman, Richard & Briggs, Charles L. 2003. *Voices of Modernity: Language Ideologies and the Politics of Inequality.* Cambridge & New York: Cambridge University Press.

Bauman, Zygmunt 1991. *Modernity and Ambivalence.* Cambridge: Polity Press.

Bausinger, Hermann 1990 [1961]. *Folk Culture in a World of Technology.* Translated by Elke Dettmer. Bloomington: Indiana University Press.

Bazegski, Dimitri & Laine, Antti 2000. Trade and Population Development across the Finnish-Russian Border. In: Pirkkoliisa Ahponen & Pirjo Jukarainen (eds.), *Tearing Down the Curtain, Opening the Gates: Northern Boundaries in Change.* SoPhi 54. Pp. 38–54. Jyväskylä: SoPhi, University of Jyväskylä.

Becker, Jane S. 1988. Revealing Traditions: The Politics of Culture and Community in America, 1988–1988. In: Jane S. Becker & Barbara Franco (eds.), *Folk Roots, New Roots: Folklore in American Life.* Pp. 19–60. Lexington, Mass.: Museum of Our National Heritage.

Bell, Daniel 1976. *The Coming of Post-Industrial Society: A Venture in Social Forecasting.* New York: Basic Books.

Belmont, Nicole 1986. Le Folklore refoulé, ou les séductions de l'archaisme. *L'homme* XXVI, 97–98 (1–2): 259–268.

Ben-Amos, Dan 1972. Toward a Definition of Folklore in Context. In: Américo Paredes and Richard Bauman (eds.), *Toward New Perspectives in Folklore.* Pp. 1–15. Austin: University of Texas Press.

Ben-Amos, Dan 1984. The Seven Strands of Tradition: Varieties in Its Meaning in American Folklore Studies. *Journal of Folklore Research* 21 (2/3): 97–131.

Ben-Amos, Dan 1989. Foreword. In: Reimund Kvideland and Henning K. Sehmsdorf (eds.), *Nordic Folklore: Recent Studies.* Pp. vii–x. Bloomington: Indiana University Press.

Ben-Amos, Dan 1990. Foreword. In: Hermann Bausinger, *Folk Culture in a World of Technology*. Pp. vii–x. Bloomington: Indiana University Press.

Ben-Amos, Dan 1998. The Name is the Thing. *Journal of American Folklore* 111 (441): 257–280.

Bendix, Regina 1992. Diverging Paths in the Scientific Search for Authenticity. *Journal of Folklore Research* 29 (2): 103–132.

Bendix, Regina 1997. *In Search of Authenticity: The Formation of Folklore Studies*. Madison: University of Wisconsin Press.

Bendix, Regina 1998. Of Names, Professional Identities, and Disciplinary Futures. *Journal of American Folklore* 111 (441): 235–246.

Bendix, Regina 2000. Heredity, Hybridity and Heritage from One *Fin de Siècle* to the Next. In: *Folklore, Heritage Politics, and Ethnic Diversity: A Festschrift for Barbro Klein*. Edited by Pertti J. Anttonen in collaboration with Anna-Leena Siikala, Stein R. Mathisen and Leif Magnusson. Pp. 37–54. Botkyrka, Sweden: Multicultural Centre.

Bendix, Regina 2002. The Uses of Disciplinary History. *Radical History Review*. Issue 84 (fall 2002): 110–114.

Bendix, Regina & Klein, Barbro 1993. Foreigners and Foreignness in Europe: Expressive Culture in Transcultural Encounters. Introduction. *Journal of Folklore Research* 30 (1): 1–14. Special Issue. Foreigners and Foreignness in Europe: Expressive Culture in Transcultural Encounters. Special Issue Editors: Regina Bendix and Barbro Klein.

Benjamin, Walter 1992. *Illuminations*. Edited with an Introduction by Hannah Arendt. Translated by Harry Zohn. London: Fontana Press/HarperCollins.

Berman, Marshall 1982. *All That is Solid Melts into Air: The Experience of Modernity*. London: Verso.

Bernstein, J. M. 1991. Introduction. In: Theodor W. Adorno, *The Culture Industry: Selected Essays on Mass Culture*. Edited with an Introduction by J. M. Bernstein. Pp. 1–25. London: Routledge.

Bernstein, Richard 1986. *Philosophical Profiles*. Philadelphia: University of Pennsylvania Press.

Bhabha, Homi K. 1994. *The Location of Culture*. London and New York: Routledge.

Birch, Anthony H. 1989. *Nationalism and National Integration*. London: Unwin Hyman.

Björn, Ismo 1993. *Ryssät ruotsien keskellä. Ilomantsin ortodoksit ja luterilaiset 1700-luvun puolivälistä 1800-luvun puoliväliin*. Karjalan tutkimuslaitoksen julkaisuja 106. Joensuu: Joensuun yliopisto, Karjalan tutkimuslaitos.

Blain, Neil & Boyle, Raymond & O'Donnell, Hugh 1993. *Sport and National Identity in the European Media*. Leicester: Leicester University Press.

Blommaert, Jan & Verschueren, Jef 1998. The Role of Language in European Nationalist Ideologies. In: Bambi Schieffelin, Kathryn A. Woolard, Paul V. Kroskrity (eds.), *Language Ideologies: Practice and Theory*. Pp. 189–210. New York & Oxford: Oxford University Press.

Blomstedt, Yrjö 1980. Yrjö Koskinen historioitsijana. *Historiallinen aikakauskirja* 4/1980: 299–306.

Boyer, Pascal 1990. *Tradition as Truth and Communication: A Cognitive Description of Traditional Discourse*. Cambridge: Cambridge University Press.

Bradley, Harriet 2000. Changing Social Structures: Class and Gender. In: Stuart Hall, David Held, Ron Hubert, and Kenneth Thompson (eds.), *Modernity: An Introduction to Modern Societies*. Pp. 122–148. Oxford: Blackwell Publishers.

Branch, Michael 1993. The Finno-Ugrian Peoples. In: Lauri Honko, Senni Timonen and Michael Branch, *The Great Bear: A Thematic Anthology of Oral Poetry in the Finno-Ugrian Languages*. Finnish Literature Society Editions 533. Pp. 25–41. Helsinki: Finnish Literature Society.

Breckenridge, Carol A. & van deer Veer, Peter (eds.) 1993. *Orientalism and the Postcolonial Predicament: Perspectives on South Asia*. Philadelphia: University of Pennsylvania Press.

Brednikova, Olga 2000. From Soviet 'Iron Curtain' to Post-Soviet 'Window to Europe'. In: Pirkkoliisa Ahponen & Pirjo Jukarainen (eds.), *Tearing Down the Curtain, Opening the Gates: Northern Boundaries in Change*. SoPhi 54. Pp. 25–37. Jyväskylä: SoPhi, University of Jyväskylä.

Briggs, Charles L. 1986. *Learning How To Ask: A Sociolinguistic Appraisal of the Use of the Interview in Social Science Research*. Cambridge: Cambridge University Press.

Briggs, Charles L. 1988. *Competence in Performance: The Creativity of Tradition in Mexicano Verbal Art*. Philadelphia: University of Pennsylvania Press.

Briggs, Charles L. 1993. Metadiscursive Practices and Scholarly Authority in Folkloristics. *Journal of American Folklore* 106: 387–434.

Briggs, Charles L. 1996. The Politics of Discursive Authority in Research on the 'Invention of Tradition'. *Cultural Anthropology* 11 (4): 435–469.

Briggs, Charles L. and Bauman, Richard 1992. Genre, Intertextuality, and Social Power. *Journal of Linguistic Anthropology* 2 (2): 131–172.

Briggs, Charles and Shuman, Amy (eds.) 1993. Theorizing Folklore: Toward New Perspectives on the Politics of Culture. Special Issue. *Western Folklore* 52 (2, 3, 4).

Brück, Ulla 1988. Identity, Local Community and Local Identity. In: Lauri Honko (ed.), *Tradition and Cultural Identity*. Pp. 77–92. Turku: Nordic Institute of Folklore.

Bryan, Dominic 2000. *Orange Parades: The Politics of Ritual, Tradition and Control*. London: Pluto Press.

Bryan, Dominic n.d.. 'The Right to March': Parading a Loyal Protestant Identity in Northern Ireland. Paper presented at the Seminar 'Les Heros Nationaux: Construction et Deconstruction', April 1, 1996 in Dresden, Germany. Manuscript.

Burke, Peter 1992. We, the People: Popular Culture and Popular Identity in Modern Europe. In: Scott Lash and Jonathan Friedman (eds.), *Modernity and Identity*. Pp. 293–308. Oxford, UK & Cambridge, USA: Blackwell.

Bustin, Dillon 1988. New England Prologue: Thoreau, Antimodernism, and Folk Culture. In: Jane S. Becker & Barbara Franco (eds.), *Folk Roots, New Roots: Folklore in American Life*. Pp. 1–6. Lexington, Mass.: Museum of Our National Heritage.

Calhoun, Craig 1993. Postmodernism as Pseudohistory. *Theory, Culture & Society* 10: 75–96.

Calinescu, Matei 1987. *Five Faces of Modernity: Modernism, Avant-Garde, Decadence, Kitsch, Postmodernism*. Durham, N.C.: Duke University Press.

Castells, Manuel 1996. *The Rise of the Network Society*. Cambridge, MA & Oxford, UK: Blackwell.

Castrén, M. A. 1857. *Nordiska resor och forskningar. 4: Ethnologiska föreläsningar öfver altaiska folken*. Helsingfors: Finska Litteratur-Sällskapets tryckeri.

Chakrabarty, Dipesh 2000. *Provincializing Europe: Postcolonial Thought and Historical Difference*. Princeton, N.J.: Princeton University Press.

Chatterjee, Partha 1986. *Nationalist Thought and the Colonial World: A Derivative Discourse?* London: Zed Books.

Chatterjee, Partha 1993. *The Nation and its Fragments: Colonial and Postcolonial Histories*. Princeton, N.J.: Princeton University Press.

Cirese, Alberto Maria 1982. Gramsci's Observations on Folklore. In: Anne Sowstack Sassoon (ed.), *Approaches to Gramsci*. Pp. 212–247. London: Writers and Readers.

Čistov, K. V. 1976. *Venäläinen perinnekulttuuri. Neuvostoliiton Pohjois-Euroopan venäläisväestön etnologiaa 1800-luvulta 1900-luvun alkuun*. Suomentanut Marjatta Ryynänen. Suomalaisen Kirjallisuuden Seuran Toimituksia 322. Helsinki: Suomalaisen Kirjallisuuden Seura.

Clifford, James 1986. On Ethnographic Allegory. In: James Clifford & George E. Marcus (eds.), *Writing Culture: The Poetics and Politics of Ethnography*. Pp. 98–121. Berkeley: University of California Press.

Clifford, James 1988a. Introduction: The Pure Products Go Crazy. In: James Clifford, *The Predicament of Culture*. Pp. 1–17. Cambridge: Harvard University Press.

Clifford, James 1988b. On Ethnographic Authority. In: James Clifford, *The Predicament of Culture*. Pp. 21–54. Cambridge: Harvard University Press.

Clifford, James 1988c. On Collecting Art and Culture. In: James Clifford, *The Predicament of Culture*. Pp. 215–251. Cambridge: Harvard University Press.

Clifford, James & Marcus, George E. (eds.) 1986. *Writing Culture: The Poetics and Politics of Ethnography*. Berkeley: University of California Press.

Cocchiara, Giuseppe 1981. *The History of Folklore in Europe*. Translated from the Italian by John N. McDaniel. Philadelphia: Institute for the Study of Human Issues.

Cohen, Anthony P. 1985. *The Symbolic Construction of Community*. Chichester and London: Ellis Horwood Limited & Tavistock Publications Limited.

Collins, Randall 1992. The Rise and Fall of Modernism in Politics and Religion. *Acta Sociologica* 35 (3): 171–186.

Collins, Randall 1994. *Four Sociological Traditions*. New York & Oxford: Oxford University Press.

Crapanzano, Vincent 1980. *Tuhami: Portrait of a Moroccan*. Chicago: University of Chicago Press.

Crapanzano, Vincent 1990. On Dialogue. In: Tullio Maranhão (ed.), *The Interpretation of Dialogue*. Pp. 269–291. Chicago: University of Chicago Press.

Crapanzano, Vincent 1992. *Hermes' Dilemma and Hamlet's Desire: On the Epistemology of Interpretation*. Cambridge: Harvard University Press.

Cronberg, Tarja 2000. Euregios in the Making: The Case of Euregio Karelia. In: Pirkkoliisa Ahponen & Pirjo Jukarainen (eds.), *Tearing Down the Curtain, Opening the Gates: Northern Boundaries in Change*. SoPhi 54. Pp. 170–183. Jyväskylä: SoPhi, University of Jyväskylä.

Dalton, Russel J. & Kuechler, Manfred (eds.) 1990. *Challenging the Political Order*. New York: Oxford University Press.

Damsholt, Tine 1995. On the Concept of the 'Folk'. *Ethnologia Scandinavica* 25: 5–24. Also available at: http://www.etn.lu.se/ethscand/text/1995/1995_5–24.PDF

DeJean, Joan 1997. *Ancients against Moderns: Culture Wars and the Making of a* Fin de Siècle. Chicago: University of Chicago Press.

Delanty, Gerard 1995. *Inventing Europe: Idea, Identity, Reality*. London: Macmillan.

Derrida, Jacques 1976. *Of Grammatology*. Translated by G. Spivak. Baltimore: Johns Hopkins University Press.

Derrida, Jacques 1981. *Dissemination*. Translated by B. Johnson. Chicago: University of Chicago Press.

Dick, Ernst S. 1989. The Folk and their Culture: The Formative Concepts and the Beginnings of Culture. In: Robert J. Smith & Jerry Stannard (eds.), *The Folk: Identity, Landscapes and Lores*. University of Kansas Publications in Anthropology 17. Pp. 11–28. Lawrence, Kansas: University of Kansas, Department of Anthropology.

Dominguez, Virginia 1986. The Marketing of Heritage. *American Ethnologist* 13 (3): 546–555.

Dorson, Richard 1950. Folklore and Fakelore. *American Mercury* 70: 335–343.

Dorson, Richard M. 1959. *American Folklore*. Chicago: Chicago University Press.

Dorson, Richard M. 1968. *The British Folklorists: A History*. Chicago: University of Chicago Press.

Dorson, Richard M. (ed.) 1978. *Folklore in the Modern World*. The Hague: Mouton.

Dorst, John 1988. Postmodernism vs. Postmodernity: Implications for Folklore Studies. *Folklore Forum* 21(2): 216–220.

Dorst, John 1990. Tags and Burners, Cycles and Networks: Folklore in the Teletronic Age. *Journal of Folklore Research* 27 (3): 179–190.

Dundes, Alan 1965. What is Folklore? In: Alan Dundes (ed.), *The Study of Folklore*. Pp. 1–3. Englewood Cliffs, N.J.: Prentice-Hall, Inc.

Dundes, Alan 1966. The American Concept of Folklore. *Journal of the Folklore Institute* 3: 226–249.

Dundes, Alan 1969. The Devolutionary Premise in Folklore Theory. *Journal of the Folklore Institute* 6: 5–19.

Dundes, Alan 1977. Who Are the Folk? In: William R. Bascom (ed.), *Frontiers of Folklore*. Pp. 17–35. Boulder, Colorado: Westview Press.

Duranti, Alessandro 1993. Truth and Intentionality: An Ethnographic Critique. *Cultural Anthropology* 8 (2): 214–245.

During, Simon 1994. Rousseau's Patrimony: Primitivism, Romance and Becoming Other. In: Francis Baker, Peter Hulme and Margaret Iversen (eds.), *Colonial Discourse / Postcolonial Theory*. Pp. 47–71. Manchester and New York: Manchester University Press.

Eco, Umberto 1986. *Travels in Hyper-Reality*. London: Picador.

Edmondson, Ricca 1984. *Rhetoric in Sociology*. Foreword by Anthony Heath. London: Macmillan.

Ehrnrooth, Jari 1996. Suomalainen itsetutkiskelu. In: Pekka Laaksonen & Sirkka-Liisa Mettomäki (eds.), *Olkaamme siis suomalaisia*. Kalevalaseuran vuosikirja 75–76. Pp. 237–243. Helsinki: Suomalaisen Kirjallisuuden Seura.

Eisenstadt, S. N. 1974. Post-Traditional Societies and the Continuity and Reconstruction of Tradition. In: S. N. Eisenstadt (ed.), *Post-Traditional Societies*. Pp. 1–28. New York: W. W. Norton & Company Inc.

Elkins, David J. 1997. Globalization, Telecommunications, and Virtual Ethnic Communities. *International Political Science Review* 18 (2): 139–152.

Engman, Max 1999. The Finland-Swedes: A Case of a Failed National History? In: Michael Branch (ed.), *National History and Identity: Approaches to the Writing of National History in the North-East Baltic Region Nineteenth and Twentieth Centuries*. Studia Fennica Ethnologica 6. Pp. 166–177. Helsinki: Finnish Literature Society.

Eriksen, Anne 1993. Den nasjonale kulturarven – en del av det moderne. *Kulturella perspektiv* 1/1993: 16–25.

Ervasti, A(ugust) V(ilhelm) 1884. *Suomalaiset Jäämeren rannalla. Matkamuistelmia*. Oulu: Wickström ja k.

*Ethnologia Europaea* 1999. Europe as a Cultural Construction and Reality. *Ethnologia Europaea. Journal of European Ethnology* 29 (2).

*Ethnologia Europaea* 2002. Getting Europe into Place. *Ethnologia Europaea. Journal of European Ethnology* 32 (2).

Fabian, Johannes 1983. *Time and the Other: How Anthropology Makes Its Object*. New York: Columbia University Press.

Featherstone, Mike 1987. Lifestyle and Consumer Culture. *Theory, Culture & Society* 4: 55–70.

Featherstone, Mike 1989. Towards a Sociology of Postmodern Culture. In: Hans Haferkamp (ed.), *Social Structure and Culture*. Pp. 147–172. Berlin and New York: Walter de Gruyter.

Featherstone, Mike (ed.) 1990. *Global Culture: Nationalism, Globalization and Modernity. A Theory, Culture & Society* special issue. London: Sage.

Featherstone, Mike & Lash, Scott & Robertson, Roland (eds.) 1995. *Global Modernities*. London: Sage.

Fernandez, James W. 1985. Folklorists as Agents of Nationalism: Legends Asturian Mountain Villagers Tell Themselves (and others) About Themselves and the Problem of Local, Regional and National Identity. *New York Folklore*. 40th Anniversary Issue. XI (1–4): 135–147.

Finnegan, Ruth 1991. Tradition, But What Tradition and For Whom? *Oral Tradition* 6 (1): 104–124.

Fiske, John 1987. *Television Culture*. London: Methuen.

Fiske, John 1989. *Reading the Popular*. Boston: Unwin Hyman.

Forsander, Annika 1999. Outsiders or Insiders? Ingrian Finns in a Context of the Finnish Immigration Policy. In: Maarit Leskelä (ed.), *Outsiders or Insiders? Constructing Identities in an Integrating Europe*. Publications of the Doctoral Program on Cultural Interaction and Integration 4. Pp. 52–73. Turku: University of Turku.

Foster, Robert J. 1991. Making National Cultures in the Global Ecumene. *Annual Review of Anthropology* 20: 235–260.

Foster, Stephen William 1982. The Exotic as a Symbolic System. *Dialectical Anthropology* 7 (1): 21–30.

189

Foucault, Michel 1972. *The Archaeology of Knowledge and the Discourse on Language*. Translated from the French by A. M. Sheridan Smith. New York: Pantheon Books.

Foucault, Michel 1980. *Power/Knowledge: Selected Interviews and Other Writings, 1972–1977*. Translated by Colin Gordon et al. New York: Pantheon Books.

Fox, Jennifer 1987. The Creator Gods: Romantic Nationalism and the En-genderment of Women in Folklore. *Journal of American Folklore* 100 (398): 563–572.

Freud, Sigmund 1962. *Civilization and its Discontents*. New translation and edited by James Strachey. New York: Morton.

Friedman, Jonathan 1988. Cultural Logics of the Global System: A Sketch. *Theory, Culture & Society* 5: 447–460.

Friedman, Jonathan 1992a. Narcissism, Roots and Postmodernity: The Constitution of Selfhood in the Global Crisis. In: Scott Lash & Jonathan Friedman (eds.), *Modernity and Identity*. Pp. 331–366. Oxford: Blackwell.

Friedman, Jonathan 1992b. The Past in the Future: History and the Politics of Identity. *American Anthropologist* 94 (4): 837–859.

Friedman, Jonathan 1994a. General Historical and Culturally Specific Properties of Global Systems. In: Jonathan Friedman, *Cultural Identity and Global Process*. 15–41. London: Sage.

Friedman, Jonathan 1994b. History and the Politics of Identity. In: Jonathan Friedman, *Cultural Identity and Global Process*. Pp. 117–146. London: Sage. A revised version of 'The Past in the Future: History and the Politics of Identity', published in *American Anthropologist* 94 (4): 837–859 (1992).

Frykman, Jonas 1979. Ideologikritik av arkivsystemen. *Norveg* 22: 231–242.

Frykman, Jonas 1995. The Informalization of National Identity. *Ethnologia Europaea* 25: 5–15.

Frykman, Jonas & Löfgren, Orvar (eds.) 1985. *Modärna tider: vision och vardag i folkhemmet*. Malmö: Liber.

Gadamer, Hans-Georg 1975. *Truth and Method*. New York: The Seabury Press.

Gadamer, Hans-Georg 1976. *Philosophical Hermeneutics*. Berkeley: University of California Press.

García Canclini, Néstor 1995. *Hybrid Cultures: Strategies for Entering and Leaving Modernity*. Translated by Christopher L. Chiappari and Silvia L. Lopéz. Minneapolis: University of Minnesota Press.

García Canclini, Néstor 2001. *Consumers and Citizens: Globalization and Multicultural Conflicts*. Translated and with an Introduction by George Yúdice. Minneapolis: University of Minnesota Press.

Gaunt, David 1992. Ethnic Relations in the Swedish Empire 1000–1800. In: Åke Daun, Billy Ehn & Barbro Klein (eds.), *To Make the World Safe for Diversity: Towards an Understanding of Multi-Cultural Societies*. Pp. 145–161. Stockholm: The Swedish Immigration Institute and Museum & The Ethnology Institute, Stockholm University.

Geertz, Clifford 1973. *The Interpretation of Cultures*. New York: Basic Books.

Geertz, Clifford 1980. Blurred Genres: The Refiguration of Social Thought. *The American Scholar* 49: 165–183.

Gellner, Ernest 1983. *Nations and Nationalism*. Oxford: Basil Blackwell.

Giddens, Anthony 1994. Living in a Post-Traditional Society. In: Ulrich Beck, Anthony Giddens, Scott Lash, *Reflexive Modernization: Politics, Tradition and Aesthetics in the Modern Social Order*. Pp. 56–109. Cambridge: Polity Press.

Gidlund, Janerik & Sörlin, Sverker 1993. *Det europeiska kalejdoskopet*. Stockholm: SNS Förlag.

Gilroy, Paul 1995. *The Black Atlantic: Modernity and Double Consciousness*. London: Verso.

Glassie, Henry 1983. The Moral Lore of Folklore. *Folklore Forum* 16 (2): 123–151.

Glassie, Henry 1988. Postmodernism. *Folklore Forum* 21 (2): 221–224.

Glassie, Henry 1995. Tradition. *Journal of American Folklore* 108 (430): 395–412.

Goffman, Erving 1959. *The Presentation of Self in Everyday Life*. New York: Doubleday.

190

Goffman, Erving 1974. *Frame Analysis: An Essay on the Organization of Experience*. New York: Harper & Row.

Goffman, Erving 1981. *Forms of Talk*. Philadelphia: University of Pennsylvania Press.

Gregory, Derek & Urry, John (eds.) 1985. *Social Relations and Spatial Structures*. London: Macmillan.

Haavio, Martti 1985 (1943). *Viimeiset runonlaulajat*. Third edition 1985. Porvoo & Helsinki: WSOY.

Habermas, Jürgen 1981. Modernity versus Postmodernity. *New German Critique* 22: 3–14.

Habermas, Jürgen 1984. *The Theory of Communicative Action, Vol. 1: Reason and Rationalization of Society*. Translated by Thomas McCarthy. Boston: Beacon Press.

Habermas, Jürgen 1989. *The New Conservatism, Cultural Criticism and the Historian's Debate*. Edited and translated by S. Nicholsen. Cambridge, Mass.: The MIT Press.

Haferkamp, Hans 1987. Beyond the Iron Cage of Modernity? Achievement, Negotiation and Changes in the Power Structure. *Theory, Culture & Society* 4: 31–54.

Hakamies, Pekka 2004. Finns in Russia, Russians in Finland: Remigration and the Problem of Identity. In: Anna-Leena Siikala, Barbro Klein & Stein R. Mathisen (eds.), *Creating Diversities: Folklore, Religion and the Politics of Heritage*. Studia Fennica Folkloristica 14. Pp. 43–53. Helsinki: Finnish Literature Society.

Hall, Stuart 1992. Introduction. In: Stuart Hall and Bram Gieben (eds.), *Formations of Modernity*. Pp. 1–16. Cambridge: Polity Press in Association with the Open University.

Hall, Stuart 2000a. Introduction. In: Stuart Hall, David Held, Ron Hubert, and Kenneth Thompson (eds.), *Modernity: An Introduction to Modern Societies*. Pp. 3–18. Oxford: Blackwell Publishers.

Hall, Stuart 2000b. The West and the Rest: Discourse and Power. In: Stuart Hall, David Held, Ron Hubert, and Kenneth Thompson (eds.), *Modernity: An Introduction to Modern Societies*. Pp. 184–227. Oxford: Blackwell Publishers.

Hall, Stuart & Held, David & McLennan, Gregor 2000. Introduction. In: Stuart Hall, David Held, Ron Hubert, and Kenneth Thompson (eds.), *Modernity: An Introduction to Modern Societies*. Pp. 425–435. Oxford: Blackwell Publishers.

Haller, Max & Richter, Rudolf (eds.) 1994. *Toward a European Nation? Political Trends in Europe – East and West, Center and Periphery*. New York: M.E. Sharpe.

Hamilton, Peter 2000. The Enlightenment and the Birth of Social Science. In: Stuart Hall, David Held, Ron Hubert, and Kenneth Thompson (eds.), *Modernity: An Introduction to Modern Societies*. Pp. 19–54. Oxford: Blackwell Publishers.

Handler, Richard & Linnekin, Jocelyn 1984. Tradition, Genuine or Spurious. *Journal of American Folklore* 97: 273–288.

Hannerz, Ulf 1990. Cosmopolitans and Locals in World Culture. In: Mike Featherstone (ed.), *Global Culture: Nationalism, Globalization and Modernity. A Theory, Culture & Society* special issue. Pp. 237–251. London: Sage.

Hannerz, Ulf 1991. Scenarios for Peripheral Cultures. In: Anthony D. King (ed.), *Culture, Globalization and the World-System: Contemporary Conditions for the Representation of Identity*. Pp. 107–128. London: Macmillan in association with Department of Art and Art History, State University of New York at Binghamton.

Hannerz, Ulf 1993. The Withering Away of the Nation? An Afterword. *Ethnos* 1993 (3–4): 377–391.

Hannerz, Ulf & Löfgren, Orvar 1992. Nationen i den globala byn. *Kulturella perspektiv* 1/1992: 21–29.

Hanson Paul W. 1993. Reconceiving the Shape of Culture: Folklore and Public Culture. *Western Folklore* 52 (2, 3, 4): 327–344. Special Issue. Theorizing Folklore: Toward New Perspectives on the Politics of Culture. Guest Editors: Charles Briggs and Amy Shuman.

Harlow, Ilana 1998. Introduction. *Journal of American Folklore* 111 (441): 231–234.

Harvey, David 1989. *The Condition of Postmodernity: An Inquiry into the Origins of Cultural Change*. Oxford: Blackwell.

191

Harviainen, Tapani 1999. Suomen juutalaiset. In: Markku Löytönen & Laura Kolbe (eds.), *Suomi. Maa, kansa, kulttuurit.* Suomalaisen Kirjallisuuden Seuran Toimituksia 753. Pp. 333–343. Helsinki: Suomalaisen Kirjallisuuden Seura.

Harvie, Christopher 1994. *The Rise of Regional Europe.* London: Routledge.

Haug, W. F. 1980. *Warenästhetik und kapitalistische Massenkultur: 'Werbung' und 'Konsum'; Systematische Einführung in die Warenästhetik.* Berlin: Argument-Verlag.

Hautala, Jouko 1954. *Suomalainen kansanrunoudentutkimus.* Helsinki: Suomalaisen Kirjallisuuden Seura.

Hautala, Jouko 1957. *Johdatus kansanrunoustieteen peruskäsitteisiin.* Tietolipas 11. Helsinki: Suomalaisen Kirjallisuuden Seura.

Heelas, Paul 1996. Introduction: Detraditionalization and its Rivals. In: Paul Heelas, Scott Lash & Paul Morris (eds.), *Detraditionalization: Critical Reflections on Authority and Identity.* Pp. 1–20. Cambridge, MA: Blackwell.

Heelas, Paul & Lash, Scott & Morris, Paul (eds.) 1996. *Detraditionalization: Critical Reflections on Authority and Identity.* Cambridge, MA: Blackwell.

Heikkinen, Kaija 1989. *Karjalaisuus ja etninen itsetajunta. Salmin siirtokarjalaisia koskeva tutkimus.* Joensuun yliopiston humanistisia julkaisuja N:o 9. Joensuu: University of Joensuu.

Heikkinen, Kaija 2003. Nationalistinen karelianismi paluumuuttajien kiusana. In: Raisa Simola & Kaija Heikkinen (toim.), *Monenkirjava rasismi.* Pp. 158–174. Joensuu: Joensuu University Press.

Held, David 2000. The 1989 Revolutions and the Triumph of Liberalism. In: Stuart Hall, David Held, Ron Hubert, and Kenneth Thompson (eds.), *Modernity: An Introduction to Modern Societies.* Pp. 436–465. Oxford: Blackwell Publishers.

Herzfeld, Michael 1982. *Ours Once More: Folklore, Ideology, and the Making of Modern Greece.* Austin: University of Texas Press.

Herzfeld, Michael 1987. *Anthropology Through the Looking-Glass: Critical Ethnography in the Margins of Europe.* Cambridge: Cambridge University Press.

Hirst, Paul 1997. Challenges of Globalization to the Nation-State. *Politiikka* 39 (1): 3–13.

Hobsbawm, Eric 1972. Some Reflections on Nationalism. In: T. J. Nossiter, A. H. Hanson & S. Rokkan (eds.), *Imagination and Precision in the Social Sciences.* Pp. 385–406. London: Faber & Faber.

Hobsbawm, Eric J. 1982. Marx, Engels and Pre-Marxian Socialism. In: Eric J. Hobsbawm (ed.), *The History of Marxism. Volume One: Marxism in Marx's Day.* Pp. 1–28. Bloomington: Indiana University Press.

Hobsbawm, E. J. 1990. *Nations and Nationalism Since 1780: Programme, Myth, Reality.* Cambridge: Cambridge University Press.

Hobsbawm, E. J. 1992. Ethnicity and Nationalism in Europe Today. *Anthropology Today* 8 (1): 3–8.

Hobsbawm, Eric & Ranger, Terence (eds.) 1983. *The Invention of Tradition.* Cambridge: Cambridge University Press.

Holbek, Bengt 1981. Tacit Assumptions. *Folklore Forum* 14 (2): 121–140. Originally published as Stiltiende forudsætninger, in *Norveg* 22: 209–221, 1979.

Holbek, Bengt 1992. Tendencies in Modern Folk Narrative Research. *NIF Papers* 4. Turku: Nordic Institute of Folklore.

Honko, Lauri 1980a. Nationella värden och internationellt forskningssamarbete. Introduktion: Nordiska institutet för folkdiktning (NIF) 1959–1979. In: Lauri Honko (ed.), *Folklore och nationsbyggande i Norden.* NIF Publications No. 9. Pp. 1–3. Turku: Nordic Institute of Folklore.

Honko, Lauri 1980b. Upptäckten av folkdiktning och nationell identitet i Finland. In: Lauri Honko (ed.), *Folklore och nationsbyggande i Norden.* NIF Publications No. 9. Pp. 33–51. Turku: Nordic Institute of Folklore.

Honko, Lauri 1980c. Kansallisten juurien löytyminen. In: Päiviö Tommila, Aimo Reitala, Veikko Kallio (eds.), *Suomen kulttuurihistoria II.* Pp. 42–62. Porvoo, Helsinki, Juva: WSOY.

Honko, Lauri 1982. Folktradition och identitet. In: Aili Nenola-Kallio (ed.), *Folktradition och regional identitet i Norden*. Pp. 11–23. Åbo: NIF.

Honko, Lauri 1983. Research Traditions in Tradition Research. In: Lauri Honko & Pekka Laaksonen (eds.), *Trends in Nordic Tradition Research*. Studia Fennica 27. Pp. 13–22. Helsinki: Finnish Literature Society.

Honko, Lauri 1987a. The Kalevala Process. In: Alan Jabbour & James Hardin (eds.), *Folklife Annual 1986*. A Publication of the American Folklife Center at the Library of Congress. Pp. 66–79. Washington, D.C.: Library of Congress.

Honko, Lauri 1987b. Kalevala: aitouden, tulkinnan ja identiteetin ongelmia. In: Lauri Honko (ed.), *Kalevala ja maailman eepokset*. Kalevalaseuran vuosikirja 65. Pp. 125–170. Helsinki: Suomalaisen Kirjallisuuden Seura. Published in English as The Kalevala: The Processual View. In: Lauri Honko (ed.), *Religion, Myth, and Folklore in the World's Epics: The Kalevala and its Predecessors*. Religion and Society 30. Pp. 181–229. Berlin & New York: Mouton de Gruyter (1990).

Honko, Lauri 1988. Studies on Tradition and Cultural Identity. An Introduction. In: Lauri Honko (ed.), *Tradition and Cultural Identity*. NIF Publications 20. Pp. 7–26. Turku: Nordic Institute of Folklore.

Honko, Lauri 1991. The Folklore Process. In: *Folklore Fellows' Summer School Programme*. Pp. 25–47. Turku: FFSS.

Honko, Lauri 1992. The Unesco Perspective on Folklore. *FF Network* 3: 1–5.

Honko, Lauri 1995. Traditions in the Construction of Cultural Identity and Strategies of Ethnic Survival. *European Review* 3 (2): 131–146.

Honko, Lauri 1999. Thick Corpus and Organic Variation: an Introduction. In: Lauri Honko (ed.), *Thick Corpus, Organic Variation and Textuality in Oral Tradition*. Pp. 3–28. Helsinki: Finnish Literature Society.

Honko, Lauri 2002. Kenen omaisuutta on suullinen perinne? *Hiidenkivi* 2/2002: 6–9.

Honko, Lauri 2003. The Five Performances of the Kalevala. *FF Network* 24 (May 2003): 6–17.

Hulme, Peter & Jordanova, Ludmilla 1990. Introduction. In: Peter Hulme & Ludmilla Jordanova (eds.), *The Enlightenment and its Shadows*. Pp. 1–15. London: Routledge.

Huntington, Samuel P. 1996a. The Clash of Civilizations? In: *The Clash of Civilizations? The Debate*. Pp. 1–25. New York: Foreign Affairs.

Huntington, Samuel P. 1996b. If Not Civilizations, What? Paradigms of the Post-Cold War World. In: *The Clash of Civilizations? The Debate*. Pp. 56–67. New York: Foreign Affairs.

Huntington, Samuel P. 1996c. *The Clash of Civilizations and the Remaking of World Order*. London: Touchstone Books.

Hurskainen, Arvi (ed.) 1992. Language, Tradition and Identity. Proceedings of the international seminar held in Dar-es-Salaam 1–3.4.1992. Special Issue. *Nordic Journal of African Studies* 1 (2).

Hymes, Dell 1975. Folklore's Nature and the Sun's Myth. *Journal of American Folklore* 88: 345–369.

Häkkinen, Kaisa 1997. Suomalaisten esihistoria kielitieteen valossa. In: Jan Rydman (ed.), *Maailmankuvaa etsimässä. Tieteen päivät 1997*. Pp. 331–345. Helsinki: WSOY.

Häkli, Jouni 1994. Territoriality and the Rise of Modern State. *Fennia* 172 (1): 1–82.

Häkli, Jouni 2000. Knowledge and the State: The Construction of Finland by Bureaucrats and Scientists. In: Pirkkoliisa Ahponen & Pirjo Jukarainen (eds.), *Tearing Down the Curtain, Opening the Gates: Northern Boundaries in Change*. SoPhi 54. Pp. 11–24. Jyväskylä: SoPhi, University of Jyväskylä.

Ilomäki, Henni 1992. Oral and Written Tradition during the Creation of the National Culture: Early fieldwork on the Kalevala Runes. In: Language, Tradition and Identity. Proceedings of the international seminar held in Dar-es-Salaam 1–3.4. 1992. Special Issue. *Nordic Journal of African Studies* 1 (2): 95–111.

Immonen, Kari 1987. *Ryssästä saa puhua... Neuvostoliitto suomalaisessa julkisuudessa ja kirjat julkisuuden muotona 1918–39*. Helsinki: Otava.

Inglehart, Ronald 1990. *Culture Shift in Advanced Industrial Society*. Princeton, N.J.: Princeton University Press.

Isaksson, Pekka 1997. Saamelaiset kansakunnan rakentamisen marginaalissa. (The Sami in the Margin of Nation-Building.) *Kosmopolis* 27 (3): 53–67.

Isaksson, Pekka 2001. *Kumma kuvajainen. Rasismi rotututkimuksessa, rotuteorioiden saamelaiset ja suomalainen fyysinen antropologia*. Inari: Kustannus Puntsi Oy.

Jaakkola, Magdalena 1999. *Maahanmuutto ja etniset asenteet. Suomalaisten suhtautuminen maahanmuuttajiin 1987–1999*. (Immigration and the Ethnic Attitudes. Finns' Attitudes towards Immigrants in 1987–1999.) Ministry of Labour, Studies in Labor Policy 213. Helsinki: Edita.

Jääskeläinen, Ari 1998. Kansallistava kansanrunous. Suomalaisuus ja folklore. In: Pertti Alasuutari & Petri Ruuska (eds.), *Elävänä Euroopassa. Muuttuva suomalainen identiteetti*. Pp. 41–82. Tampere: Vastapaino.

Jabbour, Alan 1988. Introduction. In: Jane S. Becker & Barbara Franco (eds.), *Folk Roots, New Roots: Folklore in American Life*. Pp. 7–18. Lexington, Mass.: Museum of Our National Heritage.

Jackson, Bruce 1985. The Folksong Revival. *New York Folklore* 11: 195–203.

Jallinoja, Riitta 1991. *Moderni elämä: Ajankuva ja käytäntö*. Helsinki: Suomalaisen Kirjallisuuden Seura.

Jameson, Fredric 1988. The Politics of Theory: Ideological Positions in the Postmodernism Debate. In: Fredric Jameson, *The Ideologies of Theory: Essays 1971–1986, Vol. 2: Syntax of History*. Pp. 103–113. London: Routledge.

Joenniemi, Pertti 1998. The Karelian Question: On the Transformation of a Border Dispute. *Culture and Conflict. Nordic Journal of International Studies* 33 (2): 183–206.

Jukarainen, Pirjo 2004. Tieteellinen katse ja politiikka – Tilan, identiteetin ja turvallisuuden politiikan tarkastelu. In: Jouko Huru & Tarja Väyrynen (eds.), Kadonnutta poliittista etsimässä. Kansainvälinen turvallisuus ja politiikka. Pp. 13–42. Helsinki: Yliopistopaino / Helsinki University Press.

Jussila, Osmo 1987. *Maakunnasta valtioksi. Suomen valtion synty*. Porvoo: WSOY.

Jussila, Osmo & Hentilä, Seppo & Nevakivi, Jukka 1999. *From Grand Duchy to Modern State: A Political History of Finland since 1809*. Translated from the Finnish by David and Eva-Kaisa Arter. London: Hurst.

Jutikkala, Eino with Pirinen, Kauko 1962. *A History of Finland*. Translated by Paul Sjöblom. London: Thames and Hudson.

Jutikkala, Eino with Pirinen, Kauko 1984. *A History of Finland*. Translated by Paul Sjöblom. Fourth revised edition. Helsinki: Weilin + Göös.

Jutikkala, Eino with Pirinen, Kauko 2003. *A History of Finland*. Translated by Paul Sjöblom. Sixth, revised edition. Helsinki: Werner Söderström Osakeyhtiö.

Kajanoja, Pauli 1993. Keitä me suomalaiset olemme? In: Teppo Korhonen (ed.), *Mitä on suomalaisuus?* Pp. 13–22. Helsinki: Finnish Anthropological Society.

Kalela, Jorma 1993. *Aika, historia ja yleisö. Kirjoituksia historiantutkimuksen lähtökohdista*. Julkaisuja C:44. Turku: Turun yliopisto, Poliittinen historia.

Kapchan, Deborah 1993. Hybridization and the Marketplace: Emerging Paradigms in Folkloristics. *Western Folklore* 52 (2, 3, 4): 303–326. Special Issue. Theorizing Folklore: Toward New Perspectives on the Politics of Culture. Guest Editors: Charles Briggs and Amy Shuman.

Kapchan, Deborah A. 1996. *Gender on the Market: Moroccan Women and the Revoicing of Tradition*. Philadelphia: University of Pennsylvania Press.

Kapchan, Deborah A. & Strong, Pauline Turner (eds.) 1999. Theorizing the Hybrid. *Journal of American Folklore* 111 (445). Special Issue.

Karemaa, Outi 1998. *Vihollisia, vainoojia, syöpäläisiä. Venäläisviha Suomessa 1917–1923*. English summary: Foes, Fiends and Vermin: Ethnic Hatred of Russians in Finland 1917–1923. Bibliotheca historica 30. Helsinki: Finnish Historical Society.

Karkama, Pertti 1999. The Individual and National Identity in J. V. Snellman's Young-Hegelian Theory. In: Michael Branch (ed.), *National History and Identity: Approaches to the Writing of National History in the North-East Baltic Region Nineteenth and*

*Twentieth Centuries.* Studia Fennica Ethnologica 6. Pp. 141–152. Helsinki: Finnish Literature Society.

Karkama, Pertti 2001. *Kansakunnan asialla. Elias Lönnrot ja ajan aatteet.* Suomalaisen Kirjallisuuden Seuran Toimituksia 843. Helsinki: Suomalaisen Kirjallisuuden Seura.

Karkama, Pertti & Koivisto, Hanne 1997. Johdanto. Sivistyneistö ja älymystö Suomessa. In: Pertti Karkama & Hanne Koivisto (ed.), *Älymystön jäljillä. Kirjoituksia suomalaisesta sivistyneistöstä ja älymystöstä.* Tietolipas 151. Pp. 9–29. Helsinki: Suomalaisen Kirjallisuuden Seura.

Karp, Ivan & Lavine, Steven D. (eds.) 1991. *Exhibiting Cultures: The Poetics and Politics of Museum Display.* Washington, D.C.: Smithsonian Institution Press.

Katsuta, Makoto 2002. U.S. Still Pursuing Policy of Unilateralism. (Series: Civilization in the 21ˢᵗ Century. Interview with Arthur Schlesinger, Jr.) *The Daily Yomiuri.* January 16, 2002. Edition D, Pages 1 & 3. Tokyo, Japan. Also available at: http://www.yomiuri. co.jp/dy/civil/civil013.htm.

Keane, John 1988. Introduction. In: John Keane (ed.), *Civil Society and the State: New European Perspectives.* London & New York: Verso.

Keat, Russell 1981. *The Politics of Social Theory: Habermas, Freud and the Critique of Positivism.* Oxford: Basil Blackwell.

Keesing, Roger M. 1989. Creating the Past: Custom and Identity in the Contemporary Pacific. *The Contemporary Pacific* 1: 19–42.

Kemiläinen, Aira 1980. Kansallisen tehtävän ajatus historiassa. *Historiallinen aikakauskirja* 1980 (1): 3–14.

Kemiläinen, Aira 1998. *Finns in the Shadow of the 'Aryans': Race Theories and Racism.* Studia Historica 59. Helsinki: Finnish Historical Society.

Keryell, Gaela 1999. Viini, eurooppalaisuus, sivistäminen. *Yhteiskuntapolitiikka* 64 (3): 257–269.

King, Anthony D. (ed.) 1991. *Culture, Globalization and the World-System: Contemporary Conditions for the Presentation of Identity.* London: Macmillan.

Kirkpatrick, Jeane F. 1996. The Modernizing Imperative. In: *The Clash of Civilizations? The Debate.* Pp. 50–53. New York: Foreign Affairs.

Kirshenblatt-Gimblett, Barbara 1978. Culture Shock and Narrative Creativity. In: Richard M. Dorson (ed.), *Folklore in the Modern World.* Pp. 109–122. The Hague: Mouton Publishers.

Kirshenblatt-Gimblett, Barbara 1983. The Future of Folklore Studies in America: The Urban Frontier. *Folklore Forum* 16 (2): 175–234.

Kirshenblatt-Gimblett, Barbara 1988. Mistaken Dichotomies. *Journal of American Folklore* 101: 140–155.

Kirshenblatt-Gimblett, Barbara 1991. Objects of Ethnography. In: Ivan Karp & Steven D. Lavine (eds.), *Exhibiting Cultures: The Poetics and Politics of Museum Display.* Pp. 386–443. Washington, D.C.: Smithsonian Institution Press.

Kirshenblatt-Gimblett, Barbara 1992. From Cult to Culture: Jews on Display at World's Fairs. In: Reimund Kvideland (ed.), *Tradition and Modernisation. Plenary Papers read at the 4ᵗʰ International Congress of the Société Internationale d'Ethnologie et de Folklore.* NIF Publications 25. Pp. 75–105. Turku: Nordic Institute of Folklore.

Kirshenblatt-Gimblett, Barbara 1996. Topic Drift: Negotiating the Gap between the Field and Our Name. *Journal of the Folklore Institute* 33 (3): 245–254.

Kirshenblatt-Gimblett, Barbara 1998a. Folklore's Crisis. *Journal of American Folklore* 111 (441): 281–327.

Kirshenblatt-Gimblett, Barbara 1998b. *Destination Culture: Tourism, Museums, and Heritage.* Berkeley, Los Angeles, London: University of California Press.

Kirshenblatt-Gimblett, Barbara 2000. Folklorists in Public: Reflections on Cultural Brokerage in the United States and Germany. *Journal of Folklore Research* 37 (1): 1–21.

Klein, Barbro 1993. Reflexivitet, etik och fotografi. Funderingar kring kulturvetenskapligt fältarbete. In: Ulrika Wolf-Knuts, Brittmari Wikström, Nina Hägerstrand (eds.), *Folklore & etik. Föredrag vid seminariet 'Folklore & etik' arrangerat av Ålands högskola och folkloristerna vid Åbo Akademi, 11–12 maj 1992 i Mariehamn.* Pp.

195

14–27. Mariehamn: Ålands högskola.

Klein, Barbro 1997. Tillhörighet och utanförskap om kulturarvspolitik och folklivsforskning i en multietnisk värld. (Summary: Insiders and Outsiders: Heritage Politics and Folklife Studies in a Multiethnic World.) *Rig* 1–2: 15–32.

Klein, Barbro 2000. Foreigners, Foreignness, and the Swedish Folklife Sphere. *Ethnologia Scandinavica* 20: 5–23.

Klinge, Matti 1988a. *Från lojalism till rysshat*. Svensk översättning Kerstin Smeds. Helsingfors: Söderström & C:o Förlags AB.

Klinge, Matti 1988b. Finska litteratursällskapet och lojalismen. In: *Från lojalism till rysshat*. Pp. 143–153. Helsingfors: Söderström & C:o Förlags AB.

Klinge, Matti 1997. *Krig, kvinnor, konst*. Esbo: Schildt. Published in Finnish as *Kaukana ja kotona*. Suomennos Marketta Klinge. Espoo: Schildt (1997).

Klinge, Matti 2003. *Finland in Europe*. Translated by Philip Binham, Timothy Binham and David Mitchell. Helsinki: Otava.

Knuuttila, Seppo 1989. Paluu nykyisyyteen. In: Teppo Korhonen & Matti Räsänen (eds.), *Kansa kuvastimessa. Etnisyys ja identiteetti*. Tietolipas 114. Pp. 92–102. Helsinki: Suomalaisen Kirjallisuuden Seura.

Knuuttila, Seppo 1993. Kesyn kansan juhlavuosi. In: Pekka Laaksonen & Sirkka-Liisa Mettomäki (eds.), *Kauas on pitkä matka. Kirjoituksia kahdesta kotiseudusta*. Kalevalaseuran vuosikirja 72. Pp. 65–72. Helsinki: Suomalaisen Kirjallisuuden Seura.

Knuuttila, Seppo 1994. *Tyhmän kansan teoria. Näkökulmia menneestä tulevaan*. Tietolipas 129. Helsinki: Suomalaisen Kirjallisuuden Seura.

Kodish, Debora 1993. On Coming of Age in the Sixties. *Western Folklore* 52 (2, 3, 4): 193–207. Special Issue. Theorizing Folklore: Toward New Perspectives on the Politics of Culture. Guest Editors: Charles Briggs and Amy Shuman.

Koivulehto, Jorma 1993. Suomi. *Virittäjä* 3/1993: 400–406.

Köngäs-Maranda, Elli 1982. The Roots of the Two Ethnologies, and Ethnilogy. *Folklore Forum* 15 (1): 51–68.

Korhonen, Mikko 1986. *Finno-Ugrian Language Studies in Finland 1828–1918*. Helsinki: Societas Scientiarum Fennica.

Korten, David C. 1997. *When Corporations Rule the World*. Reprint. London: Earthscan.

Kotkin, Joel 1993. *Tribes: How Race, Religion and Identity Determine Success in the New Global Economy*. New York: Random House.

Kuhn, Thomas S. 1962. *The Structure of Scientific Revolutions*. Chicago: University of Chicago Press.

Kurki, Tuulikki 2002. *Heikki Meriläinen ja keskusteluja kansanperinteestä*. Suomalaisen Kirjallisuuden Seuran Toimituksia 880. Helsinki: Suomalaisen Kirjallisuuden Seura.

Kuusi, Matti 1959. Kansanperinteen metamorfoosi. *Suomalainen Suomi* 7/1959: 395–399.

Kuusi, Matti (ed.) 1963. *Suomen kirjallisuus I. Kirjoittamaton kirjallisuus*. Helsinki: Otava.

Kuusi, Matti 1974. Kansanperinteestä populaarikulttuuriin. In: Pekka Suhonen, Pekka Haatanen, Seppo Vaittinen, Matti Kuusi, Erkki Aho, Anto Leikola, Aarne Laurila, *Sata suomalaisen kulttuurin vuotta: 1870-luvulta nykyaikaan*. Pp. 147–172. Helsinki: WSOY.

Laaksonen, Pekka & Mettomäki, Sirkka-Liisa (eds.) 1996. *Olkaamme siis suomalaisia*. Kalevalaseuran vuosikirja 75–76. Helsinki: Suomalaisen Kirjallisuuden Seura.

Laari, Outi. 1997. Suomi ja inkerinsuomalaiset – etnisyys velvoittaa? *Tiede ja edistys* 22 (4): 302–317.

Laine, Antti 1993. Tiedemiesten Suur-Suomi – Itä-Karjalan tutkimus jatkosodan vuosina. *Historiallinen arkisto* 102: 91–202. Helsinki: Finnish Historical Society.

Lash, Scott 1990. *Sociology of Postmodernism*. London: Routledge.

Länkelä, Jaako 1865. Kuvaelmia Suomen kansan tavoista. Itäsuomesta v 1865? The Finnish Literature Society Folklore Archives, Helsinki. Länkelä No. 1693. Manuscript.

Lash, Scott & Urry, John 1996. *Economies of Signs and Space*. London: Sage.

Latour, Bruno 1993. *We Have Never Been Modern*. Translated by Catharine Porter. Cambridge, Massachusetts: Harvard University Press.

Lauristin, Marju 1997. Contexts of Transition. In: *Return to the Western World: Cultural and Political Perspectives on the Estonian Post-Communist Transition*. Ed. by Marju Lauristin & Peeter Vihalemm with Karl-Erik Rosengren and Lennart Weibull. Pp. 25–40. Tartu: Tartu University Press.

Law, Vivien 1998. Language Myths and the Discourse of Nation-Building in Georgia. In: Graham Smith, Vivien Law, Andrew Wilson, Annette Bohr and Edward Allworth, *Nation-Building in the Post-Soviet Borderlands: The Politics of National Identities*. Pp. 167–196. Cambridge: Cambridge University Press.

Leach, Edmund 1970. *Claude Lévi-Strauss*. Revised Edition. Harmondsworth, England: Penguin Books.

Lears, Jackson T. J. 1985. The Concept of Cultural Hegemony: Problems and Possibilities. *American History Review* 90 (3): 567–593.

Lefèbvre, Henri 1991. *Critique of Everyday Life*. Transl. by John Moore with a preface by Michel Trebitsch. London: Verso.

Lehtola, Veli-Pekka 1997. *Rajamaan identiteetti. Lappilaisuuden rakentuminen 1920- ja 30-luvun kirjallisuudessa*. Helsinki: Suomalaisen Kirjallisuuden Seura.

Lehtinen, Ari Aukusti 1994. Neocolonialism in the Viena Karelia. In: Heikki Eskelinen, Jukka Oksa, Daniel Austin (eds.), *Russian Karelia in Search of a New Role*. Pp. 147–159. Joensuu: Karelian Institute, University of Joensuu.

Lepola, Outi 2000. *Ulkomaalaisesta suomenmaalaiseksi. Monikulttuurisuus, kansalaisuus ja suomalaisuus 1990-luvun maahanmuuttopoliittisessa keskustelussa*. Suomalaisen Kirjallisuuden Seuran Toimituksia 787. Helsinki: Suomalaisen Kirjallisuuden Seura.

Lévi-Strauss, Claude 1967. *Tristes Tropiques: An Anthropological Study of Primitive Societies in Brazil*. Translated by John Russell. New York: Atheneum.

Levine, Joseph M. 1999. *Between the Ancients and the Moderns: Baroque Culture in Restoration England*. New Haven: Yale University Press.

Liikanen, Ilkka 1995. *Fennomania ja kansa. Joukkojärjestäytymisen läpimurto ja Suomalaisen puolueen synty*. Historiallisia tutkimuksia 191. Helsinki: Finnish Historical Society.

Liikanen, Ilkka 1997. Kansalaisen synty. Fennomania ja modernin politiikan läpimurto. *Tiede & Edistys* 4/97: 342–351.

Limón, José E. 1983a. Folklore, Social Conflict, and the United States–Mexico Border. In: Richard M. Dorson (ed.), *Handbook of American Folklore*. Pp. 216–226. Bloomington: Indiana University Press.

Limón, José E. 1983b. Western Marxism and Folklore: A Critical Introduction. *Journal of American Folklore* 96: 34–52.

Linde-Laursen, Anders 1991: '...derfra min verden går' – om national identitet. In: *Nationella identiteter i Norden – ett fullbordat projekt?* Sjutton nordiska undersökningar redigerade av Anders Linde-Laursen och Jan Olof Nilsson. Nord 1991: 26. Pp. 11–18. Stockholm: Nordiska rådet.

Linke, Uli 1995. Power and Culture Theory: Problematizing the Focus of Research in German Folklore Scholarship. In: Regina Bendix and Rosemary Lévy Zumwalt (eds.), *Folklore Interpreted: Essays in Honor of Alan Dundes*. Pp. 417–447. New York and London: Garland Publishing.

Linnekin, Jocelyn 1983. Defining Tradition: Variations on the Hawaiian Identity. *American Ethnologist* 10: 223–234.

LiPuma, E. & Meltzoff, S. K. 1990. Ceremonies of Independence and Public Culture in the Solomon Islands. *Public Culture* 3 (1): 77–92.

Löfgren, Orvar 1989. The Nationalization of Culture. *Ethnologia Europaea* XIX (1): 5–24.

Löfgren, Orvar 1991. Att nationalisera moderniteten. In: *Nationella identiteter i Norden – ett fullbordat projekt?* Sjutton nordiska undersökningar redigerade av Anders Linde-Laursen och Jan-Olof Nilsson. Nord 1991: 26. Pp. 101–115. Stockholm: Nordiska rådet.

Löfgren, Orvar 1993a. Nationella arenor. In: Billy Ehn, Jonas Frykman, Orvar Löfgren, *Försvenskningen av Sverige: Det nationellas förvandlingar.* Pp. 21–117. Stockholm: Natur och kultur.

Löfgren, Orvar 1993b. The Cultural Grammar of Nation-Building: The Nationalization of Nationalism. In: Pertti J. Anttonen and Reimund Kvideland (eds.), *Nordic Frontiers: Recent Issues in the Study of Modern Traditional Culture in the Nordic Countries.* NIF Publications No. 27. Pp. 217–238. Turku: Nordic Institute of Folklore.

Löfgren, Orvar 2001. The Nation as Home or Motel? Metaphors and Media of Belonging. In: Gran, Hougen, Kasin (eds.), *Sosiologisk Årbok* 2001.1 / *Yearbook of Sociology* 1–34.

Löfgren, Orvar 2003. The New Economy: A Cultural History. In: Globalization, Creolization, and Cultural Complexity: Essays in Honor of Ulf Hannerz. *Global Networks: A Journal of Transnational Affairs* 3 (3): 239–254.

Lombardi-Satriani, Luigi 1974. Folklore as Culture of Contestation. *Journal of the Folklore Institute* 11(1–2): 99–121.

Lönnqvist, Bo 1989. Minne och glömska: Om etnologens identitet. In: Teppo Korhonen & Matti Räsänen (eds.), *Kansa kuvastimessa. Etnisyys ja identiteetti.* Tietolipas 114. Pp. 29–41. Helsinki: Suomalaisen Kirjallisuuden Seura.

Lopez, Barry 1986. *Arctic Dreams: Imagination and Desire in a Northern Landscape.* London: Picador.

Lyotard, Jean-François 1984. *The Postmodern Condition: A Report on Knowledge.* Translated by Geoff Bennington and Brian Massumi. Minneapolis: University of Minnesota Press.

MacCannell, Dean 1989 [1976]. *The Tourist: A New Theory of the Leisure Class.* With a New Introduction by the Author. New York: Schocken Books.

MacDonald, Dwight 1957. A Theory of Mass Culture. In: Bernard Rosenberg & David Manning White (eds.), *Mass Culture: The Popular Arts in America.* Pp. 59–73. Glencoe, Illinois: The Free Press.

Macdonald, Sharon (ed.) 1993. *Inside European Identities: Ethnography in Western Europe.* Providence & Oxford: Berg.

MacKeith, Peter B. & Smeds, Kerstin 1993. *The Finland Pavilions: Finland at the Universal Expositions 1900–1992.* Translations from the Finnish by John Arnold. [Helsinki]: City.

Madison, G. B. 1988. *The Hermeneutics of Postmodernity: Figures and Themes.* Bloomington: Indiana University Press.

Maffesoli, Michel 1996. *The Times of the Tribes. The Decline of Individualism in Mass Society.* Translated by Don Smith. London: Sage.

Majander, Mikko 2000. Yrjö Koskisen suuri kertomus Suomen kansan historiasta. Postmoderni luenta. In: *Jäljillä. Kirjoituksia historian ongelmista. Juhlakirja Jorma Kalelalle hänen 60-vuotispäivänään 12.11. 2000.* Toimituskunta: Pauli Kettunen, Auli Kultanen, Timo Soikkanen. Osa 1. Pp. 497–517. Turku: University of Turku: Department of Political History and Kirja-Aurora.

Manninen, Juha 2000. *Valistus ja kansallinen identiteetti. Aatehistoriallinen tutkimus 1700-luvun Pohjolasta.* Historiallisia tutkimuksia 210. Helsinki. Suomalaisen Kirjallisuuden Seura.

Manninen, Juha 2002. Kansakunnan aatteen synty Ruotsissa ja Suomessa. *Tieteessä tapahtuu* 1/2002: 6–13.

Manninen, Ohto 1980. *Suur-Suomen ääriviivat.* Helsinki: Kirjayhtymä.

Maranhão, Tullio 1990. Introduction. In: Tullio Maranhão (ed.), *The Interpretation of Dialogue.* Pp. 1–22. Chicago: University of Chicago Press.

Marcus, George E. 1980. Rhetoric and the Ethnographic Genre in Anthropological Research. *Current Anthropology* 21 (4): 507–510.

Marcus, George E. & Cushman, Dick 1982. Ethnographies as Texts. *Annual Review of Anthropology* 11: 25–69.

Marcus, George E. & Fischer, Michael M. J. 1986. The Repatriation of Anthropology as Cultural Critique. In: George E. Marcus & Michael M. J. Fischer, *Anthropology as*

*Cultural Critique: An Experimental Moment in the Human Sciences.* Pp. 111–136. Chicago: University of Chicago Press.

Mathisen, Stein R. 2000. Travels and Narratives: Itinerant Constructions of a Homogenous Sami Heritage. In: *Folklore, Heritage Politics, and Ethnic Diversity: A Festschrift for Barbro Klein.* Edited by Pertti J. Anttonen in collaboration with Anna-Leena Siikala, Stein R. Mathisen and Leif Magnusson. Pp. 179–205. Botkyrka, Sweden: Multicultural Centre.

Mathisen, Stein R. 2004. Hegemonic Representations of Sámi Culture: From Narratives of Noble Savages to Discourses on Ecological Sámi. In: Anna-Leena Siikala, Barbro Klein & Stein R. Mathisen (eds.), *Creating Diversities: Folklore, Religion and the Politics of Heritage.* Studia Fennica Folkloristica 14. Pp. 17–30. Helsinki: Finnish Literature Society.

Mattila, Markku 1999. *Kansamme parhaaksi. Rotuhygienia Suomessa vuoden 1935 sterilointilakiin asti.* (Summary: In Our Nation's Best Interest – Eugenics in Finland until the promulgation of the Sterilization Law of 1935.) Bibliotheca Historica 44. Helsinki: Suomen Historiallinen Seura.

Maure, Marc 1996. Le Paysan et le Viking au musée. Nationalisme et patrimoine en Norvège au XIXe siècle. In: Daniel Fabre, Claudie Voisenat and Eva Julien (eds.), *L'Europe entre Cultures et Nations: Actes de Colloque de Tours, Décembre 1993.* Collection Ethnologie de la France Regards sur l'Europe. Cahier 10. Éditions de la Maison des sciences de l'homme. Paris: Mission du Patrimoine Ethnologique.

McCarthy, Thomas 1985. Reflections on Rationalization in the Theory of Communicative Action. In: Richard J. Bernstein (ed.), *Habermas and Modernity.* Pp. 176–191. Cambridge: Polity Press & Oxford: Basil Blackwell.

McGrew, Anthony 2000. The State in Advanced Capitalist Societies. In: Stuart Hall, David Held, Ron Hubert, and Kenneth Thompson (eds.), *Modernity: An Introduction to Modern Societies.* Pp. 239–279. Oxford: Blackwell Publishers.

McLellan, David 1982. The Materialistic Concept of History. In: Eric J. Hobsbawm (ed.), *The History of Marxism. Volume One: Marxism in Marx's Day.* Pp. 29–46. Bloomington: Indiana University Press.

McLennan, Gregor 2000. The Enlightenment Project Revisited. In: Stuart Hall, David Held, Ron Hubert, and Kenneth Thompson (eds.), *Modernity: An Introduction to Modern Societies.* Pp. 635–663. Oxford: Blackwell Publishers.

Mechling, Jay 1985. Introduction. Special Section: William James and the Philosophical Foundations for the Study of Everyday Life. *Western Folklore* 44: 301–310.

Mechling, Jay 1991. Homo Narrans Across the Disciplines. *Western Folklore* 50: 41–51.

Mikkeli, Heikki 1994. *Euroopan idea. Eurooppa-aatteen ja eurooppalaisuuden pitkä historia.* Helsinki: Suomen Historiallinen Seura.

Mikkeli, Heikki 1998. *Europe as an Idea and an Identity.* London: Macmillan.

Mills, Margaret A. 1990. Critical Theory and the Folklorist: Performances, Interpretative Authority, and Gender. *Southern Folklore* 47: 5–15.

Mills, Margaret 1993. Feminist Theory and the Study of Folklore: A Twenty-Year Trajectory toward Theory. *Western Folklore* 52 (2, 3, 4): 173–192. Special Issue. Theorizing Folklore: Toward New Perspectives on the Politics of Culture. Guest Editors: Charles Briggs and Amy Shuman.

Mongardini, Carlo 1992. The Ideology of Postmodernity. *Theory, Culture & Society* 9: 55–65.

Morley, David and Kevin Robins 1995. *Spaces of Identity: Global Media, Eletronic Landscapes and Cultural Boundaries.* London: Routledge.

Morris-Suzuki, Tessa 1998. *Re-Inventing Japan: Time, Space, Nation.* Armonk, New York & London, England: M. E. Sharpe.

Myerhoff, Barbara & Ruby, Jay 1982. Introduction. In: Jay Ruby (ed.), *A Crack in the Mirror: Reflexive Perspectives in Anthropology.* Pp. 1–35. Philadelphia: University of Pennsylvania Press.

Mäkelä, Klaus 1985. Kulttuurisen muuntelun yhteisöllinen rakenne Suomessa. Summary: Social Structure of Cultural Variation in Finland. *Sosiologia* 22 (4): 247–260.

Nadel-Klein, Jane 1991. Reweaving the Fringe: Localism, Tradition, and Representation in British Ethnography. In: Representations of Europe: Transforming State, Society, and Identity. *American Ethnologist* 18 (3): 500–517.

Naithani, Sadhana 1997. The Colonizer-Folklorist. *Journal of Folklore Research* 34 (1): 1–14.

Newell, William Wells 1888. On the Field and Work of a Journal of American Folk-Lore. *Journal of American Folklore* 1: 3–7.

Nieminen, Markku 1995. *Vienan runokylät. Kulttuuriopas.* Suomalaisen Kirjallisuuden Seuran Toimituksia 618. Helsinki: Suomalaisen Kirjallisuuden Seura.

Nisbet, H. B. 1999. Herder: The Nation in History. In: Michael Branch (ed.), *National History and Identity: Approaches to the Writing of National History in the North-East Baltic Region Nineteenth and Twentieth Centuries.* Studia Fennica Ethnologica 6. Pp. 78–96. Helsinki: Finnish Literature Society.

Norrback, Ole 1998. Globalisaatio vaatii uutta yhteistyötä. *Helsingin Sanomat,* September 25, 1998.

Noyes, Dorothy 1991. The Satisfactions of Reproduction: A Baroque Painter in Italian Philadelphia. In: James Hardin (ed.), *Folklife Annual 90.* A Publication of the American Folklife Center at the Library of Congress. Pp. 58–69. Washington, D.C.: Library of Congress.

Noyes, Dorothy 1995. Group. *Journal of American Folklore* 108 (430): 449–478.

Nygård, Toivo 1978. *Suur-Suomi vai lähiheimolaisten auttaminen. Aatteellinen heimotyö itsenäisessä Suomessa.* Helsinki: Otava.

Ó Giolláin, Diarmuid 1990. Folklore, the Nation and the State. *Suomen Antropologi* 15 (4): 29–38.

Ó Giolláin, Diarmuid 2000. *Locating Irish Folklore: Tradition, Modernity, Identity.* Cork: Cork University Press.

Ó Giolláin, Diarmuid 2003. Tradition, Modernity and Cultural Diversity. In: Lotte Tarkka (ed.), *Dynamics of Tradition: Perspectives on Oral Poetry and Folk Belief. Essays in Honour of Anna-Leena Siikala on her 60th Birthday 1st January 2003.* Studia Fennica Folkloristica 13. Pp. 35–47. Helsinki: Finnish Literature Society.

Oring, Elliott 1994. The Arts, Artifacts, and the Artifices of Identity. *Journal of American Folklore* 107: 211–233.

Østergaard, Uffe 1991. 'Denationalizing' National History – The Comparative Study of Nation-States. *Culture & History* 9/10: 9–41.

Paasi, Anssi 1994. The Changing Meanings of the Finnish-Russian Border. In: Heikki Eskelinen, Jukka Oksa, Daniel Austin (eds.), *Russian Karelia in Search of a New Role.* Pp. 26–40. Joensuu: Karelian Institute, University of Joensuu.

Paasi, Anssi 2000. The Finnish-Russian Border as a Shifting Discourse. In: Pirkkoliisa Ahponen & Pirjo Jukarainen (eds.), *Tearing Down the Curtain, Opening the Gates: Northern Boundaries in Change.* SoPhi 54. Pp. 85–100. Jyväskylä: SoPhi, University of Jyväskylä.

Peltonen, Ulla-Maija 1996. *Punakapinan muistot. Tutkimus työväen muistelukerronnan muotoutumisesta vuoden 1918 jälkeen.* Suomalaisen Kirjallisuuden Seuran Toimituksia 657. Helsinki: Suomalaisen Kirjallisuuden Seura.

Peltonen, Ulla-Maija 2003. *Muistin paikat. Vuoden 1918 sisällissodan muistamisesta ja unohtamisesta.* Suomalaisen Kirjallisuuden Seuran Toimituksia 894. Helsinki: Suomalaisen Kirjallisuuden Seura.

Pentikäinen, Juha 1997. Castrénilainen 'pohjoisen etnografian' paradigma. In: Anna Maria Viljanen & Minna Lahti (eds.), *Kaukaa haettua. Kirjoituksia antropologisesta kenttätyöstä.* Pp. 224–236. Helsinki: Suomen Antropologinen Seura.

Pentikäinen, Juha (ed.) 1999a. *'Silent as Waters We Live': Old Believers in Russia and Abroad: Cultural Encounter with the Finno-Ugrians.* Studia Fennica Folkloristica 6. Helsinki: Finnish Literature Society.

Pentikäinen, Juha 1999b. Pohjoisten vähemmistökansojen uskonnot kolonialismin paineessa. In: Heikki Palva & Juha Pentikäinen (eds.), *Uskonnot maailmanpolitiikassa.* Pp. 315–351. Porvoo, Helsinki, Juva: Werner Söderström Osakeyhtiö.

Pentikäinen, Juha & Hiltunen, Marja (eds.) 1997. *Suomen kulttuurivähemmistöt*. Suomen Unesco-toimikunnan julkaisuja No 72. Helsinki: Suomen Unesco-toimikunta.

Pimiä, Tenho 2003. Ethnologists on the Warpath: Finno-Ugric Research and the Finno-Ugric Collections During the Period 1941–1944. *Ethnologia Scandinavica* 33: 74–83.

Pöllä, Matti 1991. Vienan Karjala perinnealueena. In: Pekka Laaksonen & Sirkka-Liisa Mettomäki (eds.), *Kolme on kovaa sanaa. Kirjoituksia kansanperinteestä*. Kalevalaseuran vuosikirja 71. Pp. 168–183. Helsinki: Suomalaisen Kirjallisuuden Seura.

Pöllä, Matti 1995. *Vienan Karjalan etnisen koostumuksen muutokset 1600–1800-luvulla*. Suomalaisen Kirjallisuuden Seuran Toimituksia 635. Helsinki: Suomalaisen Kirjallisuuden Seura.

Pöysä, Jyrki 1994. Nykyperinteen tutkimus. In: Jari Kupiainen & Erkki Sevänen (eds.), *Kulttuurintutkimus. Johdanto*. Tietolipas 130. Pp. 226–248. Helsinki: Suomalaisen Kirjallisuuden Seura.

Pöysä, Jyrki 2004. 'Finnishness' and 'Russianness' in the Making: Sport, Gender and National Identity. In: Anna-Leena Siikala, Barbro Klein & Stein R. Mathisen (eds.), *Creating Diversities: Folklore, Religion and the Politics of Heritage*. Studia Fennica Folkloristica 14. Pp. 54–68. Helsinki: Finnish Literature Society.

Raivo, Petri J. 2000. Landscaping the Finnish Past: Finnish War Landscapes as a National Heritage. *Fennia* 178 (1): 139–150.

Rasila, Viljo 1986. Kansa ja kansakäsitys historiassa. In: Leena Viitanen (ed.), *Kadotettu kansa. Oulussa 1983 pidetyn kansaseminaarin esitelmiä*. Oulun yliopisto, Kirjallisuuden laitos. Julkaisuja 12. Pp. 8–25. Oulu: Oulun yliopisto.

Reitala, Aimo 1983. *Suomi-neito. Suomen kuvallisen henkilöitymän vaiheet*. Helsinki: Otava.

Ricoeur, Paul 1986. *The Rule of Metaphor: Multi-disciplinary Studies of the Creation of Meaning in Language*. London: Routledge & Kegan Paul.

Rihtman-Auguštin, Dunja 2000. Ethnology and the Ethnomyth. In: *Volkskultur und Moderne: Europäische Ethnologie zur Jahrtausendwende. Festschrift für Konrad Köstlin zum 60. Geburtstag am 8. mai 2000*. Hrsg. vom Institut für Europäische Ethnologie der Universität Wien. Veröffentlichungen des Instituts für Europäische Ethnologie der Universität Wien, Band 21. Pp. 329–340. Wien: Selbstverlag des Instituts für Europäische Ethnologie.

Ritzer, George 1996. *The McDonaldization of Society: An Investigation into the Changing Character of Contemporary Social Life*. Revised Edition. Thousand Oaks, Calif.: Pine Forge Press.

Robertson, Roland 1987. Globalization and Societal Modernization: a Note on Japan and Japanese Religion. *Sociological Analysis* 47 (S): 35–43.

Robertson, Roland 1990. After Nostalgia? Wilful Nostalgia and the Phases of Globalization. In: Bryan S. Turner (ed.), *Theories of Modernity and Postmodernity*. Pp. 45–61. London: Sage Publications.

Rommi, Pirkko 1980. Yrjö-Koskinen fennomaanisena poliitikkona. *Historiallinen aikakauskirja* 78: 307–314.

Rorty, Richard 1979. *Philosophy and the Mirror of Nature*. Princeton, N.J.: Princeton University Press.

Rorty, Richard 1985. Habermas and Lyotard on Postmodernity. In: Richard J. Bernstein (ed.), *Habermas and Modernity*. Pp. 161–175. Cambridge: Polity Press & Oxford: Basil Blackwell.

Rosenberg, Harold 1959. *The Tradition of the New*. New York: Horizon Press Inc.

Ruokanen, Tapani 1996. 1916–1996. *Suomen Kuvalehti* 48/1996.

Rusi, Alpo 1998. Myrskyn jälkeen. *Suomen Kuvalehti* 39/1998.

Ruuska, Petri 1998. Mennyt tulevaisuutena. In: Pertti Alasuutari & Petri Ruuska (eds.), *Elävänä Euroopassa. Muuttuva suomalainen identiteetti*. Pp. 281–311. Tampere: Vastapaino.

Ryymin, Teemu 1998. 'Bein av vårt bein, kjøtt av vårt kjøtt'. Finske nasjonalisters og norske myndigheters kvenpolitikk i mellomkrigstiden. Upublisert hovedoppgave i historie, Universitetet i Bergen.

201

Ryymin, Teemu 2003. 'De nordligste Finner'. Fremstillingen av kvenene i den finske litterære offentligheten 1800–1939. Dr.art.-avhandling, Institutt for historie, Det samfunnsvitenskapelige fakultet, Universitetet I Tromsø, Juni 2003. Manuscript.

Saari, Mirja 1999. Kieli, kulttuuri, identiteetti. In: Markku Löytönen & Laura Kolbe (eds.), *Suomi. Maa, kansa, kulttuurit.* Suomalaisen Kirjallisuuden Seuran Toimituksia 753. Pp. 266–277. Helsinki: Suomalaisen Kirjallisuuden Seura.

Said, Edward W. 1978. *Orientalism.* New York: Vintage Books.

Sajantila, Antti 1997. Suomalaisten geneettinen historia. In: Jan Rydman (ed.), *Maailmankuvaa etsimässä. Tieteen päivät 1997.* Pp. 346–357. Helsinki: WSOY.

Salminen, Timo 2003. *Suomen tieteelliset voittomaat. Venäjä ja Siperia suomalaisessa arkeologiassa 1879–1935.* (Lands of Conquest: Russia and Siberia in Finnish archaeology 1879–1935.) Suomen muinaismuistoyhdistyksen aikakauskirja 110. Helsinki: Suomen muinaismuistoyhdistys.

Sammallahti, Pekka 1999. Saamen kielen ja saamelaisten alkuperästä. In: Paul Fogelberg (ed.), *Pohjan poluilla. Suomalaisten juuret nykytutkimuksen mukaan.* (The Roots of the Finns in the light of present-day research.) Bidrag till kännedom av Finlands natur och folk 153. Pp. 70–90. Helsinki: Societas Scientiarum Fennica / Finnish Society of Sciences and Letters.

Sampat, Payal 2001. Last Words. *World Watch* May/June 2001: 34–40.

Sangren, P. Steven 1988. Rhetoric and Authority of Ethnography: 'Postmodernism' and the Social Reproduction of Texts. *Current Anthropology* 29 (3): 405–435.

Sanjek, Roger (ed.) 1990. *Fieldnotes: The Makings of Anthropology.* Ithaca, N.Y.: Cornell University Press.

Sarajas, Annamari 1962. *Viimeiset romantikot. Kirjallisuuden aatteiden vaihtelua 1880-luvun jälkeen.* Porvoo: WSOY.

Sarajas, Annamari 1982 [1956]. *Studiet av folkdiktning i Finland intill slutet av 1700-talet.* (Kungl. vitterhets historie och antikvitets akademiens handlingar, Filologisk-filosofiska serien 19). Stockholm: Almqvist & Wiksell International. Originally published as: *Suomen kansanrunouden tuntemus 1500–1700 -lukujen kirjallisuudessa.* Helsinki: WSOY (1956).

Sarmela, Matti 1979. *Paikalliskulttuurin rakennemuutos. Raportti Pohjois-Thaimaan riisikylistä.* (Structural Change in Local Culture. De-Localization and Cultural Imperialism in Rural North Thailand.) Helsinki: Finnish Anthropological Society.

Saukkonen, Pasi 1996. Identiteetti ja kansallinen identiteetti. *Kosmopolis* 26 (4): 5–19.

Saukkonen, Pasi 1998a. Kansallisvaltion identiteettipolitiikka. Kansallinen identiteetti politiikan tutkimuksen käsitteenä. *Politiikka* 40 (3): 212–225.

Saukkonen, Pasi 1998b. Porvari ja talonpoika. Kansanluonteen 'kansa' Zachris Topeliuksella ja Robert Fruinilla. In: Marja Keränen (ed.), *Kansallisvaltion kielioppi.* Pp. 27–48. Jyväskylä: SoPhi.

Saukkonen, Pasi 1999. *Suomi, Alankomaat ja kansallisvaltion identiteettipolitiikka. Tutkimus kansallisen identiteetin poliittisuudesta, empiirinen sovellutus suomalaisiin ja hollantilaisiin teksteihin.* (Summary: Finland, the Netherlands and the Politics of a Nation-State Identity: A Study on the Political Aspects of National Identity. An Empirical Application to the Dutch and Finnish Cases.) Suomalaisen Kirjallisuuden Seuran toimituksia 752. Helsinki: Suomalaisen Kirjallisuuden Seura.

Saukkonen, Pasi n.d. Finland and the Netherlands: The Politics of Nation-State Identity. Manuscript.

Sedergren, Jari 1996. Nationalismeista identiteetteihin: suomalainen nationalismi hobsbawmilaisittain. *Kosmopolis* 26 (4): 21–33.

Shils, Edward 1981. *Tradition.* Chicago: University of Chicago Press.

Shore, Chris 2000. *Building Europe: The Cultural Politics of European Integration.* London & New York: Routledge.

Shore, Chris 2001. Nation and State in the European Union: Anthropological Perspectives. In: Réka Kiss & Attila Paládi-Kovács (eds.), *Times, Places, Passages: Ethnological Approaches in the New Millennium.* Seventh International Congress of International Society for Ethnology and Folklore (Société International d'Ethnologie et de Folklore,

SIEF), 23–28 April 2001. Plenary Papers. Pp. 25–53. Budapest: Hungarian Academy of Sciences, Institute of Ethnology.

Shuman, Amy 1993. Dismantling Local Culture. *Western Folklore* 52 (2, 3, 4): 345–364. Special Issue. Theorizing Folklore: Toward New Perspectives on the Politics of Culture. Guest Editors: Charles Briggs and Amy Shuman.

Shuman, Amy & Briggs, Charles L. 1993. Introduction. *Western Folklore* 52 (2, 3, 4): 109–134. Special Issue. Theorizing Folklore: Toward New Perspectives on the Politics of Culture. Guest Editors: Charles Briggs and Amy Shuman.

Sider, Gerald M. 1986. *Culture and Class in Anthropology and History: A Newfoundland Illustration*. Cambridge: Cambridge University Press.

Sihvo, Hannes 1969. *Karjalan löytäjät*. Helsinki: Kirjayhtymä.

Sihvo, Hannes 1973. *Karjalan kuva. Karelianismin taustaa ja vaiheita autonomian aikana*. Helsinki: Suomalaisen Kirjallisuuden Seura.

Sihvo, Hannes 1994. Karjalaisuus, Karjala ja muu Suomi. Oma ja muiden näkökulma karjalaiseen identiteettiin. In: Väinö Jääskeläinen and Ilkka Savijärvi (eds.), *Tieten Tahtoen*. Studia Carelia Humanistica 3. Pp. 23–44. Joensuu: University of Joensuu Faculty of Arts.

Sihvo, Hannes 1999. Karelia: A Source of Finnish National History. In: Michael Branch (ed.), *National History and Identity: Approaches to the Writing of National History in the North-East Baltic Region Nineteenth and Twentieth Centuries*. Studia Fennica Ethnologica 6. Pp. 181–201. Helsinki: Finnish Literature Society.

Siikala, Anna-Leena 1994. *Suomalainen šamanismi – mielikuvien historiaa*. Suomalaisen Kirjallisuuden Seuran Toimituksia 565. Helsinki: Suomalaisen Kirjallisuuden Seura.

Siikala, Anna-Leena 1997. Toisiinsa virtaavat maailmat. In: Anna Maria Viljanen & Minna Lahti (eds.), *Kaukaa haettua. Kirjoituksia antropologisesta kenttätyöstä*. Pp. 46–68. Helsinki: Suomen Antropologinen Seura.

Siikala, Anna-Leena 1998. Etninen uskonto ja identiteetti. Udmurttien uhrijuhlat traditiona. In: Pekka Hakamies (ed.), *Ison karhun jälkeläiset. Perinne ja etninen identiteetti yhteiskunnallisessa murroksessa*. Pp. 194–216. Helsinki: Suomalaisen Kirjallisuuden Seura.

Siikala, Anna-Leena 2000. From Sacrificial Rituals into National Festivals: Post-Soviet Transformations of Udmurt Tradition. In: *Folklore, Heritage Politics, and Ethnic Diversity: A Festschrift for Barbro Klein*. Edited by Pertti J. Anttonen in collaboration with Anna-Leena Siikala, Stein R. Mathisen and Leif Magnusson. Pp. 57–85. Botkyrka, Sweden: Multicultural Centre.

Siikala, Anna-Leena 2002a. The Singer Ideal and the Enrichment of Poetic Culture: Why Did the Ingredients for the Kalevala Come From Viena Karelia? In: Lauri Honko (ed.), *The Kalevala and the World's Traditional Epics*. Studia Fennica Folkloristica 12. Pp. 26–43. Helsinki: Finnish Literature Society.

Siikala, Anna-Leena 2002b. Elias Lönnrot etnografina. *Tieteessä tapahtuu* 4/2002: 5–12.

Siikala, Anna-Leena 2003. Elias Lönnrot the ethnographer. *FF Network* No. 25 (December 2003): 12–17.

Skyttä, Kyösti & Skyttä, Päivi 1981. *Tuntematon Snellman*. Helsinki: Kirjayhtymä.

Smart, Ninian 1983. Religion, Myth, and Nationalism. In: Peter H. Merkl & Ninian Smart (eds.), *Religion and Politics in the Modern World*. Pp. 15–28. New York: New York University Press.

Smeds, Kerstin 1996. *Helsingfors – Paris. Finlands utveckling till nation på världs-utställningarna 1851–1900*. Helsinki: Society of Swedish Literature in Finland.

Smith, Anthony D. 1990: Towards a Global Culture? In: Mike Featherstone (ed.), *Global Culture: Nationalism, Globalization and Modernity. A Theory, Culture & Society* special issue. Pp. 171–191. London: Sage.

Smith, Anthony D. 1991. *National Identity*. London: Penguin Books.

Smith, Neil 1987. Of Yuppies and Housing: Gentrification, Social Structuring, and the Urban Dream. *Environment and Planning D: Society and Space* 5: 151–172.

Snellman, J. V. 1928. *Kootut teokset. II. Valtio-oppi, Oikean ehdoton pätevyys, Kansallisuus ja kansallisuusaate*. Suomentanut Heikki Lehmusto. Porvoo: WSOY.

Snellman, J. V. 1931. *Kootut teokset. 12. Kirjeitä.* Suomentanut Heikki Lehmusto. Porvoo: WSOY.

Soja, Edward W. 1985. The Spatiality of Social Life: Towards a Transformative Retheorisation. In: Derek Gregory & John Urry (eds.), *Social Relations and Spatial Structures.* Pp. 90–127. London: Macmillan.

Soja, Edward W. 1989. *Postmodern Geographies: The Reassertation of Space in Critical Social Theory.* London: Verso.

Sörlin, Sverker 1986. Framtidslandet. Norrland och det nordliga i svensk och europeiskt medvetande. In: Ingmar Karlsson (ed.), *I kontinentens utkant.* Pp. 109–167. Uppsala: Forskningsnämnden. FRN-Framtidsstudier.

Sörlin, Sverker 1992. Regioner och regionalism. Tankar kring ett nytt forskningsområde. *Kulturella perspektiv* 1: 48–50.

Spengler, Oswald 1959 [1926–28]: *The Decline of the West.* Authorized transl. with notes by Charles Francis Atkinson. London: Allen & Unwin.

Sperber, Dan 1987. *On Anthropological Knowledge: Three Essays.* Cambridge: Cambridge University Press.

Stark, Laura 2002. Ethnic Dynamics and the Finnish Factor: the View from a Post-Soviet Karelian Village. *Ethnologia Fennica.* 30: 63–76.

Stenius, Henrik 1995. Yhdenmukaisuus on perintöosamme. *Helsingin Sanomat,* July 30, 1995.

Stewart, Susan 1991. Notes on Distressed Genres. *Journal of American Folklore* 104: 5–31.

Stewart, Susan 1993 [1984]. *On Longing: Narratives of the Miniature, the Gigantic, the Souvenir, the Collection.* First paperback edition. Durham, N.C.: Duke University Press.

Stolcke, Verena 1995. Talking Culture: New Boundaries, New Rhetorics of Exclusion in Europe. *Current Anthropology* 36 (1): 1–24. A shorter version published in French in: Daniel Fabre, Claudie Voisenat and Eva Julien (eds.), *L'Europe entre Cultures et Nations.* Collection Ethnologie de la France Regards sur l'Europe. Cahier 10. Éditions de la Maison des sciences de l'homme. Paris: Mission du Patrimoine Ethnologique, 1996.

Stråth, Bo 1994. The Swedish Path to National Identity in the Nineteenth Century. In: Øystein Sørensen (ed.), *Nordic Paths to National Identity in the Nineteenth Century.* Nasjonal identitet nr. 1/94: 55–63. KULTs skriftserie nr. 22. Oslo: The Research Council of Norway.

Sulkunen, Irma 2004. *Suomalaisen Kirjallisuuden Seura 1831–1892.* Suomalaisen Kirjallisuuden Seuran Toimituksia 952. Helsinki: Suomalaisen Kirjallisuuden Seura.

Survo, Arno 2001. *Magian kieli. Neuvosto-Inkeri symbolisena periferiana.* Suomalaisen Kirjallisuuden Seuran Toimituksia 820. Helsinki: Suomalaisen Kirjallisuuden Seura.

Tarasti, Eero 1990. *Johdatusta semiotiikkaan. Esseitä taiteen ja kulttuurin merkki-järjestelmistä.* Helsinki: Gaudeamus.

Tarkiainen, Kari 1986. *Se vanha vainooja. Käsitykset itäisestä naapurista Iivana Julmasta Pietari Suureen.* Historiallisia tutkimuksia 132. Helsinki: Suomen Historiallinen Seura.

Tarkka, Lotte 1989. Karjalan kuvaus kansallisena retoriikkana. Ajatuksia karelianismin etnografisesta asetelmasta. In: Seppo Knuuttila & Pekka Laaksonen (eds.), *Runon ja rajan tiellä.* Kalevalaseuran vuosikirja 68. Pp. 243–257. Helsinki: Suomalaisen Kirjallisuuden Seura.

Tarkka, Lotte 1993. Intertextuality, Rhetorics, and the Interpretation of Oral Poetry: The Case of Archived Orality. In: Pertti J. Anttonen & Reimund Kvideland (eds.), *Nordic Frontiers: Recent Issues in the Study of Modern Traditional Culture in the Nordic Countries.* NIF Publications 27. Pp. 165–193. Turku: Nordic Institute of Folklore.

Tengström, Juhana Jaakko 1931. Muutamista Suomen kirjallisuuden ja kulttuurin esteistä. In: *Suomen kansalliskirjallisuus VII. Kansallisia herättäjiä, romanttisia runoilijoita, tiedemiehiä ja tutkimusmatkailijoita 1800-luvun alkupuolelta.* Edited by E. N. Setälä, V. Tarkiainen, Vihtori Laurila. Helsinki: Otava. Ruotsin kielestä suomentanut E. V. I. Karjalainen. Originally published as Om några hinder för Finlands litteratur och cultur. *Aura* I 1817, Pp. 69–90, *Aura* II 1818, Pp. 93–129.

Thoms, William 1965. Folklore. In: Alan Dundes (ed.), *The Study of Folklore.* Pp. 4–6. Englewood Cliffs, N. J.: Prentice-Hall, Inc.

Tiilikainen, Teija 1998. *Europe and Finland: Defining the Political Identity of Finland in Western Europe.* Aldershot, Brookfield USA & Singapore & Sydney: Ashgate.

Tiitta, Allan 1994. *Harmaakiven maa. Zacharias Topelius ja Suomen maantiede.* Bidrag till kännedom av Finlands natur och folk 147. Helsinki: Societas Scientiarum Fennica / Finnish Society of Sciences and Letters.

Tilly, Charles 1990. *Coercion, Capitalism, and European States, AD 900–1990.* Oxford: Basil Blackwell.

Tiryakian, E. A. 2001. Traditions in Sociology. In: Neil J. Smelser & Paul B. Baltes (eds.), *International Encyclopedia of the Social and Behavioral Sciences*, Volume 23: 15824–15833. Amsterdam: Elsevier.

Todorov, Tzvetan 1984a. *Mikhail Bakhtin: The Dialogical Principle.* Translated by Wlad Godzich. Minneapolis: University of Minnesota Press.

Todorov, Tzvetan 1984b. *The Conquest of America: The Question of the Other.* New York: Harper & Row.

Tommila, Päiviö 1983. Taiteilija ja hänen teoksensa. In: Aarno Karimo, *Kumpujen yöstä. Suomalaisia vaiheita, tekoja ja oloja kivikaudesta nykyaikaan.* Pp. v–ix. Porvoo, Helsinki, Juva: WSOY.

Tonkin, Elizabeth & Bryan, Dominic 1996. Political Ritual: Temporality and Tradition. In: Åsa Boholm (ed.), *Political Ritual.* Pp. 14–36. Gothenburg: Institute for Advanced Studies in Social Anthropology (IASSA).

Topelius [Z.]. 1985 [1875]. *Maamme kirja.* Toimittanut Vesa Mäkinen. Porvoo, Helsinki, Juva: WSOY.

Topelius, Zachris 1845. Äger finska folket en historie? *Joukahainen II*: 189–217. Helsingfors: Österbotniska Afdelningen.

Turner, Bryan S. 1984. *Body and Society: Explorations in Social Theory.* Oxford: Blackwell.

Turner, Bryan S. 1987. A Note on Nostalgia. *Theory, Culture & Society* 4 (1): 147–156.

Turner, Bryan S. 1990. Two Faces of Sociology: Global or National? In: Mike Featherstone (ed.), *Global Culture: Nationalism, Globalization and Modernity. A Theory, Culture & Society* special issue. Pp. 343–358. London: Sage.

Turner, Victor 1969. *The Ritual Process: Structure and Anti-Structure.* Ithaca, N.Y.: Cornell University Press.

Turner, Victor 1974. *Dramas, Fields, and Metaphors: Symbolic Action in Human Society.* Ithaca, N.Y.: Cornell University Press.

Tuulentie, Seija 2001. *Meidän vähemmistömme. Valtaväestön retoriikat saamelaisten oikeuksista käydyissä keskusteluissa.* Suomalaisen Kirjallisuuden Seuran Toimituksia 807. Helsinki: Suomalaisen Kirjallisuuden Seura.

Vahtola, Jouko 1999. Saamelaisten esiintyminen Suomessa varhaishistoriallisten lähteiden ja paikannimien valossa. In: Paul Fogelberg (ed.), *Pohjan poluilla. Suomalaisten juuret nykytutkimuksen mukaan.* (The Roots of the Finns in the light of present-day research.) Bidrag till kännedom af Finlands natur och folk 153. Pp. 109–116. Helsinki: Societas Scientiarum Fennica / Finnish Society of Sciences and Letters.

Valenius, Johanna 1998. Suomi neidon silmin. In: Johanna Valenius (ed.), *Kertomuksia Suomesta. Historiankirjoitusta sanan voimalla ja kuvan keinoin.* Turun yliopiston poliittisen historian tutkimuksia 11. Pp. 14–70. Turku: Turun yliopisto, Poliittisen historian laitos.

Valenius, Johanna 2004. *Undressing the Maid: Gender, Sexuality and the Body in the Construction of the Finnish Nation.* Bibliotheca Historica 85. Helsinki: Suomalaisen Kirjallisuuden Seura.

Vansina, Jan 1985. *Oral Tradition as History.* Madison: University of Wisconsin Press.

Varpio, Yrjö 1997. *Matkalla moderniin Suomeen. 1800-luvun suomalainen matka-kirjallisuus*. Suomalaisen Kirjallisuuden Seuran Toimituksia 681. Helsinki: Suomalaisen Kirjallisuuden Seura.

Vattimo, Gianni 1988. *The End of Modernity: Nihilism and Hermeneutics in Post-modern Culture*. Translated and with an Introduction by Jon R. Snyder. Cambridge: Polity Press.

Vesa, Unto 2000. Historian- ja rauhantutkimuksen suhteesta. Tapaustutkimus: mitä mieltä on tarkastella ristiretkiä rauhantutkimuksessa. In: *Jäljillä. Kirjoituksia historian ongelmista. Juhlakirja Jorma Kalelalle hänen 60-vuotispäivänään 12.11. 2000*. Toimituskunta: Pauli Kettunen, Auli Kultanen, Timo Soikkanen. Osa 1. Pp. 485–494. Turku: University of Turku: Department of Political History and Kirja-Aurora.

Vihavainen, Timo 1999. To whom does the Kalevala belong? *Books from Finland* 1999 (2): 119–122.

Viljanen, Anna Maria 1994. Etnisyys = rotu = kulttuuri? In: Jari Kupiainen & Erkki Sevänen (eds.), *Kulttuurintutkimus. Johdanto*. Tietolipas 130. Pp. 143–163. Helsinki: Suomalaisen Kirjallisuuden Seura.

Virtanen, Leea 1993. Is the Comparative Method Out of Date? In: Michael Chesnutt (ed.), *Telling Reality: Folklore Studies in Memory of Bengt Holbek*. Copenhagen Folklore Studies 1 / NIF Publications 26. Pp. 255–271. Copenhagen & Turku: Nordic Institute of Folklore.

Virtanen, Leila 1999. Discursive Tensions: The Quest for an Imagined Past and Heritage Tourism. Paper given at the American Folklore Society annual meeting in Memphis, TN, USA, on October 21, 1999. Manuscript.

Vuorela, Toivo 1977. *Ethnology in Finland Before 1920*. Helsinki: Societas Scientiarum Fennica.

Wallace, Anthony F. C. 1956. Revitalization Movements. *American Anthropologist* 58 (2): 264–281.

Wallgren, Thomas 1989. Moderni ja postmoderni käsitteinä ja tapoina kokea aikaa. In: Pirkko Heiskanen (ed.), *Aika ja sen ankaruus*. Pp. 35–53. Helsinki: Gaudeamus.

Wallgren, Thomas 1999. The Modern Discourse of Change and the Periodization and End of Modernity. In: Anne Ollila (ed.), *Historical Perspectives on Memory*. Studia Historica 61. Pp. 195–220. Helsinki: Finnish Historical Society.

Waris, Heikki 1952. *Suomalaisen yhteiskunnan rakenne*. Helsinki: Otava.

Warshaver, Gerald E. 1991: On Postmodern Folklore. *Western Folklore* 50: 219–229.

Weber, Eugen 1976. *Peasants into Frenchmen: The Modernization of Rural France 1870–1914*. Stanford: Stanford University Press.

Weber, Max 1964. *The Theory of Social and Economic Organization*. Translated by A. M. Henderson and Talcott Parsons. New York: The Free Press.

*Webster's* 1984: *Webster's II New Riverside University Dictionary*. Boston: Riverside Publishing Company.

Wellmer, Albrecht 1985. *Zur Dialektik von Moderne und Postmoderne*. Frankfurt/M.: Suhrkamp.

Welz, Gisela 2001. Multiple Modernities and Reflexive Traditionalization: A Mediterranean Case Study. *Ethnologia Europaea* 30 (1): 5–14.

Westerholm, John 1999. Kansa ja alue. Suomenruotsalaiset osana kansakuntaa ja valtiota. In: Markku Löytönen & Laura Kolbe (eds.), *Suomi. Maa, kansa, kulttuurit*. Suomalaisen Kirjallisuuden Seuran Toimituksia 753. Pp. 278–289. Helsinki: Suomalaisen Kirjallisuuden Seura.

Westerlund, David (ed.) 1996. *Questioning the Secular State: The Worldwide Resurgence of Religion in Politics*. London: C. Hurst & Company.

White, Hayden 1987. *The Content of Form: Narrative Discourse and Historical Representation*. Baltimore: Johns Hopkins University Press.

Williams, Raymond 1976. *Keywords: A Vocabulary of Culture and Society*. London: Fontana.

Williams, Raymond 1977. *Marxism and Literature*. New York: Oxford University Press.

Willis, William S. Jr. 1974. Skeletons in the Anthropological Closet. In: Dell Hymes (ed.), *Reinventing Anthropology*. Pp. 121–152. New York: Vintage Books.

Wilson, William A. 1973. Herder, Folklore and Romantic Nationalism. *Journal of Popular Culture* 6: 819–835.

Wilson, William A. 1976. *Folklore and Nationalism in Modern Finland*. Bloomington: Indiana University Press.

Wilson, William A. 1987. Partial Repentance of a Critic: The Kalevala, Politics, and the United States. In: Alan Jabbour & James Hardin (eds.), *Folklife Annual 1986*. A Publication of the American Folklife Center at the Library of Congress. Pp. 81–91. Washington, D.C.: Library of Congress. Published in Finnish as: Kriitikon osittainen katumus: Kalevala, politiikka ja Yhdysvallat. In: Lauri Honko (ed.), *Kalevala ja maailman eepokset*. Kalevalaseuran vuosikirja 65. Pp. 404–416. Helsinki: Suomalaisen Kirjallisuuden Seura.

Wilson, William A. 1996. Sibelius, the Kalevala, and Karelianism. In: Glenda Dawn Goss (ed.), *The Sibelius Companion*. Pp. 43–60. Westport, Conn.: Greenwood Press.

Wilson, William A. 1998. Nationalism. In: Mary Ellen Brown and Bruce A. Rosenberg (eds.), *Encyclopedia of Folklore and Literature*. Pp. 441–444. Santa Barbara, Calif.: ABC-CLIO.

Wintle, Michael (ed.) 1996. *Culture and Identity in Europe: Perceptions of Divergence and Unity in Past and Present*. Aldershot: Avebury.

Wolf, Eric R. 1982. *Europe and the People Without History*. Berkeley & Los Angeles: University of California Press.

Workman, Mark E. 1989. Folklore in the Wilderness: Folklore and Postmodernism. *Midwestern Folklore* 15 (1): 5–14.

Zeitlin, Steven J. 2000. I'm a Folklorist and You're Not: Expansive versus Delimited Strategies in the Practice of Folklore. *Journal of American Folklore* 113 (447): 3–19.

Zewail, Ahmed 2002. Ahmed in Femtoland. Nobel Chemist Takes an Ultra-Fast Look at a Fleet-Footed World. *Penn Arts & Sciences*. Spring 2002. Philadelphia: University of Pennsylvania. Also available at: http://www.sas.upenn.edu/sasalum/newsltr/spring2002/femtoland.html.

# Subject Index

# Name Index

www.ingramcontent.com/pod-product-compliance
Lightning Source LLC
Chambersburg PA
CBHW081739270326
41932CB00020B/3327